Reference Services Today: From Interview to Burnout

Forthcoming topics in *The Reference Librarian* series:

•International Aspects of Reference Services, Number 17
•Current Trends in Information: Research and Theory, Number 18
•Reference Services Administration and Budget, Number 19
•Reference Services and Public Policy, Number 20
•Information and Referral, Number 21
•Information Brokers and Consultants, Number 22

Published:

Reference Services Today: From Interview to Burnout

Edited by
Bill Katz and Ruth A. Fraley

School of Library & Information Science
State University of New York at Albany

The Haworth Press
New York • London

Reference Services Today: From Interview to Burnout has also been published as *The Reference Librarian,* Number 16, Winter 1986.

The Haworth Press, Inc., 12 West 32 Street, New York, NY 10001
EUROSPAN/Haworth, 3 Henrietta Street, London WC2E 8LU England

Library of Congress Cataloging-in-Publication Data

Reference services today.

Has also been published as The Reference Librarian, Number 16, Winter 1986—T.p. verso.
Includes bibliographies.
1. Reference services (Libraries) 2. Librarians—Psychology. I. Katz, William A., 1924- .
II. Fraley, Ruth A.
Z711.R454   1987   025.5'2   86-29481
ISBN 0-86656-572-8

Reference Services Today: From Interview to Burnout

The Reference Librarian
Number 16

CONTENTS

REFERENCE SERVICES WITH SPECIAL FUNCTIONS AND SUBJECTS

REFERENCE SERVICES AND STAGES
OF AUTOMATION

Reference Services Today: From Interview to Burnout

Today Is the Same
Yet Different

Ruth A. Fraley

Reference service in a time of small budgets and expanded auto-mation capabilities is complex, exciting, and exasperating. As the members of the information society begin to realize the value of the resources and organizational skills in the library when they search for information, the pressure increases, the pace becomes more in-tense, and the ability to accurately disassemble and reassemble a query to respond correctly increases in value. Reference librarians have an opportunity to enhance the public image. This collection of articles offers advice for improving service and raises questions that require thought on the part of every individual reference librarian.

Gothberg talks about "the beginnings" or the evolution of refer-ence theory. Her work traces early theories on aspects of the com-munications process as it relates to library reference work. The ref-erence communication process can be accurately described as one on one communication between librarian and patron. The typology of questioning is reviewed by Ross and she provides guidance for structuring interviews at the reference desk. She is an advocate of the "open" question designed to elicit the information need of the patron in an effective and timely manner. Naiman, Hauptman, and Oser use practical experience to look closely at some of the gener-ally accepted views of a proper reference interview and occasionally disagree with Ross. The practice of making an analogy and relating the reference interview to a practice of another profession is still in use and several authors choose to do this. Arguments are presented for comparison with shop clerks and with people in the helping pro-fessions. It is a reflection on the status of the profession that we look for these analogies. No one indicates a belief in the unique nature of the reference interview—that is unique in the sense that it is a feature of librarianship, no other profession. Perhaps enhancing our self image can lead to some positive conclusions.

The focus on communication in reference services continues as several people examine special aspects of the process. Reference services is sometimes carried out at the desk and at other times carried out in relation to another library function or service. Special functions, clientele, and subject areas influence the service and the nature of the communications process. There are echos of the pre-technology era in the discussions of the independent scholar project by Lindauer and the lifelong learner by Heiser. The independent scholar, for example, brings to mind the Chataqua circuits of the 1900s. Each of these "special" clientele require different skills and knowledge on the part of the reference librarian. The examinations of the telephone interview and of the interlibrary loan interview review the special interview and information needs affiliated with a certain library function. Sommerville and Paterson talk about the special skills and techniques required for services to science researchers and to the public in search of medical information.

Technology is part of reference services in 1986. One interesting aspect of the subject is the varied level of technological implementation in libraries. Some libraries are seriously considering or actually implementing end user searching of the major data bases while others are in the beginning phases and are determining the optimal way to introduce automation beginning with the catalog and other functions. Roberts and Jensen present the results when a computer knowledgeable person attempts to search data bases as an end user without the aid of an experienced reference librarian. The result of their study is a resounding endorsement for librarian mediated searching. Stachacz and King write about the introduction of technology in the library and the role of reference librarians in the process, while Lamprecht examines the factors to consider in the traditional online search interview.

As the complexities of reference services increase, the training and education of staff serving at the reference desk is important. Vavreck has suggestions for incorporating the microcomputer into the process of education for reference work in graduate school. Young has done a great deal of work developing a training program for reference librarians new to a particular library. Preparation of preprofessionals and a suggested training program is discussed by Woodard and Van Der Laan.

The reference librarian can draw upon several theories in order to determine the best technique for the job. Penland and Mathai suggest the best source for theory is psychology and the optimal technique is to apply some of the precepts of this body of knowledge to reference communication techniques. The discussion of theories includes possible explanations for burnout. The need for continued courtesy in reference work is outlined by Alloway.

Reference services today involve complexities brought about by automation and the growth of specialized subject information. The situation is further compounded by the diversity of clientele and the ever changing types of questions asked. It is different than it was in the early days of the profession but it can never be said to be boring. Instead it can be viewed as a series of challenges to be conquered without losing perspective.

THE REFERENCE
INTERVIEW
AND COMMUNICATION
CHALLENGES

The Beginnings

Helen M. Gothberg

The study and research into the reference process based on specific communication constructs evolved out of the profession's attempt to develop a theory of reference service. The growth of reference theory spanned the last hundred years or more, and at best, remains nebulous and debatable even today. The foundations of reference, as a service unique to libraries, were laid in 1876 with the creation of the American Library Association. ALA provided a formal organization and an official journal through which librarians could formulate their theories and discuss shared concerns. Other contributing factors included the publication of the Cutter and Dewey Decimal Classification schemes and Poole's *Index to Periodical Literature*. Together, these three events led to the professionalization of reference librarianship. This meant that patrons were viewed differently, which led in turn to the emergence of theory.

There are at least seven identifiable constructs which have contributed at one time or another to the formation of reference theory. Three of the seven are directly concerned with human communication:

1. The quantity, quality and use of the collection
2. Levels of service
3. Human relations awareness between librarian and patron
4. Question/negotiation in information seeking
5. Specific communication/relationship models
6. Research
7. Education/training

QUANTITY, QUALITY AND USE OF THE COLLECTION

One of the ways reference service was defined initially was through the collection of descriptive statistics: How many books,

The author is Associate Professor, Graduate Library School, University of Arizona, Tucson, AZ 85719.

what percentage of the collection was made up of reference materials, how many questions were answered, how much seating space allowed, how many personnel employed and their qualifications, comprehensiveness of the collection based on recommended sources and currency were some of the kinds of data collected within this framework. The collection of statistics provided a necessary but limited picture of what reference was or attempted to be. In recent years there has been less concern with quantitative and more emphasis on qualitative methods in developing a theoretical construct that adequately reflects reference librarianship.

LEVELS OF SCIENCE

In 1915 W. W. Bishop,[1] superintendent of the Reading Room at the Library of Congress, undertook the first serious effort at developing a theory of reference. To this extent Bishop defined reference as a service provided by librarians "in aid" of some type of study or research. He also introduced the concept of the self-denying ordinance which recognized that, in some cases, specialists in a field would be necessary to provide a high level of service. He defined "theory" not only as the work which a librarian might do in aid of a reader—plus staff qualifications, materials and work environment—but also the *attitude* of the librarian.

The link between attitude and interpersonal communication was not made for a long time; rather, a concern for the various levels of service was expanded by both Wyer and Butler in the years that followed Bishop's initial theoretical statement. Wyer published his book *Reference Work* in 1930,[2] which was the standard text for library school students for many years. Wyer took issue with Bishop's concept of aiding the library user and believed that a more accurate interpretation of reference was "to help" or "assist" the reader. Wyer's contribution to a theory of reference was to define three levels of reference work as: conservative, moderate, and liberal or ideal. He described these levels as follows: Conservative provided minimum assistance; moderate meant that the actual answer was found for the library patron; and liberal or ideal went beyond the collection at hand for information. Today we could consider Wyer's ideal level as akin to interlibrary loan or information and referral services in the modern library. We are indebted to Wyer for his interest in the educational or instructional aspects of reference. He felt that no theory of reference work was complete that did not recognize the library's obligation to educate patrons in its use.

Pierce Butler also defined reference in terms of levels of service. In 1943 his book, *Reference Function of the Library*,[3] he chided librarians for not taking reference theory more seriously. It is important to note here that Butler viewed reference as a "function" as opposed to "work." This difference is not incidental, for it was the first step in the evolution of reference theory which moved away from a primary concern with the practice of reference toward a greater interest in its philosophical foundations. Butler, for the most part, remained focused on levels of service which he defined as: elementary, or answering a factual, readily answered question; intermediate, a more detailed search which involved the relationship of human values between persons, things, or events; and advanced, wherein the librarian actually provided the answer either orally or in written form.

In his *Introduction to Reference Work*,[4] Katz defined reference as the "art of finding information" and moved reference theory a step beyond the notion of "work" or "function" when he described reference as a process. "Process" is defined in one sense as, "a natural progressively continuing operation or development marked by a series of gradual changes that succeed one another in a relatively fixed way and lead toward a particular result or end."[5] Katz defined reference in terms of four types of questions: Directional, or telling patrons where certain features of the library were located; ready reference, which was similar to Butler's elementary level, or locating the factual easily answered question. Specific search questions involved the librarian in pulling together a number of sources on a given topic for the library patron and was not unlike Butler's intermediate level. Finally, there were research questions where the type of inquiry was more scholarly and involved locating resources outside the library—a description closely related to Wyer's ideal and Butler's advanced levels of service. Clearly, the type of question and the level of service had become interwoven constructs in reference theory.

The notion of levels of service in reference theory led to the debate over instructing the user vs. providing the answer. Librarians were always concerned with educating the user, but in the 1960s, Anita Schiller[6] led the crusade against library instruction. Schiller regarded instruction as minimal reference service and pointed out the dichotomy that existed when librarians accepted two antagonistic philosophies. Proponents of library instruction persisted and brought new meaning to the position of "orientation librarian" in the academic setting. Today, many college and university libraries have developed sophisticated instructional modules for freshman classes and made greater efforts to consult with university classes at the request of faculty. When Schiller looked back on the old debate in 1981, she found the major issues had changed. With the growth of electronic networks, she believed the primary concern now was with "who shall control and who shall have access to society's information resources."[7] She felt that the crucial issue libraries were facing was the public's right to know.

Levels of service are variable; they are based to a considerable extent on the type of library. For example, a special library with its limited clientele may find it more expedient to provide the answer—just as may a public library but for different reasons. Libraries located in educational institutions place a greater emphasis on educating the user to answer his/her own questions at the basic level of information need; yet, there needs be nothing minimum about the type of instruction provided. Professional staff time can then be spent in other ways, such as answering research questions and helping the user to access computerized databases.

It is traditional to speak of the modern library as being on the cutting edge of the new technology, yet libraries have always been part of the technological revolution, from the invention of type and printing to the use of computers and interactive videodiscs. In an article written in 1922 that described the "Psychological Moment" between patron and librarian, Marilla Waite Freeman[8] noted that it was the age of electricity, double entendre intended, and the tremendous development of mechanical and industrial arts that presented an opportunity to be seized by librarians. What is different today is that new technologies are proliferating at a faster pace, and Anita Schiller's concerns about access to electronic information should be taken seriously by the profession. "User-friendly" systems will have an impact on reference service in the future, but for now there remains a need for person-to-person encounters as the librarian conducts a pre-search interview before doing an on-line search or explains the use of the ROM reader. This situation may not always be the case, and minimum-maximum levels of service will be redefined in ways we can only speculate about at this point in time. As a theoretical construct for reference service, levels of service provided the profession with a forum for discussion that helped to shape attitudes. Like other descriptive standards of service, it provided an incomplete picture of that complex human communication process called "reference."

HUMAN RELATIONS AWARENESS

It is traditional in the literature on reference librarianship to give credit to Samuel S. Green for being the first to recognize that there were "Personal Relations Between Librarians and Readers."[9] His article, published in the *American Library Journal* in October 1876, advised librarians that:

> A hearty reception by a sympathizing friend, and the recognition of some one at hand who will listen to inquiries, even although he may consider them unimportant, make it easy for such persons to ask questions, and put them at once on a home footing.[10]

While Green's advice is acceptable decades later, not all his methods would receive wholehearted endorsement today. For instance, he believed that the librarian should be as persistent as a shopkeeper in not permitting the patron to leave without an answer. He had difficulty dealing with the spirit of democracy. At one point Green noted its importance in dealing with readers in popular libraries, but a few sentences later continued that the librarian, "runs little risk in placing readers on a footing of equality with himself. The superiority of his culture will always enable him to secure respectful treatment . . ."[11] Nor did women fare much better, for he viewed them as primarily useful as volunteers in small public libraries.

Green did not overlook the public relations aspects of "hearty receptions" and "personal relations" with library users. He closed his classic article with the following advice:

> The more freely a librarian mingles with readers, and the greater amount of assistance he renders them, the more intense does the conviction of citizens, also, become that the library is a useful institution, and the more willing do they grow to grant money in larger sums to be used in buying books and employing additional assistants.[12]

Some of this author's prose conjures up Dickensian scenes of this librarian pursuing the reader while rubbing his hands in gleeful anticipation of what may be future rewards for the library. The significance of humanism in reference, and its contribution to theory building had to wait. Still, Green's was a pioneering paper, at least in terms of its title—and basic goodness of intent. The reader must consider the milieu in which it was written.

Writers continued to see the role of the librarian as that of host or hostess as late as 1942. Interaction with the public was governed more by a philosophy of social etiquette than humanism. However, in her article, "The Reader as a Person,"[13] Alice Bryan suggested that psychology could be useful to librarians. The modern day reader may be amused that Bryan's source for her article and the discussion that followed was a book entitled, *The Unadjusted Girl.* Nonetheless, it was a beginning for this author to call to the attention of the profession four human drives identified as: security, a desire for new experiences, a need for recognition and the desire for response, as a framework for improving reference services. Samet, a psychiatrist and former librarian, would probably have applauded Bryan's interest. He encouraged librarians to gain a better understanding of those individuals with emotional problems who sought help initially through the use of library resources. He noted that authoritarian attitudes on the part of the librarian or smug superiority would push such patrons into withdrawal, as would a patronizing overconcern. Samet closed his article with the following critical comment: "Perhaps we reject the 'odd' library patron because he is too much like us."[14]

The degree, if any, to which librarians are responsible for counseling services in a library is a matter of debate. That the reference or public service librarian should like and understand people is not. It is a philosophy that has long been held by many informed professionals. Sarah Reed's article published in the *Library Journal* on January 1, 1956,[15] stressing the need for human qualities, brought the following response from a reader:

> It was Professor Reed's remarks on the human qualities of a reference librarian that particularly arrested my attention, however. She indicated that part of the basic tools of the trade are "understanding, interest, tact, and patience." To this I nod assent, but then ask, how do librarians, especially reference librarians, acquire these so-called basic tools of the trade?[16]

A reasonable question asked by an aware reader, but unfortunately one that would not be answered with any certainty for another 20 years or more.

The primary contributor to humanistic thought in the evolution of a theory of reference services was the East Indian scholar, S. R. Ranganathan. He, more than any other writer before his time, understood reference service as a philosophical concept that went considerably beyond having good manners or being gracious toward the reading public for the sake of library progress. Ranganathan defined humanism as, ''A system, mode or attitude of thought or action centering upon distinctively human interests or ideas as contrasted with other interests or ideas.''[17] Citing Walter Lippmann, Ranganathan pointed out that human interests should not be taken for social interests. While they might, in many situations be the same, in others, they could be at crossed purposes. He felt that modern humanism was flouted in libraries because of the artificiality of their organization.

In this context bringing book and reader together is reference service; it is an activity based on humanistic principles—that is, human individual growth. On the other hand, the library and its growth is based on societal needs and concerns. Ranganathan's answer to the dilemma can be found in this frequently quoted gem:

''When the reader comes amidst the library,'' the profession says, ''he will meet a person, who with radiant geniality whispers into his ears,

Take my hand;
For I have passed this way,
And know the truth.''[18]

Ranganathan believed that modern humanism would transform librarianship at all levels of service. He was possibly overly idealistic, but a concern for people coupled with humanistic philosophy led in time to the profession's desire to better understand the complex communication process of question/negotiation in the reference interview.

QUESTION/NEGOTIATION

Fred Mosher used to tell his reference classes at Berkeley that it was easier to locate the answer among the books in the library than to discover what it was that the reader really wanted. Students took this comment as more of the famous Mosher wit until their first day on the reference desk. Although recognized, the communication gap between the question asked and the ultimate answer was not studied seriously by librarians in the beginning. Margaret Hutchins was probably the first to christen the communication process between the reference librarian and the patron with a question, as "The Reference Interview." In her book, *Introduction to Reference Work*[19] published in 1944, she devoted an entire chapter to the subject. Another librarian, Jack Delaney, discussed the process of interviewing as something akin to salesmanship and advised librarians that, "Patrons are not expected to be practiced in self-expression."[20]

Serious inquiry into "The Process of Asking Questions" was initiated by Robert Taylor.[21] Taylor's four levels of information need —visceral, conscious, formalized and compromised—provided the incentive for much of the study and research into the nature of the reference interview that would follow. He challenged librarians to think more seriously about the barriers to successful question/negotiation than they had in the past. Taylor's work gave a major thrust to human communication as a scientific construct which could be studied within the research paradigm of reference theory.

The library literature on the reference interview that followed Taylor's seminal work comprised one or both of two aspects of the process. First, meeting user information needs by working through the barriers which prevented a successful outcome by following a series of prescribed steps. Second, the reference interview was studied as a problem in human communication or interpersonal relationships. The interview process and the search for information were clearly described in much of this literature as was the fact that human communication played a significant role. Yet, specific communication models were not proposed or investigated at this point in the development of a theory of reference service. Librarians were left with the former reader's lament as to what the communication tools were that facilitated information seeking.

SPECIFIC COMMUNICATION/RELATIONSHIP MODELS

The need to know more about how to communicate effectively with a wide variety of patrons led to the identification and study of a number of human relations and or communication models. Many of these models had their origins in either the psychology of human behavior or the study of non-verbal communication. Alice Bryan's suggestion that psychological concepts would be useful to librarians was not a misplaced notion. No matter what the content of the message, human beings are always talking about how they feel about themselves; how they feel about the situation they are in; and how they feel about the person or persons with whom they are communicating. These feelings can not be ignored. They are part of the interview process just as much as reflecting the user's question and locating the desired information.

"What we need," Charles Bunge wrote, "are researchable hypotheses predicting relationships among the variables involved in the reference situation."[22] A practical minded librarian might ask why all the bother with reference theory—why not just get on with doing the job? It may not always seem so, but theory building serves a number of useful purposes—the bottom line of which is to help reference librarians do their jobs better. Information about the reference process is generated through theory building which leads to researchable hypotheses. In looking back over the evolution of reference theory, four functions which have served the profession well have resulted:

1. First, theory has provided a forum for discussion. Out of the debates that inevitably followed, there evolved testable hypotheses.
2. Research followed theory and provided the profession with valid data which could be generalized to different kinds of libraries or library users.
3. The findings of research helped to set standards for performance measurement in reference departments.
4. Lastly, the education of new librarians and the in-service training of existing professionals were greatly enhanced by all of the above—debate, research, and ultimately the generation of data which could be used to educate library personnel and set measurable standards which went beyond purely quantifiable measures.

New trends in examining the reference interview continue to emerge, including an increased interest in unobtrusive measurement. Research in this area has involved determining whether librarians adequately answer questions put to them by a person who is unknown as a researcher. The results of many of these studies have been shocking, and the reported poor performance on the part of reference staff must rest in part with the education they received, along with questions about continued in-service training and adequate supervision or performance standards. Whether poor performance in finding information is due to a lack of communication skills, knowledge of reference books and automated databases or inadequate collections—or all three—should be seriously addressed by the profession. Another area of recent research interest has focused on cognitive aspects of information transfer.[23] The aim of such study has been to better understand human information processing. Perhaps investigating into this area will help to shed additional light on the problem of inaccurate responses to reference questions.

EDUCATION AND TRAINING

Research very often raises more questions than it answers—such is the nature of empirical or other types of investigation. The educational environment is conducive to carrying out continued study and research, although such activity is not limited to students and faculty in Graduate Library and Information Science or other degree programs. Many practitioners in the profession have made important contributions. Today when a student or reference librarian asks how to be more approachable to the user—there *is* an answer: "Come out from behind the desk, make frequent but not prolonged eye contact, and maintain a pleasant facial expression and an open body posture." These skills are easily learned and even though such initial contact is only one step in a very complicated and involved process, the opening encounter in the reference interview is quite often a significant one.

Education helps the student or professional to put the role of human communication into perspective. Learning to interact effectively on a one-to-one basis with another human being is not only a matter of learning body postures or appropriate phrases. Although these skills are a part of handling the interview in a meaningful way, it is important to remember that we are dealing with humanism in bringing people and information together. Librarians should not regard the development of interpersonal communication skills solely as a means to further library public relations. The focus must be on establishing genuine human relationships with users, or all that may have been learned will result in a backlash. The difference between the two approaches is analogous to that which exists between the used car salesperson and the sensitive physician or caring nurse. Humanism, coupled with technical skills, is what puts the "professional" in librarianship; otherwise, we are merely shop keepers promoting our wares. Effective public relations may very well be a side benefit of a staff trained in effective human relations skills, but personal growth and philosophical attitude, in addition to interviewing skills and a knowledge of resources MUST be taught as an integrated cohesive whole. To fail to understand interpersonal communication in reference service as humanistic theory is to fail those individuals who come to the library seeking knowledge.

NOTES

1. W. W. Bishop, "The Theory of Reference Work." *Bulletin of the American Library Association* (June 1915): 134-139.

2. Jame I. Wyer, *Reference Work* (Chicago: American Library Association, 1930).

3. Pierce Butler, *The Reference Function of the Library* (Chicago: University of Chicago Press, 1943).

4. William A. Katz, *Introduction to Reference Work,* v. 1 (New York: McGraw-Hill Book Company, 1982).

5. *Webster's New International Dictionary of the English Language* (Springfield, Massachusetts: G & C Merriam Company, 1961): 1808.

6. Anita R. Schiller, "Reference Service: Instruction or Information?" *Library Quarterly* (January 1965): 52-60.

7. Ibid., p. 9.

8. Marilla Waite Freeman, "The Psychological Moment," *The Library Journal* (February 1911): 55-62.

9. Samuel S. Green, "Personal Relations Between Librarians and Readers," *American Library Journal* (October 1876): 74-81.

10. Ibid., p. 74.

11. Ibid., p. 80.

12. Ibid., p. 81.

13. Alice I. Bryan, "The Reader as a Person," *The Library Journal* (February 15, 1942): 137-141.

14. Norman T. Samet, "Why Does That Man Stare at Me?" *Library Journal* (January 1968): 156-157.

15. Sarah Rebecca Reed, "The Reference Librarian." *Library Journal* (January 1, 1956): 21-23.

16. L. W. Anderson, "Reference Librarians and Psychology," *Library Journal* (May 1956): 1058.

17. S. R. Ranganathan, "Reference Service and Humanism," in Arthur Ray Rowland, comp., *Reference Services* (Hamden, Connecticut: The Shoe String Press, Inc., 1964): 31.

18. Ibid., p. 33.

19. Margaret Hutchins, *Introduction to Reference Work* (Chicago: American Library Association, 1944).

20. Jack Delaney, "Interviewing," *Wilson Library Bulletin* (December 1954): 317-318.

21. Robert S. Taylor, "The Process of Asking Questions." *American Documentation* (October 1962): 391-393.

22. Charles A. Bunge, "Research in Reference." *RQ* (Summer 1972): 373.

23. Peter Ingwersen, "Search Procedures in the Library—Analyzed From the Cognitive Point of View." *Journal of Documentation* (September 1982): 165-191.

How to Find Out
What People Really Want to Know

Catherine Sheldrick Ross

The following reference requests, which were made in various public libraries in Ontario, look diverse but they all have something in common:

1. I'm looking for books on ethnic arts and crafts.
2. Where could I find information on a particular company—what they make?
3. Do you have the district business directory?
4. Can you tell me where I'd find a directory of museums?
5. What I'm looking for is information on stockbrokers. Articles that have been written about stockbrokers in Canada.
6. Do you have any idea when the next *Vancouver Sun* will be coming out?

The element linking these questions is that all six were asked by people who needed help with a job search.[1] The user asking the question about ethnic arts and crafts turned out to be preparing for a job interview involving programming for children; she wanted to find out how to make a piñata in order to sound knowledgeable talking about crafts at the interview. Questions two, three, and four were asked because job-hunters needed names and addresses of potential employers to whom they could send resumes. The question about stockbrokers was really a request for something describing what stockbrokers do; the user wanted to decide whether he himself would be suited to stockbroking. The user asking for the next *Vancouver Sun* wanted to see listings of job openings in Western Canada.

There are three points suggested by this juxtaposition of reference requests. First is the way that the users have chosen to formulate

The author is at the School of Library and Information Science, Elborn College, The University of Western Ontario, London, Ontario, Canada N6G 1H1.

19

their questions. None of the users said, "I'm job hunting and I want . . ." Rather, the three users with questions about ethnic crafts, companies, and stockbrokers transformed their particular question into a request for information on a broad general topic. The other three users asked questions one step more remote from their original question. Starting with their job-hunting problem, they translated their need into a general topic and then *prescribed* the reference source that they thought most appropriate for their topic— business directories, a directory of museums, and the *Vancouver Sun*. Unfortunately, the further away the presenting question gets from the original information need, the greater the chance of mistranslation, misunderstanding, and mistaken requests for inappropriate reference sources. The second point to notice is the improbability that, on the basis of these initial questions, the librarians would be able to guess what the original information need was or what kind of help the user really wanted. And the third point becomes apparent as soon as one asks, "Would it make any difference to the librarian's handling of the question to know *why* the user is asking it?" Surely with at least some of these six questions, the answer must be that, yes, it would make a difference to know the particular context of the question.

Before returning to these points, it may be fruitful to explore why users tend to formulate questions in terms of general topics and prescribed sources and why librarians choose, very often, to accept these questions at face value. It seems that the way users ask questions and the way librarians answer them are grounded in how we think about information.

TWO WAYS OF THINKING ABOUT INFORMATION

In the profession of librarianship, several factors combine to make us think of information as a commodity. Most pervasive of all is the language we share, which provides us with a way of talking and thinking about information that is essentially metaphoric: we "store" information; we "retrieve" it; and so on. These metaphors for information are subsumed by what Michael Reddy has called the "conduit metaphor" for language.[2] He has argued that the way we talk about language is structured by the following metaphors: ideas are *objects*; linguistic expressions are *containers*; communication is a process of putting idea-objects into linguistic containers and sending them along a *conduit* to a listener, who takes the idea-objects out of their word-containers.

Normally, of course, we are not aware of the metaphors we use. But once we start paying attention to them we can see how strongly what we think of as ordinary reality is structured by metaphor.[3] George Lakoff and Mark Johnson have analyzed the entailments of the conduit metaphor as follows. If we think of ideas as objects, then we think of meanings as existing independently of people and contexts. Moreover if words are thought of as containers for meanings, then we think of words and sentences as having meanings *in themselves*, independent of any context or speaker.[4]

Likewise, if we think of information as a commodity, it too can be thought of as existing apart from people or contests—an object to be transferred, retrieved, exchanged, and stored. This way of conceptualizing information makes it seem "natural" to think that a question can be posed and can be answered correctly with no reference to its context in the life of the asker. That is, no matter who asks the question and in no matter what context, the answer to the question, "How did Senator Williams of New Jersey vote on the Panama Canal treaties?" always remains, "He voted 'Yes' on both treaties."

This brings us to the second and third factors that strengthen librarians' tendency to conceptualize information as a commodity with no context: the way reference is taught and the way it is evaluated. Library schools typically have taught basic reference courses by giving students questions to answer: How many goats are there in Bangladesh? What was Alice Munro's first published short story? The evaluative studies of reference service that have had the most methodological prestige have followed Terrence Crowley and Thomas Childers in using proxies who pose as real users, ask questions, and unobtrusively measure how correctly libraries provide answers to queries like "Where is the nearest airport to Warren, Pennsylvania?"[5] In both these situations, it is understood that there *is* a correct answer (in fact the way one develops such questions is to work backwards from a known answer to a question that will elicit this answer). Being tested is whether or not the M.L.S. student or librarian, as the case may be, has succeeded in discovering this one pre-determined correct answer. Again, here are cases in which questions and answers can be held to exist independently, apart from their contexts. And precisely because these contrived questions truly are decontextualized (no real person ever asked them), the paradigm of information as commodity is appropriate for them.

QUESTIONS IN CONTEXTS

Now we come to a different situation—that of a real user asking a genuine question in a library. Whereas contrived questions have no context and no history, real questions are embedded in the context of users' day-to-day lives. Users ask questions out of the contexts of their immediate concerns. They don't ask questions in libraries for the fun of it; they ask questions as a means to an end important to them. They are trying to *do* something—apply for a job, make a decision, complete a school project, remodel their kitchen, make a complaint, get some ideas, get in touch with other people.[6] They ask questions to fill in gaps in their understanding so that they can get on with these concerns. Therefore, a necessary part of understanding the question is knowing the situation out of which the question arose. The question is meaningful in its context, and its context is part of its meaning. We understand the question when we recover its framework.

The user may ask, "Do you know when the next *Vancouver Sun* is coming out?" and the librarian may choose to treat it as a decontextualized question requiring the answer, "The *Vancouver Sun* is still on strike and no one knows when it will be out." But a more appropriate way of thinking about information and information-seeking in this case would be to think of the question as having a context in the life of the person who asked it. And a more helpful answer to this question, when it is asked because the user is job-hunting, may be "The *Vancouver Sun* is on strike just now, but we do have other sources for job listings in western Canada." More generally, a helpful answer for job hunters is one that helps them, in their own terms, to get on with the business of job-hunting. Users are helped to the extent that the answers they get in libraries help them to do something that they want to do. Hence it is conceptually useful to distinguish between the *"correct"* answer for the disembedded, contextless question and the *helpful* answer for a particular person in a particular situation. The librarian who answers a question without knowing anything about the context in which the question became a question may provide an answer that is correct but unhelpful.

Now we come to the hard part. To be able to provide this helpful answer, the librarian needs to know the question's context. But users normally do not, without encouragement from the librarian, volunteer the context for the questions they ask. They also, to a greater or lesser degree, have learned to think of information as a commodity that must be asked for in libraries in decontextualized terms. Rather than saying, "Next week I'm going on a holiday to Hawaii, and I want to know what the temperature is likely to be, so I can pack appropriate clothes," a user may ask, "Where is your travel section?" Users, as we have seen, often translate their questions into what they think are library classifications or ask for the specific reference source that they think (often wrongly) will contain the answer.

Moreover they are unlikely to understand the full complexity of how information is organized in libraries. A user who wanted names and prices of ski resorts in the Laurentian Mountains where his family might holiday said, "I'm interested in your ski section." We can assume that he had a rather nebulous view of what the "ski section" might include. He had probably not considered the differences among such aspects of skiing as ski resorts, learning how to ski, buying ski equipment, biographies of famous skiers, sports injuries connected with skiing, etc. or among such formats as vertical file materials, books, periodical articles, etc. Librarians know all this, but can't use their professional expertise without more to go on than just "ski section." So how is the librarian to find out, quickly and tactfully, the context for the user's question?

A WORKSHOP ON COMMUNICATION SKILLS

For the past several years, Patricia Dewdney and I have been giving a workshop in which we teach interviewing and communication skills. The focus is on finding out what the real question is, and this often means going from the translated question back to the question in its context. The workshop, though rooted in a sense-making theory of information and based on current research in reference, is essentially practical in emphasis. Through a combination of methods including small lectures, modelling, group exercises, role plays, and discussion, the workshop explores communication problems occurring between library users and library staff and presents some skills for coping with these problems.[7] Among the skills taught are avoiding premature diagnosis, acknowledgement or restatement, open questioning, and neutral questioning. In various forms, the workshop has been presented to about thirty groups of participants in Canada and the United States, numbering some nine hundred librarians and library assistants in public, academic, and special libraries, and community information centres.

We call this workshop "How to Find Out What People Really Want to Know" although privately we think of it as "Why Didn't You Say So in the First Place?" Both these titles acknowledge the phenomenon, familiar to practising librarians, that users often ask initial questions that bear little resemblance to what it is they really want to know. We have asked workshop participants for examples from their own experience of cases in which the real question has turned out to be different from the question as initially presented. Here are some of the examples offered: the initial question (in a school library) was "Do you have a biography of Catherine the Great?" but the user wanted information on Mennonites in Russia for a school paper (because someone had told her that Mennonites were a big problem during the reign of Catherine the Great, she thought that biographies of Catherine would discuss Mennonites). The initial question was "Where are your encyclopedias?" but the user wanted to find out about the availability of jobs in Australia because she wanted to go there. The initial question (in a very large library) was "How extensive is your library?" but the user wanted a book on wedding etiquette that would tell him what he should do as best man at a wedding. The initial question was "Do you have a formula on noise decibels?" but the user wanted to make a complaint to City Hall about noisy trucks speeding past her house. The initial question was "Do you have a copy of the Ocala, Florida newspaper?" but the user wanted to know whether Ocala, Florida had a car rental agency that he could contact.

Users, apparently, often don't understand what the librarian needs to know before she can answer their information needs most efficiently. It sometimes seems that the user is like the unhelpful witness in the murder story who doesn't tell the detective the crucial clue until it is almost too late, on the grounds that he didn't think there was any importance to that detail about the barking dog (or the postman coming early or the clock that runs slow). The librarian, like the good detective, has to know what questions to ask. Users will not volunteer information that they do not perceive as relevant. Fortunately, librarians who realize that they cannot answer the question without knowing more about its context can develop effective questioning techniques to ask for the information they need. In the workshop, we emphasize two skills that can be learned by librarians and can be incorporated into their repertoire for negotiating the reference interview: open questioning and neutral questioning.[8]

OPEN QUESTIONING

Most readers will be familiar with definitions for open and closed questions. Whereas an open question allows the user to respond in her own terms, a closed question limits responses to one of several presented options: yes or no; this or that; A or B or C. A useful rule of thumb is that a question beginning with Is, Was, Do, or Does is very likely to be a closed question. Librarians find it easy to ask closed questions,[9] as the following example would suggest:

User:	Do you have anything on computers?
Librarian:	Do you need something to take home or do you want to use it in the library? [Closed]
User:	Oh, something to take home.
Librarian:	Do you want mainframes or microcomputers? [Other likely closed questions are: Do you want hardware or software? Do you want something on how to program a computer or do you want to know how computers work?]
User:	Well, I'm not sure.
Librarian:	Have you checked the catalogue? [Closed]

These questions are like the ones on multiple choice examinations or structured questionnaires. The respondent is allowed to choose from the answers provided but from no others. Researchers posing closed questions on questionnaires conduct pretests to make sure that the range of answers provided is exhaustive and does not leave out anything important. But librarians who ask closed questions are in the position of guessing. They play Twenty Questions: Is it American or Canadian? Is it nineteenth cenury or twentieth century? Is it this? Is it that? With closed questions, the questioner takes the initiative in selecting the aspects of the topic to be considered. The librarian who asks closed questions gets to choose the conversational ground. And the ground chosen turns out, more often than not, to be home territory for the librarians: questions about how the user's request fits into the library's system for organizing and disseminating knowledge. Hence, when the user asks for something on publishing, the librarian may ask, "Do you want a magazine article or do you want addresses of publishers?" or "Is this for a school project?"

Asking closed questions at the beginning of the reference interview almost always involves the librarian in making assumptions. Sometimes, when questions such as "Is this something for your child?" turn out to be based on false assumptions, the patron may be offended. More often, closed questions involve the librarian in making an assumption of the following sort: this aspect of topic X is most important to *me* and therefore it must be the most important thing for the user too. Such assumptions, when they are mistaken (as so often they are), lead to questions that are not salient for the user and hence not readily answered. Most librarians can recall the frustration of a reference interview that has developed along these lines: "You're looking for a song. Do you know if it was written recently?" (No, I'm afraid I don't), "Was it written by an American?" (Sorry, I don't know), "Is it a popular song?" (I think so. No, I'm not sure. I'm terribly sorry. I guess I shouldn't really bother you about this. I can come back later.) As this example illustrates, catechising the user with questions he can't answer may make him feel inadequate, as if he ought to have researched the topic far more thoroughly before bothering the librarian.

It appears that asking closed questions has two effects of consequence for the interview: closed questions restrict the user's response; and second they restrict the response to aspects of the topic that concern the librarian but not necessarily the user. A further characteristic of closed questions is that they do not invite users to talk freely. Usually they elicit very short answers. Since sometimes short answers are wanted, there is a place for closed questions in the reference interview. Closed questions are effective in focussing wandering conversation and can also be useful, at the end of the interview, to verify that the librarian understands what really is needed. But at the beginning it is usually preferable to get users talking, and this can be done best by asking open questions. The user looking for a song in the above example would probably be able to say something helpful in response to an open question like: "What can you tell me about this song?" Asking open questions encourages the user to say in his or her own words what is wanted.

One way of identifying open questions is to look at their beginnings: questions starting with Who, What Why, Where, and When are apt to be open. So, for example, open questions suitable for the user who wanted information on computers would include:

— What type of computer interests you?
— What sort of thing are you looking for?
— Perhaps if you could tell me more about what interests you, I could make some suggestions. [Not strictly speaking a question but it functions as a question]

An open question does not limit the range of responses and it does not impose any assumptions on the user. What it boils down to is that instead of making assumptions and guessing (Is it this? Is it that?), the librarian is essentially saying, though not in so many words, "Please tell me what is important *to you* about this topic." Open questioning may reassure a user who has been asking questions as if information were an impersonal commodity that it is OK to ground his question in the context of his own particular concerns.

After this explanation of the value (especially during the initial part of the reference interview) of open questions, workshop participants sometimes protest that all this would take too long: they are busy people who must get to the point quickly without hearing user's life stories. It should therefore be emphasized that open questions don't take longer; usually they save time in the long run. One librarian, reporting her success with using open questions, said that a user asked, "Do you have cookbooks from different lands?" An open question elicited the further information, "I have a grade seven project on special Christmas recipes and I'm supposed to do *bûche de Noël.*" The librarian's summary of the transaction: "We had two books for her in one minute." Open questions save time because they give users the chance to focus immediately on whatever is important to *them.* Guessing with a series of closed questions that also may be making assumptions takes longer and can be frustrating for both the librarian and the user. Open questions, on the other hand, are questions that users can answer because they allow users to select the conversational ground. Therefore they are questions that encourage the user to talk.

NEUTRAL QUESTIONS

With open questions, we can get the user talking. But what was said earlier about the contextualized nature of people's questions implies that librarians have to do more than just get users talking. They have to get them to talk about the context of the question. Sometimes asking an open question is all that is needed to encourage the user to talk about contexts, but often users need more guidance. They need to be told what information the librarian needs to know to do his job. A good way of guiding the reference interview along useful channels is to ask a special form of open question called by Brenda Dervin a neutral question.

For a question to be neutral, it must both be open *and* ask about some aspect of the context of the user's query. To explain this latter point, it is necessary to return to something said earlier about how users ask questions. We have been developing a model of the user as actively engaged in constructing his or her life. In the course of this everyday living, the user has gaps in understanding that must be filled in before she can do whatever it is she is trying to do. There are three elements here that together make up the question's context: (1) the user's *situation,* (2) the *gaps* in her understanding, and (3) *uses* or what she would like to do as a result of having this gap filled. In order fully to understand the question, the librarian needs to know all three of these elements. So, to go back to the user who asked where the travel books are kept, the librarian needs to know the situation (the user is going to Hawaii next week), the gap (she wants to know the temperature typical of Hawaii this time of year), and how the information would be used (it will help her pack appropriate clothes).

Suppose a user asks, "Do you have anything about crime?" The librarian can ask *closed* questions, that involve making assumptions and that invite short answers: "Do you want criminal law? Do you want a crime story? Do you want statistics?" The librarian can ask an *open* question, that encourages the user to talk: "What are you interested in?" "What more can you tell me about your question?" Or the librarian can ask a *neutral* question focussed on the situation, gap, or use such as "What have you done so far about this question?" "What would you like to know about crime?" or "How would you like the information to help you?" The user answering the neutral question might respond, "I want the address of the Crime Writers of America" or "I need statistics of the crime rate in Florida over the past ten years." Following up with a second neutral question, "And how would *that* help you?" will elicit more of the context of the question: "I want to write them to find out the name of a book they published giving tips for writing mystery stories" or "It's for a speech I have to make for my communication class."

Workshop participants sometimes report reservations about asking for the context of a question when the situation might turn out to be personal and/or embarrassing. Potentially embarrassing situations include, unfortunately, most of the human situations in which people desperately need help: situations of bereavement, loss, serious illness, and approaching death; situations of needing sexual information; of coping with economic failure, and so on. Something worth asking parenthetically is this: whose embarrassment are we as librarians really concerned about—the user's embarrassment in revealing something personal about himself or our own in hearing it? If it is our own, then we will be more comfortable not asking neutral questions and simply saying to the user, "We have some materials on crime over there and if you just look through those you might find something." But if it is the user's embarrassment that solely concerns us, it may be reassuring to remember that neutral questions leave the user in control. In response to a neutral question, the user can say as much or as little as he chooses. He can say, "My son has just been charged with a crime and I want to find out about the Young Offenders Act." But he doesn't have to. He need not reveal any more about his situation than he feels comfortable revealing.

Another obstacle to asking neutral questions is that, because it means thinking about reference in a new way, it requires an initial commitment. Asking closed questions comes naturally, participants at workshops often tell us, but asking open or neutral questions seems somehow artificial. An answer to this may be that any new skill takes practise before it can be used with confidence. Some librarians have reported good success with starting by asking just one neutral question such as "If you could have the perfect material (book, article, help with your project), what would it be?" After they feel comfortable asking their one question, they can expand their repertoire. Eventually this repertoire consists of a set of neutral questions, each of which focusses the user's response on some aspect of the context of their request.

A final objection to asking neutral questions must be acknowledged. As one librarian astutely put it, after you have asked neutral questions and found out what the person really wants to know, you are stuck doing something about it. It is as if the stakes are raised once you think about the user's question not as a request for information as commodity but as a question with a context in a human life. Obligations come with the recognition that the answers we give can either help or fail to help users to construct their lives. Now it will be harder simply to say, "Our encyclopedias are over there."

NOTES

1. These reference questions were collected on tape by Patricia Dewdney in the course of her data collection for a doctoral dissertation undertaken at the School of Library and Information Science at the University of Western Ontario. We know more than usually is known about the context of these questions because follow-up interviews were conducted in which the users were asked, among other things, how they had hoped the information requested would help them.

2. Michael Reddy, "The Conduit Metaphor," in A. Ortony, ed. *Metaphor and Thought* (New York: Cambridge, 1979).

3. For a fuller discussion of this idea, see George Lakoff and Mark Johnson, "Conceptual Metaphor in Everyday Language," in *Philosophical Perspectives on Metaphor,* ed. Mark Johnson (Minneapolis: University of Minnesota Press, 1981).

4. Lakoff and Johnson, pp. 292-293.

5. See, for example, Terrence Crowley and Thomas Childers, *Information Service in Public Libraries: Two Studies* (Metuchen, N.J.: Scarecrow, 1971) and Marcia J. Myers and Jassim M. Jirjees, *The Accuracy of Telephone Reference/Information Services in Academic Libraries* (Metuchen, N.J.: Scarecrow, 1983).

6. A study, *How Libraries Help*, by Brenda Dervin and Benson Fraser (a research report published by the Department of Communication, University of the Pacific, Stockton, California, October, 1985) reported the results of a telephone questionnaire administered to 1005 randomly selected Californians, stratified by county. The 81% of respondents who could recall their last library visit answered a question about how that library visit had helped them as follows: slightly more than 90% said they got support/emotional control; 89% said they found directions/got skills/reached a goal; 83% got ideas/understandings; 72% got happiness/pleasure; 54% got rest/relaxation; and 30-34% said they felt connected/not alone (p. 11).

7. Material for this workshop has been adapted from numerous studies of human communication. Neutral questioning is a technique developed by Dr. Brenda Dervin, School of Communications, University of Washington. The microskills of avoiding premature diagnosis, acknowledgement, and open questioning are derived from microcounseling, a communication model first tested in a library context by Dr. Elaine Jennerich at the University of Pittsburgh. We have modified these models as a result of our own research and teaching experiences.

8. For a helpful article on open questioning, see Geraldine B. King, "The reference interview: open and closed questions," *RQ*, 12, 2(Winter 1972), 157-60. Neutral questioning is a technique developed by Dr. Brenda Dervin and taught in her workshop "Turning Public Libraries Around." A full discussion of the theory and technique of neutral questioning will become available with the publication of the article, "Neutral Questioning: A New Approach to the Reference Interview," by Brenda Dervin and Patricia Dewdney.

9. Mary Jo Lynch has reported that 90 per cent of the questions asked by librarians in her study were closed questions while only 8 per cent were open ("Reference Interviews in Public Libraries," *Library Quarterly*, 48, 2, April 1978, 131). It should be noted that the example that Lynch gives of an open question "Have you found anything at all?" is technically a closed question, answerable by yes or no. However, it is likely to be interpreted by the user as a polite equivalent to the open question, "What have you found?"

The Unexamined Interview
Is Not Worth Having

Sandra M. Naiman

When I was doing the research for my dissertation, I came across a reference to a very long article I wanted to read. Unable to borrow it, not wanting to have it photocopied, I drove to the nearest college that subscribed to the journal in which it had appeared. The woman behind the circulation desk may not have been a librarian, but she was the only visible person in the library. "Could you tell me where you keep your bound periodicals?" I asked. "You mean you want me to show you how to use the card catalog," she retorted, zooming out from behind the desk to the card catalog.

"No, I do not want you to show me how to use the card catalog," I wanted to say, "I AM A LIBRARIAN!" Instead, I thanked her for locating the call number of the periodical I wanted to examine. She may have considered that a successful interview, but I was prepared to go to extraordinary lengths to avoid asking her another question.

That incident reenforced my belief that the most important factor in a reference interview is the librarian's empathy. Empathy requires the ability to suspend one's own frame of reference and the willingness to enter into the client's frame of reference (which includes the experiences he has had with people in general and librarians in particular). It would have helped if the person I asked about the bound periodicals had suspected that I had never been in that library and had no reason to expect that the periodicals were cataloged. Librarians sometimes have a disconcertingly elitist attitude toward directional questions. Most people would not hesitate to ask the world's most famous brain surgeon where the bathroom was, if the occasion presented itself.

Sandra M. Naiman is subject specialist in English and American literature at Northern University Library, DeKalb, IL 60115. Previously, she was a reference librarian at Elmhurst Public Library in Elmhurst, Illinois, and her observations are based on that experience.

EMPATHY IS EXHAUSTING

Empathy thrives on energy, patience, imagination, tolerance, and a high degree of self-awareness. In order to suspend one's own frame of reference, one has to have a clear picture of what is included in it. A librarian's includes more information about library collections and how they are organized than most users will ever want to know (and still never enough). A librarian also knows, and takes for granted unless she makes a deliberate, ongoing effort not to do so, the idiosyncrasies of her particular library, such as that the library owns millions of microforms which are not listed in the card catalog or that the very latest books are shelved apart from the rest of the collection. It is exhausting to keep all the possibilities for confusion in mind all the time, but it is essential to try. Many of the decisions librarians, or administrators, make about collections are expedient rather than logical, and therefore we are doubly bound to suspend our own expectations to try to learn what the expectations of our users are. This involves shifting back and forth between a "tabula rasa" mode of apperception and an "encyclopediac" mode, and it requires energy, good will, and practice. What helps? It helps me to use other libraries and analyze my experiences in them. It also helps to be involved always in some kind of personal research, even if it is preparing for a class. To the extent that librarians fall into the habit of making remarks such as, "You might find that information in *Monthly Labor Review*" without actually looking in *MLR* to see what it contains and how the material is organized, we can become increasingly remote from the problems and frustrations of our clients, who may legitimately suspect that we are not wholeheartedly committed to a lifetime of learning. We really do need to be committed to that.

KNOW THYSELF

As a result of analyzing my own behavior as a library user, I have greater insight into the reluctance of my patrons to tell me, up front, exactly what they want. I found, for example, that if I wanted to locate a specific short story by Henry James over the phone, I asked, "Do you have Henry James's collected stories?" (And that woman is a librarian!) Forced to account for my own behavior, I concluded I must have involuntarily assumed this was the most efficient question, since it would be easy to answer, and it would be easy for me to locate the story if I had the collected stories in hand. On the other hand, if I asked for a specific story and was told, "No, we don't have that story," I would not know whether to believe it, knowing there are many possible sources for a short story and knowing nothing about the quality of the search. Furthermore, if I asked for a specific title, I might forget to indicate it was a short story, and then be embarrassed later to admit this. All this ambiguity can be avoided by asking for Henry James's collected stories, so I conclude that for a patron, that probably really is more efficient.

Of course, it is not efficient for the librarian to get up, walk to the card catalog, walk back, and then discover that the patron wants only one story. Alternatively, she can ask cheerfully, "Do you want some particular story by Henry James?" but this involves some risk-taking. The patron may really want the collected stories; he may be impatient to have his question answered with a question. My experience is that it pays to devote some thought to how I can gracefully share my own needs with the patron. I try to introduce a different model of efficiency: "In case we don't have Henry James's collected stories, is there anything else you'd like for me to look for while I'm up?" and I am no longer surprised if he replies: "Yes, do you have *The One-Minute Manager*?"

WHY? WHY? WHY?

There are cultural constraints on questioning. Somewhere (in *Green Hills of Africa*, I think) Hemingway commented that in the environment in which he was raised, it was impolite to ask questions. I grew up in a similar environment; therefore, while it has been difficult to learn the right questions to ask, it has been even harder to internalize the absolute necessity of asking questions at all. Too much emphasis has been placed in discussions of the reference interview on asking, "Why?" "*Why* do you want this information?" "*How* are you going to use this information?" From the patrons' point of view, why he wants the information and how he plans to use it are his concern, not the librarian's. It has helped me significantly to convert the question into a statement about my own needs: "Hmm . . . I think I could help you better if I understood how you're going to use this information." This shift has several advantages:

1. It avoids answering a question with a question. The danger in using questions to clarify a request is that "Helpees often feel interrogated, and, as a result, threatened."[1] In particular, "why" sounds like a question about the patron's motivation. While questions may put a stranger on the defensive, he is more likely to accept a statement about one's own needs in the situation. Moreover, it is easier to make a statement in a calm, friendly manner than to ask a question.
2. It furnishes the librarian's motive for prolonging the interview instead of rushing off to answer the question ("I need time to understand this better").
3. It clearly conveys the message: "I want to help you."
4. It effectively reverses our roles; in effect, I ask for his help, thereby involving him in the transaction. The ball is in his court. From being a passive consumer of my services, he is encouraged to take some responsibility for how the dialogue turns out.

Some of my most successful interviews have ended in giving a patron almost no "information" at all. For example, a student recently came to me with an art history assignment that resembled a treasure hunt. I had some reservations about whether I should give him "the answer," but I didn't know the answer, so I told him that. Spontaneously, with complete sincerity, I said something like: "I honestly don't know the answer to that question. If I had to answer it, I think I would start by looking in some bibliographies (here I took some down). It might help to consult a book like *Timetables of History*, too. If I understand the question, you need to identify a person who flourished in a particular place at a particular time." Weeks later, I met that student outside the library, and he stopped to reveal with satisfaction that he had found the answer to "that question." Although he made a point of thanking me for "getting him started," it was clear that he was proud of himself for finding the answer, as he was entitled to be. Whether this strategy would be equally appropriate with a professor of art history the reader is invited to decide.

One reason I consider that interview must have been successful is that the student voluntarily renewed our relationship. Another reason I feel good about it is that I am satisfied I did no harm. I think I came across the way I want to be perceived—not, certainly, as a person who knows everything, very far from that, but as a person who values knowledge, is willing to make an effort to acquire it, and enjoys sharing the efforts other people make to acquire knowledge.

We may have done a disservice to ourselves as well as our clients by the extent to which we have carried the notion that if you want information, all you have to do is call the library. We may have trivialized the pursuit of knowledge. Is it really so difficult to "stump the librarian"? How many three-year-old children know how to read? How many people have seriously considered not registering for military service? Do elderly people live longer in nursing homes affiliated with religious institutions than in secular nursing homes? Most librarians still do not have access to online information, and I suspect their patrons can stump them without even trying to.

ASK AN EXPERT

Lawrence M. Brammer points out that "Behaving like an "expert" . . . is important to the helping relationship . . . helpers must consider how they are perceived . . . and what kinds of models they are presenting." But what behavior is perceived as "expert"? Brammer cites some intriguing research which indicates that helpers who were regarded by students as "experts" treated students "as equals, with friendly attentive behavior. They spoke with confidence and liveliness." Paradoxically, "less experienced and less professionally trained" helpers were often viewed as more "expert" because of their "more enthusiastic responsiveness."[2] These results bear thinking about. Evidently it is more important to be regarded by our clients as friendly, self-confident, trustworthy, and dependable than to be regarded as "walking encyclopedias." Besides, the behaviors involved in being friendly, self-confident, trustworthy, and dependable are useful in all areas of our lives, so they are well worth practicing. To succeed, however, we need to avoid promising more than we can deliver and making claims that we cannot substantiate.

ELIMINATE THE NEGATIVE

The worst thing that can happen is not that the patron may discover the librarian's ignorance. People can usually cope well with the discovery that the librarian doesn't know something, unless it is accompanied by the implication that she doesn't care, either. It may even be constructive, especially in a public library, to be able to perceive the librarian as somewhat ignorant, since it makes her more like a peer and less like an authority figure. Patrons have sometimes blossomed when, completely baffled by a question, I have temporized by replying, "Well, tell me what you already know about it." The worst thing that is likely to happen, in my experience, is that the librarian says, "That information isn't available" or "You're never going to find that out." I have been told that by a librarian before finding the information by myself a few minutes later; no doubt other patrons (maybe some of my own) have had the same experience. That undermines trust far more than a confession of ignorance would. Since it is notoriously difficult to admit defeat gracefully, we should rehearse doing it, and we should avoid saying "never." To assert that information doesn't exist implies a degree of certainty that we have no right to claim. If a librarian can't answer a question, she can at least share the gift of her own humanity by saying sincerely, "I wish I could answer that question, but I don't know how." Better still, no doubt, is a sincere offer of further effort: "Right now I can't come up with an answer, but I'd like to try again later. Would you leave your name and phone number so I can let you know if I find something?" or "I'd like to call somebody for help with this question; can you wait, or do you want me to call you?" To practice that kind of openness with patrons, however, requires sturdy self-esteem and a supportive environment.

GETTING TO CARNEGIE HALL

Writers about self-hypnosis claim that the reason it is so easy (they say it is easy) is that most people are in something like a trance much of the time—"on automatic pilot," as it were. To test this idea, one has only to picture how a doctor behaves when he is consulted about an upper respiratory infection. Some doctors act so bored that they make their patients feel guilty. The bane of reference work for an inexperienced librarian is that virtually nothing can be done "on automatic pilot." (This is the beauty of reference work for an experienced reference librarian.)

If only library users would make a habit of consistently asking questions like, "How many soldiers died in World War I?" "Who said, 'To the victors belong the spoils'?'' ''When was the first dirigible launched?'' for several hours every day, new librarians could readily develop the speed, efficiency, and self-assurance they ought to have in dealing with questions such as these, and reference desk duty would not be as taxing and inaccurate as it is. During my first two years as a reference librarian, I worked in a very small library which was not being bombarded by ''real'' reference questions, and it seemed to me that I never received the same question twice. Every question, therefore, became a new crisis (''Will I be able to answer this question?'' ''Where will I look?'' ''*Is* there an answer to this question?''). My mental picture of striding purposefully to the reference collection, seizing unerringly on one book out of hundreds, opening it to the correct page, and handing ''the right answer'' to the patron disintegrated in face of a reality that was more like being a contestant on ''The $100,000 Question.'' Fortunately, the patrons were very supportive.

The model for improving in an activity, of course, is to practice it, but this presupposes a continuity that reference work in the real world tends not to have. The keys on a piano are invariably in the same place, and, individually at least, always sound pretty much the same, but reference questions have an astonishing capacity for uniqueness. As it is not even the case that people become better piano players by playing the piano five days a week, it is impossible to credit the idea that people automatically become better reference librarians as a result of doing reference work.

DEVELOPING SELF-CONFIDENCE

Since it is plainly impossible to train our patrons to ask us questions we can answer effortlessly, library school has to do this. Following the directions for an assignment to look up answers in almanacs and yearbooks is patently unlike dealing with a stranger with a question. An oral drill would be more like it. Students need opportunities to practice the skills involved in reference work, and they need role models to imitate. Library schools should try harder to arrange for students of reference to intern alongside experienced reference librarians. What other profession (or skilled trade) does not have its recruits practice their skills in a supervised arena? Internship would have the added advantage of putting the experienced librarian on her mettle to analyze, articulate, perhaps even improve her own behavior. Why is it so rare (in my experience, it is) to hear people agree that somebody is "a great reference librarian"? One hears that Harry knows everything about tax shelters, or Pete can back a sixteen-wheeler into the garage with his eyes closed, or Sam can apply wallpaper so that a seam never shows; George knows "all about books"; but how often does one hear that "Rosemary sure knows how to answer a reference question"? Why is that?

It is almost axiomatic that a profession, or a skilled trade, is an activity whose practitioners are certified or licensed on the basis of their demonstrated proficiency. Other professions can and do agree that there is a basic core of information and/or skills that their members must have to begin with. It would be unacceptable for a doctor, no matter what his specialty, not to be able to recognize the symptoms of an upper respiratory infection. It ought to be unacceptable for a patron to know more about the *World Almanac* or the *O.E.D.* or *Bartlett's Familiar Quotations* than a librarian knows. Writing in 1979, John Larsen reported that "today no practicing reference librarian or reference instructor is actively advocating the development of a core list of reference sources to be used in all library schools to train new reference professionals. . . . At present more than half (55.66 percent) of the 2,014 titles appearing on reference course syllabi or booklists are listed by only one library school."[3] I have no reason to imagine that the diversity has decreased; I have never been in a group of librarians who were willing to reach a consensus on the indispensable reference sources. Yet why should this be the case, if we are professionals? The dazzling unpredictability of reference questions should not lead us to fantasize that we have to be equally prepared for everything; that is impossible.

There should be enough rehearsal and enough redundancy built into the experience of training for reference work that the librarian graduates with a genuine mastery of a predictable corpus of information and with a repertoire of behaviors (including knowledge of her own values and biases) such that she will have, and deserve to have, a significant measure of genuine self-esteem and self-confidence. This will communicate itself to library users, who will as a result find it easier to approach librarians and to trust them.

The agonized, organized self-doubt of librarians is too well documented for me to document it here. Many of the behaviors of librarians that make us unapproachable, unreliable, inconsistent and glib can be imputed to inadequate training and anxiety. While anxiety is an understandable response to the unpredictability and the conflicts of reference desk duty, I think it can be significantly mitigated if a new librarian is deservedly confident of her ability to answer accurately and efficiently a predictable range of questions and to accept responsibility for what she communicates to library users. Even if she has to wait months or years for some of the questions she is prepared to answer in two minutes flat, she should know those answers so well that she will be able to remember them years later, and she should know that she knows them, and bye and bye (or sooner, if reference departments will publicly describe what services they will perform accurately), patrons will know what to expect. Many of the communication problems in reference interviews can be attributed to the fact that patrons do not know what they can reasonably, legitimately expect, and neither do librarians.

Freed from some of the anxiety of being a contestant on a quiz show, fortified with an earned reserve of mastery and self-confidence, the librarian will have more available psychic energy for negotiating the reference interview. Available psychic energy is a *sine qua non*. The patron approaching the reference desk may have a question one has never heard before and will never hear again. The potential for failure is omnipresent. In addition, the patron may be tense or suspicious or confused or hostile or all of the above, and the librarian should be able to recognize those feelings without being thrown off balance or reflecting them back, so she needs to be a reasonably stable person with a reasonably satisfying personal life. Of course, the question the patron asks may be the question he really wants an answer to, or it may be a wild stab in the dark. This fact is reported repeatedly in the professional literature without being accompanied, in my experience, by an adequate acknowledgment of the psychic cost involved in performing an activity that is routinely non-routine and resists being reduced to a routine.

SHOULD EVERY QUESTION BE NEGOTIATED?

Should old acquaintance be forgot? How does the reference librarian know when the client is asking for what he really wants? I wish I knew for sure. On a busy reference desk it is not possible to negotiate every question even if it is desirable, and it probably is not; and my completely unscientific observation is that people who attempt to negotiate every question develop mechanical, stereotyped behaviors that are unattractive, yet it is probably too much to expect a librarian to react to every user with unstudied artfulness. I engage in a pretty steady state of introspection that can be pretty painful at times, asking myself: why did you say that? how did the other person respond to that? I find it helpful to remember interviews as well as I can so that I can analyze them later, trying to identify the unsuccessful aspects as well as the successful ones. I also try to remember, when other people help me, what they say or do that seems to be particularly effective or that makes me "feel good."

The issue is complicated by the possibility that the patron is just "testing the water." One of my most illuminating interviews was with a patron who asked me for consumer information about vacuum cleaners, to which I spontaneously replied, "Gee, I'm glad you asked that question! I've been thinking about getting a new vacuum cleaner, and now I'll find out about it while I'm helping you." A couple of weeks later, the patron returned to the library with details about the prices of different models at different stores. This was deeply touching, but it also made me examine my assumptions. I would have assumed that it was not "professional" to imply to a patron that I had a personal motive for finding an answer to his question; but when I thought about it, I realized that a personal motive makes my helpfulness more credible. Besides, "It is not easy to receive help,"[4] especially from a stranger, and it may be presumptuous to trust a patron to have faith in the librarian's altruism. Since then, I have made a conscious effort to imply, whenever I sincerely can, that I have some personal reason to be interested in the questions I receive, and this seems to be helpful.

There are some clues that negotiation is necessary, of course. It is improbable, for example, that anybody really wants to know "all" about a subject. I remember someone who asked for "everything" about Kurt Vonnegut—"biography, criticism, the names of all his books and what they are about, all the prizes he's won"—and left the library a few minutes later, smiling broadly, with a photocopy of the *Masterplots* summary of *Slaughterhouse Five*. I doubt whether it would have helped to ask him why he wanted to know everything about Kurt Vonnegut. My initial response was to take down a summary of *Cat's Cradle* and say, "You might be interested in reading about some of Vonnegut's novels while I'm looking for the information you want."

One of my memorable failures to negotiate a reference question occurred when a very patient gentleman asked me: "How many people in the United States work crossword puzzles?" Alas, I was deceived by the syntax into thinking I should be able to jump up and answer that question the way I would jump up and answer the question, "How many practicing physicians are there in the United States?" First I thought of the *Encyclopedia of Associations* and the list of clubs in the *World Almanac*, in case there was a society of crossword enthusiasts whose membership I could ascertain. Then I thought of looking in the card catalog, in case we might have a book on the history of crossword puzzles that might begin, as such a book often does, with some intimation of great significance such as "It is estimated that twenty million Americans regularly work crossword puzzles." Then I thought of *Ayer's, etc.*, in case there might be periodicals for crossword fans; and as soon as I thought of *Ayer's*, I remembered that there is a crossword puzzle in the newspaper every day; how would one know how many people work it? At that point, I realized I have to negotiate the question, if only to find out how accurate the answer needed to be, so I told the patron what was going through my mind and asked him why he wanted to know. He replied that he wanted to investigate the market for a crossword puzzle game. Within seconds I had found a relevant analysis in Standard and Poor's *Industry Surveys*.

If I could relive that encounter, I would respond (after asking myself: "Who would collect that information and why?"): "What an interesting question! What made you think of it?" On the other hand, it would obviously be fatuous and rude to respond to the question: "What is the population of Kentucky?" by saying: "What an interesting question! What made you think of it?" Unfortunately, the substantive difference may just be that it is so easy to picture sources for the population of Kentucky! Probably an online search would turn up statistics on crossword puzzle fans. Information sources have proliferated so rapidly, so much information has been collected and stored, it is so easy to retrieve information from a data base and so difficult to be aware of its existence, much less remember its location, that it is becoming increasingly difficult for me to imagine doing reference work without access to an online data base. Yet that raises questions about cost that still have not been answered and cannot be answered without an "agonizing reappraisal" of our assumptions about reference service.

In the meantime, everybody has the experience of finding the answer to an apparently straightforward question such as "What is the population of Kentucky?" only to have the patron say, or otherwise convey by his lack of enthusiasm, "Actually, that wasn't what I wanted to know." My "quick and dirty" way of dealing with this dilemma is that if I can find the answer instantly, I find it and then study the patron's reaction. If I don't know how to find the answer instantly, sometimes I temporize by saying something like: "Well, I think I can find that information, but it may take a while." My experience is that the prospect of waiting for an answer often inspires the patron to refine the question.

Saying almost anything that is relevant to what the patron said may inspire him to refine the question. However, not only does one have to listen very attentively, but one has to focus on how the patron's words can be translated into information the system can supply. Because it is important and valuable to be friendly, it is also necessary to guard against having a conversation instead of a reference interview. This also requires practice; the more open the librarian is, the more she risks losing control of the direction of the interview. If the patron says, "I want some information on Lou Gehrig's disease," it is not relevant to respond, "Oh, yes, my uncle had that." Asking "Why do you want information on Lou Gehrig's disease?" may elicit the response, "My daughter has just been diagnosed as having it," which will color the rest of the transaction substantially.

It would be possible to say facetiously that one should never ask a question unless one is fully prepared to hear the answer, but the fact is that patrons sometimes reveal startling personal information, such as "I am an ex-convict and I want to know whether I can vote," without being asked for it. Some people can deal with personal information more easily than other people can; at the very least, it helps to be aware of one's own strengths and limitations in dealing with personal information, especially if it is painful.

PARAPHRASING

Paraphrasing the patron's request can be useful. Its most obvious advantage is that it gives the patron feedback and gives him immediate gratification in the form of evidence that the librarian is listening to him, while the librarian has time to search her mental files for a match between the collection and the request. Its most obvious disadvantage is that it can be very annoying to listen to a paraphrase. I try to paraphrase in terms of possible information sources. Thus, if a patron says, "I want a list of the car dealers within a fifteen-mile radius of Elmhurst," and I examine my mental files and fail to find an object that matches this, I may say: "A list of the car dealers in

DuPage county would not help you because some of them are more than fifteen miles away and some of the ones that are less than fifteen miles away are in Cook County." The patron is at least reassured that I am paying attention to him, and at best he will review this statement thoughtfully to see whether his felt need is being described and may even decide to revise his request. If he says, "Yes, that's right," I may introduce some variation such as: "And a list of the Ford dealers would not help you, because you want to know all the dealers." To this he may say, "Yes, that's right," or he may say, "No, actually, what I'm interested in is Chevrolet dealers." Since he started over, I might start over, too: "You want to know all the Chevrolet dealers within a fifteen-mile radius of Elmhurst," to which he may reply, "Yes, that's right" or "No, actually, I just want to know the closest ones." Whatever he says, by this time at least one of us should have realized that it is simple to figure out what car dealers are within a fifteen-mile radius of Elmhurst even though I don't have a list of them.

IS THE CUSTOMER ALWAYS RIGHT?

Now comes the sticky part. Suppose the patron really does want a list of the car dealers within a fifteen-mile radius of Elmhurst, and I can't furnish it but I can explain how to figure out who they are, and suppose he is unwilling to do that. This kind of impasse is not uncommon. The library user may categorically refuse to modify his request so that it meets the constraints of the system. He may insist on having material that he can take out of the library, when the material that most effectively matches his request is programmed to stay in the library. He may insist on having his answer "packaged" in exactly the terms in which he raised it, whereas the librarian has been able to locate pieces of information in several sources. He may present a question that requires real research to find the answer, and he may be unwilling to do real research.

ARE WE DOING RESEARCH?

A perennial source of ambiguity is the line between reference work and research. What is the librarian supposed to say to a patron who calls on the phone with this request: "I am taking a graduate course in education, and I have to write a fifteen-page paper on computer-assisted instruction in elementary schools. I'll stop by this afternoon around 4:00 and pick up the material''? Exactly how is this different from responding to a patron who says simply, ''I need all the information I can get on computer-assisted instruction in elementary schools; I am a teacher''? The invidiousness of the question, ''Why?'' becomes quite apparent here, since it sounds like a question about motivation. If the patron's motive is to target a market for his products, is that more acceptable than writing a paper for a course? Why? If the patron is an inventor and he wants to design a new computer-assisted program, is that more acceptable? Why? What is the librarian supposed to do when a child calls with a question that constitutes his ''homework assignment''? What if his mother calls instead?

Is the patron entitled to place constraints on how the information is to be delivered to him? Librarians, in my experience, deny that he is. They want to take the position that their role is fulfilled when they have identified a likely source for the information or a way of figuring it out. The rest, they reason, should be the patron's responsibility. ''After all, it is his question.'' Yet their behavior is at clear variance with what they profess to believe, since it is obvious that sometimes they get up to find the answer, and sometimes they do not. How do they decide which to do? How should they decide?

Through the professional literature runs the refrain that only the patron can say when his request for information has been satisfied. Does this mean that he can hold out for a neatly typed list of car dealers within a fifteen-mile radius of Elmhurst?

Unless questions such as these are addressed in a reference service policy, different clients will continue to get different levels of service from different librarians at different times. Librarians will experience confusion and conflict, and library users will remain confused about what to expect and what to ask for.

Our advertising implies that we can do everything, while surveys of our performance indicate that we are right only half the time when we are asked factual questions in a value-free manner by people who are poised to offer immaculate motives. The cognitive dissonance is unbearable. We promise pie in the sky and fail to deliver hot pizza. Is it realistic, for example, to demand that libraries provide professional reference service every moment they are open? Of course, it is desirable; so is pie in the sky. Why do we demand from ourselves more hours of service than physicians provide, or lawyers, or automobile mechanics? Are our services more essential? Surely they are not, or we have a fantastic case for retroactive wages. The conundrum is that whether our services are that essential or not, they are difficult and challenging to perform. Librarians need to recharge their batteries; they need occasions for personal and professional growth; they need regular opportunities to associate with other professionals who have similar values, skills, ethics— who subscribe to the same "code." The more isolated they are, the more they need these opportunities, and the harder it is to absent themselves from the reference desk.

I know why it is desirable to provide 72 hours of reference service every week, but I wonder whether our insistence on doing it reflects a lack of confidence in our services, rather than the reverse. Psychiatrists do not have office hours during the night, even though three o'clock in the morning is probably the time people are most likely to feel the need for a psychiatrist. If someone has an important felt need for information, he can probably defer gratification of that need the way he defers gratification in other areas of his life. If he were convinced that our services are valuable, he would be prepared to wait. If we were convinced our services are valuable, we would be comfortable about asking him to wait.

To a disturbing extent, I think, our problems can be attributed to lack of confidence. Library schools ought to address this lack. They should be able to say truly, when a student graduates, "This person knows this and that and has these skills and those attitudes." Truly well trained reference librarians can then become role models for people out in the field. Our profession does not have enough good role models.

Whether or not one believes that librarianship is a "helping profession," it is quite clear that many of the skills and characteristics required from good reference librarians are required in the "helping professions." They have learned how to teach, and learn, those skills, and we can learn how, too. Self-confidence is high on the list. Accountability is another key concern. In the helping professions, "most authorities view this issue as a shared responsibility,"[5] but until we have become more specific and more consistent about how much responsibility we will assume for the outcomes of reference interviews, it is unreasonable to expect our clients to take any responsibility for them.

NOTES

1. Lawrence M. Brammer, *The Helping Relationship: Process and Skills*, 3rd ed. Englewood Cliffs, NJ: Prentice-Hall, Inc., 1985, p. 50.

2. Brammer, p. 28.

3. John C. Larsen, "Information Sources Currently Studied in General Reference Courses," *RQ* 18:4 (Summer 1979) 341-48, rptd. in *Reference and Information Services: A New Reader*, comp. by Bill Katz and Anne Clifford (Metuchen, NJ: Scarecrow Press, 1982), pp. 407, 414.

4. Brammer, p. 49.

5. Brammer, p. 30.

The Myth
of the Reference Interview

It is an obvious truism to every librarian who works at an information or reference desk that inquirers seldom ask at first for what they want.

Robert S. Taylor

There are times, in fact some claim more times than librarians are willing to admit, when a person asks a question—just a question, no more, no less.

Bill Katz

Most of the library users who put questions to the librarian know exactly what they need and ask for it clearly.

Denis Grogan

The amount of research done on the reference or information interview is staggering.[1] Innumerable commentators, from different fields, have mused, felt, discovered, theorized, opined, and suggested that library users are shy, confused, deceptive, or inarticulate, and they are therefore basically incapable of indicating their real needs. Beleaguered reference librarians are further distracted from their appointed tasks by authors who have insisted that although information is certainly important, creative impetus or experience is as well. Here patrons not only cannot formulate their needs, they also really do not know what they want. And so the librarian is called upon to appreciate "a personal gestalt" in an open-ended, creative session, analogous, apparently, to a stint with one's analyst.[2] All of this is compounded by those who note that the nonverbal aspects of communication are as important as the articulated query. Furthermore, the reference librarian too must be careful with

---

The author is Reference Librarian and Assistant Professor, Learning Resources Services, St. Cloud State University, St. Cloud, MN 56301.

facial expressions, head and hand gestures, and even make sympathetic clucking noises when appropriate![3] Nevertheless, it is virtually impossible to accept the assertion that sixty-five percent of the "social meaning" of a conversation is relayed nonverbally.[4] This means that the patrons' paralinguistic and kinesic responses are *twice* as important as their articulated queries. Furthermore, as Lewis Thomas points out,

> There may even be odorants that fire off receptors in our olfactory epithelia without our being conscious of smell, including signals exchanged involuntarily between human beings. Wiener has proposed, on intuitive grounds, that defects and misinterpretations in such a communication system may be an unexplored territory for psychiatry. [And library science, presumably.][5]

Readers may object that Thomas is stretching things almost beyond endurance, but all of the material on defective patrons, creativity, paralinguistics, and kinesics is equally exaggerative. There can be little doubt that patrons' queries must sometimes be clarified through concise questioning. This, however, is a far cry from a full-fledged, complex reference interview. It is, additionally, difficult to understand Geraldine B. King's insistence on discovering patrons' motivations and objectives. (Why they are interested in a topic. What use they will make of the information.) In fact, King's probing about Dick Turpin and highwaymen, in her example of correct interviewing technique, only squelches the patron's creativity.[6] As Fred Batt perceptively observes, "Sometimes the reference interview impedes the flow of information."[7]

THE MYTH REVEALED

Because the reference interview comes up frequently in the literature, is highly touted, and appears to be both practically and theoretically justified, it comes as a disconcerting intellectual shock to discover that it is, as least partially, a myth. During the course of answering tens of thousands of queries at two academic research libraries, I was struck by the infrequent necessity of posing a complex series of questions in order to ascertain the patrons' real needs. To confirm this general impression, I kept careful track of 1,074 questions asked during a 101 hour period (5/9/83-7/27/83). The results were revelatory. Some questions, to be sure, required brief discussion, but only *six* queries demanded extensive interviewing.[8] Patrons who asked for library locations were satisfied with the directions. Those who needed a biographical source for Martin Luther King manifested delight in the tendered material.

There are, of course, patrons who request *The Encyclopedia Americana* in order to do a survey of Oklahoma state statutes, but clients only infrequently cite inappropriate sources or really do not know what they want. The misleading implication of the literature is that a long-winded, convoluted reference interview, complete with nonverbal observations, is a mandatory part of virtually every exchange. My experience indicates that this is simply untrue.

Because the evaluation of the reference interview is so overwhelmingly positive, it occurred to me that I might be doing an inadequate job. Perhaps all of those patrons who asked for the *MLA International Bibliography* really wanted the *Humanities Index* or *Grzimek's Animal Life Encyclopedia*; those who needed film reviews of *Annie Hall*, really were looking for quotations of Robert Hall stock; and those who needed straight-forward facts—like how many 1978 foreign automobiles were sold to punk rockers—naturally had ulterior motives, which only a carefully orchestrated interview could elicit. One possible solution to this dilemma was to bother patrons with inquisitive probes: "Are you really looking for a history of Colombia? Perhaps you would find a list of cocaine dealers more useful? Why are you interested in buttermilk?" But such a superfluous procedure would only alienate patrons.

Instead of teasing people, I decided to observe a diversified group of reference librarians at work. I, therefore, visited eight libraries in order to learn just how one should utilize the reference interview effectively.[9] I learned very little. During the eight hours of observation librarians conducted no interviews. The closest anyone came was an exchange concerning a demand for a "list of books on fashion" by which the librarian immediately discovered the patron meant a computer-produced bibliography. Similarly, a "catalogue" was transmogrified into an index through one simple question. This type of inarticulate confusion occurred only three or four times out of a total of 229 questions.

It should also be noted that librarians may pose many counter-questions simply because they are inept, inefficient, incapable of answering, or unable to locate material. For example, one librarian did not know what GNP meant, and even after finding out led the patron to the wrong tool. One suggested the card catalog for *articles* on music! She was unfamiliar with *The Music Index*. Another, upon being told that *Journalism Quarterly* could not be located in the serials microform listing, asked what periodical index the patron had used. The relevancy of this query escapes me; the listing was apparently simply faulty. Sometimes the patron knows more than the librarian: an extremely inarticulate person asked me for an almanac. I wondered why, and he indicated that he was looking for the marriage laws of each state. I mentioned that the almanac was an inappropriate tool, but that he was welcome to try. He returned, and I asked if I could help him further. He said no and walked away. I looked in the almanac and there they were!

ROADS TO ERROR

After begrudgingly conceding that brief questioning or even a full-fledged interview is, at times, useful, it is necessary to emphasize that too much misleading, abstract, and theoretical material on the subject is published. It is time for those involved in reference work to concentrate on substantive multidisciplinary knowledge. Then they could provide responses, preferably correct ones, to carefully articulated queries. There is an increasing consensus (with which I agree) that reference librarians are doing an inadequate job. Ten years ago, David E. House described an experiment in which twenty librarians were asked for information on the artist David Shepherd. When one considers the general nature of the sources, the sixty percent rate of failure to provide any information at all is extremely disheartening.[10]

More recently, Marcia J. Myers and Jassim M. Jirjees have put together a collaborative volume consisting of material excerpted from their dissertations. The researchers posed a total of forty-nine telephone queries in each of forty-five academic libraries. About fifty percent of the responses were acceptable. This is certainly a dismal showing.[11] Examples could be multiplied easily, but there is really no need to do this; the results are invariably the same: reference librarians fail to provide adequate answers in about half the cases. Perhaps they are too busy interviewing patrons.

Very few investigations of the reference interview conclude that it is often unnecessary or even counterproductive. Thus, we should be grateful to two authors who disagree with the accepted point of view. In Mary Jo Lynch's experiment, interviews occurred in less than one half of all possible instances. Furthermore, the interviews resulted in important changes in only thirteen percent of the cases.[12] Samuel Rothstein, in his extensive historical overview, sums up the situation nicely:

> I suggest that we may have gone too far in the direction of self-consciousness and elaboration. Too much of our research confirms the obvious, and some of the training programs, with their emphasis on surface mannerisms, seem more suitable for telephone operators and encyclopedia sales people than for members of a learned profession.
>
> Above all, I charge that we keep complicating where we should be simplifying.[13]

NOTES

1. See, for example, two lengthy and only partially overlapping bibliographical surveys: Wayne W. Crouch, "The Information Interview: A Comprehensive Bibliography and an Analysis of the Literature," ERIC Document, ED 180 501 (1979) and O. Gene Norman, "The Reference Interview; An Annotated Bibliography," *Reference Services Review*, 7 (1) (Jan/Mar 1979), 71-77. Bill Katz allocates part of a chapter in the second volume of his *Introduction to Reference Work* (New York: McGraw Hill, 1982) to the interview: Denis Grogan devotes an entire thirty-five page chapter to it (*Practical Reference Work* [London: Clive Bingley, 1979]); and Gerald Jahoda, et al. think that it merits two chapters in their *Librarian and Reference Queries; A Systematic Approach* (New York: Academic Press, 1980).

2. Don McFadyen, "The Psychology of Inquiry: Reference Service and the Concept of Information/Experience," *Journal of Librarianship*, 7 (1) (January 1975), 2-11 passim.

3. Virginia Boucher, "Nonverbal Communication and the Library Reference Interview," *RQ*, 16 (1) (Fall 1976), 27-32, passim.

4. Joanna López Muñoz, "The Significance of Nonverbal Communication in the Reference Interview," *RQ*, 16 (3) (Spring 1977), 220.

5. Lewis Thomas, "Vibes," in his *The Lives of a Cell: Notes of a Biology Watcher* (New York: Viking, 1974), p. 40. (Those who are impressed by this sort of thing might also consider chronemics, haptics, proxemics, etc.)

6. Geraldine B. King, "The Reference Interview," *RQ*, 12 (2) (Winter 1972), 158-159.

7. Fred Batt, oral communication. Consider, for example, the following overheard interchange: Patron: "Where are the encyclopedias?" Reference librarian: "There are, of course, a great many encyclopedias, arranged by call number on the shelves. The general encyclopedias are on the table over there." Patron: "I'm looking for the *Encyclopedia Britannica*." Reference librarian (Pointing to the table): "It's over there."

8. A patron requested a specific reference title; he really was seeking bibliographical information on a journal. The book, however, was an appropriate source for this. Another patron asked for an almanac, which was inappropriate, since he was searching for a map of Annapolis. A third needed phone books and phonefiche; both of these did help him locate

radio stations, but ultimately he had to turn to other sources. A fourth desired an index to French magazines; he was looking for duck hunting journals. Next, there was a broad question on Ian Fleming's novels and the derived films. It turned out that the patron wished to know something quite specific about six of these films, but I had automatically answered his question. Finally, a general query concerning the oil industry hid the true question, which dealt with the business of oil wells.

9. The eight major academic libraries are at North Texas State University: one hour of observation, 51 questions posed, no interviews; Texas Woman's University: one and a half hours, 22 questions, no interviews; University of Oklahoma: one half hour, 24 questions, no interviews; Central State University (Oklahoma): one hour, 20 questions, no interviews; Washburn University: one hour, 18 questions, no interviews; University of Kansas: one hour, 22 questions, no interviews; Iowa State University: one hour, 32 questions, no interviews; University of Minnesota: one hour, 40 questions, no interviews. These statistics do not include telephone queries nor four exchanges that I was unable to hear.

10. David E. House, "Reference Efficiency or Reference Deficiency," *Library Association Record*, 76 (11) (November 1974), 222-223.

11. Marcia J. Myers, Jassim M. Jirjees, *The Accuracy of Telephone Reference/Information Services in Academic Libraries: Two Studies* (Metuchen, NJ: Scarecrow, 1983).

12. Mary Jo Lynch, "Reference Interviews in Public Libraries," *The Library Quarterly*, 48 (2) (April 1978), 133-134, 137.

13. Samuel Rothstein, "Across the Desk: 100 Years of Reference Encounters," *Canadian Library Journal*, 34 (5) (October 1977), 397.

Referens Simplex or the Mysteries of Reference Interviewing Revealed

Fred Oser

The scene is the reference room of a large academic library in Florida with an extensive collection of Floridiana.

> Freshman: Good morning, ma'am. I want everything you have on Florida.
> Reference Librarian: Of course. Is there any particular book you have in mind?
> Freshman: Oh no, just bring me everything you have. I can find what I want.
> Reference Librarian: It might save time if we knew what field you are interested in—Florida's history? Politics? Biography?
> Freshman: No, not exactly . . .
> Reference Librarian: Perhaps some unusual features of Florida—Silver Springs? Alligators? Claude Kirk?
> Freshman: No—what I actually want is a book with lots of pictures in it.
> Reference Librarian: Of course! Seminole Indian headdress? Fort San Marco? Bok Tower?
> Freshman: What I want is a picture of a cypress tree![1]

The preceding dialog along with several other examples from the library literature are suitable illustrations of what might with a little imagination be called the "tormented" or "tragic sense" of the reference interview.[2]

The reference interview has been described as drama: "The diagram can be considered as symbolizing the opening of a reference drama . . . as with a play, the stage is set and ready for action. The curtain is about to go up . . ."[3] Just dim the stack lights, please, and

---

The author will be found interviewing at the Monmouth County Library, Eastern Branch, Rt. No. 35, Shrewsbury, NJ 07701.

bring up the reference area spot. Picture our protagonists about to prepare for a long elaborate, verbal ritual replete with strophe, anti-strophe, anagnorisis, peripeteia, and, of course, catharsis.

Over there is the inquirer, wrestling with a powerful but unarticulated need for "information" and struggling with subconscious feelings of anxiety at the prospect of entering the surreal, Piranesian library landscape and facing its bibliographic labyrinths.

Here, stage front, we have our hero or heroine, querulous and uncertain under the influence of the negative image—timid, bookish bachelor or prim, bespectacled spinster—imposed upon him or her by the misconceptions of a society which persistently, despite the ministrations of Johnny Carson and the ALA, belittles his or her crucial role in the information society of our time.

Enter then the quivering, abject soul who presumes to disturb the sanctuary of the librarian. Summoning all the skills of the wise, patient counselor and also armed with a full quiver of correct kinesic attributes, the librarian—body poised at a proper angle, nodding encouragingly, and smiling broadly—is prepared for "the next element, one very important in this drama . . . the opening line."[4]

"May I please . . . I mean . . . would you mind . . . terribly . . . telling me where the . . . uh, mmm . . . ba—. . . that is, the REST room is?" Actually, adept reference librarians will immediately recognize this as a cleverly disguised ploy, that conceals the real question for a current, comprehensive, fully annotated bibliography on the subject of the patterns of etiquette in post-Sumerian middle class society for the purpose of preparing a talk for next week's luncheon meeting of the local chapter of the Sons of Liberty. The intricacies of the requisite negotiation or clarification (using Benson's and Katz's improved term) I shall leave to the imagination of the reader.

The "tragic sense" of reference interviewing derives actually from two quite respectable traditions in the library literature; the analysis of content emphasizing the intellectual component on the one hand and the analysis of the interpersonal aspect emphasizing counseling, communication, and non-verbal considerations on the other.

For the former the seminal and unquestionably indispensable contributions have been those of Robert Taylor[5] and Ellis Mount[6] with Taylor's "probably the most frequently cited investigation of the reference interview."[7] Along with this abstract analysis of the interview were the numerous articles appearing in the sixties and seventies, which have emphasized the disciplines of counseling, communications, and behavioral studies including non-verbal behavior and how information from these fields could be applied to the understanding, analysis, and improvement of the reference interview. Charles Bunge's literature review mentioned above lists all the important articles in this tradition.[8] Although more concerned with the search itself, the analyses of Jahoda, Olson, and Braunagel are significant parts of this tradition, too.[9] I must declare that I do not want to be misunderstood. I firmly believe that every librarian working today at a reference desk anywhere should be familiar with the essential and vital contributions these writings have made to the understanding of the reference interview and reference process.

Nevertheless, their powerful influence has had the effect of helping to create a model of reference work which stresses the complexity of the process. It is no accident, it seems to me, that this earlier writing on the subject of the reference interview and on the reference process had its origins in the work of special libraries and librarians. In scientific and technical subject areas there is good reason to suggest that both the inquirer and the librarian are involved in a dialectical encounter whose objective can be the elucidation of a subject which even the inquirer himself/herself has not been able to fully define. This is precisely the situation described as commonplace by N. J. Crum, who worked as an information specialist for the General Electric corporation.[10] In situations where highly educated and trained individuals are doing research and/or development on complicated matters at advanced levels there is considerable validity in a conception or model of the reference process that emphasizes difficulty, uncertainty, and complication.

TAYLOR'S NOTION

In particular Taylor's notion regarding the various "levels" of question articulation, while surely an accurate description for questions of a certain level of complexity, is too elaborate a theory for large segments of the spectrum of actual reference questions. Even subject requests of a perfectly ordinary nature—e.g., moderate amount of information on a disease; material for reports and papers at all academic levels on perennial topics; and information for practical purposes like appliance repair and other mechanical arts needs do not necessarily develop in the way he describes. Your toaster stops working and you want a book that shows how to fix toasters; the teacher assigns a five page paper on the causes of World War I. The four levels of the question in these cases collapse into one, and you want some authoritative writing that answers the questions.

Such a complex model, therefore, is not so appropriate it seems to me for the ordinary public, school, or college library environment. In fact I would like to propose a countervailing "comic view" of the reference interview for consideration.

Standard literary theory tells us that the rhythms and structures of comedy derive from a different perspective on human nature and action than tragedy. Comedy relies on the essentially decent and constructive impulses of human nature, allowing sufficient extents of time for these forces to heal wounds, resolve conflicts, and create bonds of amity and affection among individuals, so that in the end we have not violent confrontation, but reconciliation and reaffirmation. Comedy affirms the norm, and frequently comedy concludes by reconstituting the institutions of society in one of the rituals associated with order; the banquet or feast, the dance, and, of course, marriage, in which patience, forgiveness and love are the dominant forces at work.

Now don't snicker. Why I have personal knowledge of one reference interview that took place years ago at the New York Public Library that actually did end in marriage: I met my wife while on reference at Fifth Avenue and 42nd Street. I admit that this might be overdoing the "ad hominem" fallacy, but how often have your reference encounters ended with gifts of candy, cookies, even a bottle of wine? "They [the librarians] have enjoyed Indian, Mexican and soul food for which they'd found recipes. Another fringe benefit for being librarians who care."[11]

Seriously, though, the "comic" tradition in reference interviewing boasts an equally prestigious tradition in the library literature, too. Based on the reading I had done and the re-reading I have done for this article I share Charles Bunge's opinion that it is in fact gradually becoming the prevailing view. The literature of the reference interview in the late 1970s and early 1980s "might be characterized as a challenge to widely held assumptions about the reference interview and a sort of 'common sense backlash' against the growing literature on nonverbal communication."[12]

Let me next document this trend. We begin with William Katz's text:

Assume he or she is a normal human being, who gets along reasonably well with others [and] you now have the almost perfect librarian, who is almost always going to succeed with the user.[13]

The implication is that the typical reference transaction is more like a normal conversational experience than a therapeutic encounter.

Recently Michael McCoy has expressed the opinion that "the reference interview isn't always necessary." He gives an example of a simple exchange and then concludes:

It may be a bit simplistic . . . but very common. And while the reference interview does come in handy for anyone working on a paper . . . inter-library loans, subject requests, and data-base searches, it's likewise idiotic to question someone who comes in asking for last Sunday's edition of "The New York Times." I can't speak for academic or special libraries, but the reference interview can't—and shouldn't—be applied as readily in public libraries as we were taught. Time and common sense won't permit it.[14]

Mr. McCoy's subjective impression is substantiated by authoritative opinion and research in which I can identify four issues: the interview content, the questions themselves, the sociological setting, and the "unexpressed" interview content. Katz, Thomas-Hinckley-Eisenbach[15] and Bunge all have acknowledged the significant impact of the research conducted by Mary Jo Lynch.[16] Her analysis of transcribed interviews points strongly to the conclusion that the reference interview is not as frequent, not as necessary, or not as complex as previously believed. "Yet less than half of [reference transactions] involves an interview," she reported.[17] Further, "it has been assumed that library patrons do not ask for what they 'really' want . . . but the query changed substantially in only 13 per cent of the transactions observed,"[18] i.e., only 13 percent of her 309 interviews revealed that the person was not asking for what s/he "really" wanted.

Regarding the second issue of the questions themselves evidence is accumulating that the majority of questions received are not particularly complicated, can be answered in a comparatively short time, and do not require elaborate searches to find answers, and hence do not normally require extensive interviews. The Lynch data support these notions. Also, in a 1982 survey of 1400 transactions "about three-fourths" had a "short duration."[19] At Northwestern another study reached the conclusion that "the overall level of complexity of questions received is of a very low order."[20] In another study it was suggested that the bulk of reference questions are relatively easy since most require only a limited number of "steps" to answer.[21]

THE THIRD ISSUE

A third issue in the "comic" or simplified tradition of the literature on the reference interview concerns the psychological and sociological preoccupations of the earlier period. The whole idea of the reference librarian as counselor which Bunge identifies as a dominant theme[22] has been subjected to steady questioning during the same period. In his third edition Katz says:

> Useful as kinesic analysis may be at the reference desk, it often comes close to the ridiculous. In so far as a good-intentioned kinesic study helps the reference librarian arrive at an accurate picture of what the user sees, fine. When it goes beyond that to ponderous, sometimes fatuous, conclusions it is time to move on to other areas.[23]

In his fourth edition this becomes "too much may be made of how the librarian smiles, stands, or places his hands on the desk . . . Too much of the growing literature on this topic borders on the satirical."[24] I noticed that a number of the more enthusiastic of these articles were written by people who were not librarians.

In my own view the turning point came with David Isaacson's masterful antidote to the enthusiasm for the interpersonal or psychological aspect of the reference interview.[25] In "Library Inreach" his persuasive and perceptive analysis shows that the "helping" motivation may be misguided and in some cases even harmful to the reference process. The zeal with which that motivation sometimes proceeds can invade privacy and overreach the bounds of a librarian's competence, placing him or her in potentially difficult circumstances. In any event too great an emphasis on this aspect of the interview and reference encounter generally exaggerates the psychological aspect out of proportion.

Another observation made by Mary Jo Lynch that relates to this matter was that the number of questions that librarians needed to ask in order to conclude an interview were few in number compared to the typical interviews of other helping professions, so that comparisons of librarians' role to that of physicians, attorneys, or social workers had to be "seriously questioned."[26] In fact both she and a writer named Norma J. Shosid proposed on different occasions the idea that the library reference situation's closest analogy in its relative lack of ambiguity and brief duration is that of the sales clerk and customer.[27]

The fourth issue is that of "unexpressed" content. Another result of Mary Jo Lynch's study was to call into question the long standing deference to Taylor's concept of the interview. "It seems clear, however, that future commentary on the reference interview should consider the models which emerged from this study as supplements or alternatives to the Taylor model."[28] With her observation that "the reference librarian probably also gains information from such clues as how the patron is dressed, what objects he or she is carrying, how confident he or she seems to be about using the library,"[29] Lynch raises a significant cluster of ideas that indeed may signal an area of concern that will establish the "comic" view of reference interviewing as the dominant conception in the eighties.

The extensive writing of Marilyn Domas White seems to draw inspiration from just such views expressed by Lynch. Given this development I find in White's writing a sort of theoretical formulation of the requirements for the "comic" view of simplicity in the reference situation. It is the area of the non-verbal but not the kinesic aspects of the situation.

Paradoxically her model of the reference encounter is intellectually formidable and somewhat intimidating, so that at first glance she seems to be preserving the idea of complexity arising from Taylor's analysis.[30] At the same time especially in an earlier article where she identifies the key elements of structure and coherence, pace and length,[31] and then later employs these for evaluation,[32] she is clearing the air for close observation, and reminding us about what really goes on in the interview.

Sometimes her examples of interviews are relatively simple and straightforward. She takes her rather abstract communications model for the interview from the writing of one Marvin Minsky.[33]

This model includes the crucial concept called a ''frame'' which allows for the inclusion in the interview process of all relevant data that the librarian might possess from prior experience or derive from careful observation as well as learn directly from conversation with the inquirer. ''When one encounters a new situation (or makes a substantial change in one's view of the present problem) one selects from memory a substantial structure called a frame.''[34]

In the case of a librarian in the reference situation this ''frame'' may include the following ''nodes'': ''intelligence, reading skill, age, level of motivation, manner, library experience, common problems or tasks, and likely time constraints.''[35] Ms. White points out that the actual content of these frames can be anticipated in many cases. ''In an academic library, for example, librarians often face students.''[36] What she is saying, very simply, is that in some library situations the librarian knows pretty well what to expect regarding questions that will be asked in advance, based on prior experience; and in others the librarian can easily deduce important information from the combination of prior experience and close observation.

LITERATURE SUMMARY

To conclude the literature survey and summarize the trends observed I can perceive an emerging picture of the reference situation in which inquirers often ask for what they want; what they want in the ordinary library situation is not all that complicated; the tone and atmosphere of the exchange is pitched at the psychological level of an ordinary conversation (even though the pace might be quite busy); and finally, there is a large area of situational content, both prior and immediate, that can be of great use to the librarian in conducting an efficient and rapid interview.

Based on both my reading and on my experience in various types of libraries it is my firm conviction that the above description is indeed the case, and that it is time for a reevaluation of the problem of reference interviewing. At one point I believed that the approach I advocate was quite original, but after carefully reviewing so much of what has already been written on the reference interview, I now consider what I have to propose as more of an arrangement into a coherent, systematic program of approaches and techniques that have already been described by various commentators.

Having agreed upon an attitude toward the reference interview which treats it as merely a conversational exchange between two individuals requiring only a normal level of politeness and pleasant demeanor on the librarian's part, we can proceed to identify four key components in the "comic" view: the absolutely crucial importance of the librarian's initial response to a question; a "taxonomy" of reference questions kept constantly in mind for categorizing incoming questions; a keen awareness of the type of library one is in; and a heightened sense of attentiveness to all types of situational clues. I believe these elements can be combined to produce a practical methodology.

My idea lays great stress on the content of the librarian's initial reply to the original inquiry, which, if cleverly formulated, can serve as a potent factor in expediting the process. I recommend that the librarian's first remark—aside from a friendly greeting or acknowledgment, of course—be itself a question, neither "open" nor "closed" necessarily, but based on his or her estimate of the probable nature of the "real" question. "Frequently the librarian must try to imagine what the patron would do with the answer being sought."[37] Ironically, this seems an old and familiar idea: "Wyer's 'mind-reading' seems to have been a process of making guesses about the user's needs and getting the user to respond to the guesses."[38] I propose only to be more systematic in its application. Linda Callaghan gives a good example of this in solving a puzzling reference encounter.[39]

Obviously, if a person tells you that s/he is putting in a new fireplace, has just received a diagnosis of a specific disease, is writing a term paper on the *Scarlet Letter*, wants the local congressman's address, or is considering a move to a particular city, there is practically no likelihood that you will be going astray by commencing a search for the answers. Therefore, for this significant proportion of inquiries the reference interview is not even necessary. Or, as William Katz puts it, when someone asks where the telephone is you can be reasonably certain s/he has to use it.[40]

Two components of this approach are preliminary to any actual interviews. The type of library in which one is working can lead to highly predictable expectations toward the purpose, scope, and level of reference inquiries. Obviously, school librarians deal primarily with course assignments, and at another point on the educational spectrum, undergraduate or college librarians do the same. In fact all commentators and studies agree that students constitute the majority of users for reference services in all types of libraries: "student population constitutes from 50 to 80 percent of users,"[41] and "most of the factual information seeking which brings young adults into public libraries today is related to school assignments."[42]

PROPER PERSPECTIVE

I am writing this essay from the perspective of the medium-size public library in a relatively affluent suburban setting where informal surveys of my own work indicate levels of student use from 60-90 percent of inquiries varying by time of day and day of week. In the larger, more urban public library and in the university library —in both types of which I have been employed in the past—it is safe to say that the clientele and the questions would be more varied and diverse. As a general rule the higher the educational level of the population served, the greater can be expected to be the range of subject matter as well as the depth of treatment. Large public library environments will offer a higher proportion of unusual questions. However, over a period of time in any type of large library situation fairly standardized patterns of use can be observed and absorbed as an element in the consciousness of reference librarians.

A second important "background" requirement of the "comic" view of interviewing is also keeping firmly in the "foreground" of one's consciousness some useful schema of reference question types into which incoming questions can be automatically classified in order to prompt appropriate sequences of response.

In my own work I employ a conventional categorization of questions: directional; bibliographic—requests for specific items whether books, articles, documents, poems, plays, pictures, or songs; subject or substantive—requests for small or large quantities of material on a subject at whatever level is appropriate; factual—including bibliographic verifications, quotations, directory data, statistical information, as well as the obscure/trivial fact. This is similar to the sets of definitions employed by Lynch,[43] by Gary Strong,[44] and by William Jones[45] in their respective surveys. I believe that some discussions of reference work falter because of attempts to generalize about all types of reference questions under the rubric of requests for "information," thus lacking approaches based on more precise definitions of types of questions.

The remaining components of the "comic" method apply to that moment when the reference question is actually asked. At that point the librarian needs to focus intently on both the subject content and the form of the request as well as to make an effort to absorb as much relevant "situational" data as possible. With the former elements s/he is attempting to determine whether the question as asked conforms essentially to the standard question schema or is in fact an imperfect attempt on the person's part to state his need, and, therefore, corresponds only superficially to the "real" question—more on this in a moment.

Regarding the latter "situational" data Marilyn White, as noted above, has provided a useful theoretical formulation, the concept of the memory "frame" comprised of key "nodes" for incorporating "preliminary data, such as age, appearance, or demeanor."[46] I can add that manner of speech is another vital element in the preliminary impression. In the matter of assessing as many verbal and visual cues as can be deduced initially I think that the ethical considerations that the "librarian ought virtually to vanish as an individual person," and "the personal philosophies and attitudes should not be reflected in the execution of service"[47] are sometimes misconstrued to mean that one's reaction to inquirers should be so non-judgmental as to ignore the valid situational cues that are available. Insofar as this misapplication of ethical notions does exist, it should be avoided. As Thomas suggests, "the tack taken will depend on one's estimate of the inquirer."[48]

To return to the final component, the form and content of the person's initial question, we all realize that the initial question, unless it's so wildly garbled by the individual as to be totally unrelated to the "real" question, will usually define the general subject area, and establish a category of potential sources for subsequent searching.

Regarding the "form" of opening questions we already have before us thorough and careful analyses of the typical forms of initial questions. One may prefer Richard Teller's colorful terminology of "misdirected independence," "vagueness," and "abstruseness,"[49] or Marilyn White's notion of "funneling" as applied to various types of initial questions,[50] or the discussions of basic types of opening questions that appear in all three of the textbooks available today by Katz, Thomas et al., and Jahoda and Braunagel. The librarian should be alert to recognize the common types and be prepared with resources appropriate to each.

THE NOTION ILLUSTRATED

The remainder of this essay will be devoted to illustrations of the notion of a "comic" or simplified viewpoint toward reference interviewing. Having identified the major components of this approach as the librarian's primary response to the question, the library environment, the nature of the inquiry, and immediate situational cues, I shall arrange the following discussion around the major types of initial queries and suggest what seem to me to be efficient responses.

Let me repeat, I advocate that the librarian's initial response to a question that is not straightforward and apparent be itself a question, neither "open" nor "closed" necessarily, but based instead on the probable nature of the "real" question, as deduced from all the relevant data that can be assembled from the major elements in the situation. "Establishing rules about open and closed questions is difficult. . . ."[51] It has been my experience that a precisely formulated "guess" appropriate to the occasion can be found to be essentially correct in a major proportion of reference situations, and even when wrong, is a more effective and efficient stimulus to relevant conversation than the conventional idea of the open question, where long circuitous conversations can result as in the examples cited at the very beginning of this paper. The demonstration of interest in the person's question as evidenced by a thoughtful surmise is, I feel, more likely to prompt the individual to reveal enough of a context from which to conclude the interview and begin the search.

Let us examine closely (1) the general subject request, (2) the request for a specific item, (3) the request for reference sources, either general or specific, and (4) the factual question.

Of all the basic openers the general subject request is especially obvious as an immediate invitation to attempt to deduce what the inquirer wants. For example, when the request is for the location of the "library's books on art" the probabilities in my experience are nearly 100% that in the case of the student inquirer there is an assignment for a paper on an artist, a specific painting, or an art historical topic, while the same question coming from an ordinary adult whose verbal and visual cues suggest that the person is neither enrolled in a course or is likely to be knowledgeable in art history is almost always for some biographical information on an artist or an appraisal of a painting that the person has either bought at a garage sale or is contemplating for purchase. Adults who are knowledgeable collectors or dealers will usually request appropriate sources by name. I know this to be the case in the public library, and am sure it is true in college libraries and art departmental university libraries, also.

Consequently, in my view the appropriate response to such an inquiry would be a confirmation of the original surmise. If correct, then in the former case all that is further necessary to know would be exact topic, length of paper, and due date, and the search for information could begin. In the latter case the librarian can immediately accompany the person to the artists' encyclopedias and/or price guides without further delay.

Now if it happens that the original judgment were incorrect, and that the request were really, say, for a picture of some object, it has usually been the case in my experience, as I have said, that such an initial, logical question, even if wrong, is a very effective stimulus to conversation. It is certainly more direct than some "open" response about "what kind of art did you want?", which, as I have already suggested can lead to the roundabout conversations of the previously cited examples. At the same time this approach avoids the impertinence of a direct inquiry for the purpose behind the question, which itself has potential for giving offense, depending on the personality or identity of the inquirer.

This is such a very common pattern in reference work. Let me present some other examples and then analyze them for significant conclusions. The inquirer, male or female, who asks the reference librarian "where are your books on companies?" is another frequently encountered client at the reference desk. Could there be a librarian in a medium to large size library almost anywhere with more than six months' experience, who would not recognize this type of inquirer, especially, if in business attire, as someone who is probably job hunting. Further, s/he will either be at the stage of sending out letters en masse or will have an interview scheduled. Hence, I have found it expeditious to ask as my very first response, whether the person is looking for information on a specific company or wants a list of companies. If the former, then I usually just casually ask if s/he has a job interview . . . when it is . . . and the reference interview is over, for by now I know the name of the company and can begin explaining and showing how easy or difficult it will be to find information suitable for interview background depending on whether the firm is publicly or privately owned. If the inquirer had been dressed in workman's attire, however, I would have been more inclined to surmise that he either wanted (a) a specific company to locate a spare part or operating manual for a particular product or (b) wanted a list of firms making a certain type of product, and would have responded accordingly. And, I can say without reservation that most of the time I would have been right.

THE GENERAL FAULT

Another example for the "overly general" category of opening reference questions would be the request for "books on computers," which is a very common, frequent question today. The subject area defines itself in terms of hardware; software, especially computer languages; general surveys; and effects in society. Ninety-nine percent of questions will fall into one of these subdivisions with the first two categories being further subdivided by elementary, intermediate, and advanced levels of treatment. With the type of library in mind and careful observation of inquirer cues it is often possible to predict the "real" need with a high degree of accuracy and conclude the interview portion of the reference transaction with two well chosen questions such as whether the person wants to learn or review a specific language, or wants operating information on a particular personal computer model.

One last example I must mention is the request for "medical books" in a public library, which is almost always for a moderate amount of information on a specific disorder or disease that a doctor has diagnosed.

Next is the request for a specific title—book, article, document, poem, picture, song, etc. This type is immediately recognized and should activate a specific, predictable sequence of responses. It is safe to say, I believe, that only in the case of a request for a recent best seller should the librarian fail to be immediately prepared at an appropriate point later in the search to explore the distinct possibility, even probability, in certain situations that the "real" query may be a subject request. This situation is so common that it should present little difficulty in interviewing.

Even the innocent request for a classic has the potential for conversion, because at certain times of the year it is quite likely that the student inquirer has a list of classic fiction tucked away from which s/he is to choose one or more titles.

The main clue in this category of openers is a title in any traditional academic discipline that sounds or looks like a standard work or else a scholarly, esoteric or sophisticated treatment. Especially, if the person—whether obviously a student or just an ordinary adult—seems at first glance to lack the sophistication required for understanding such a work, perhaps s/he pronounced a word in the title or the author's name incorrectly, then immediately be alerted to the possibility of eventual conversion to a subject request.

Of course, it is necessary and only polite to begin the search for the requested item, but as complications arise—the library doesn't own it, the author's name is misspelled, it can't be verified readily in BIP or OCLC—a pleasantly phrased remark about the potential difficulty in actually obtaining the item should lead naturally to offering the observation that the library owns other books, more recent books, etc. on the subject. This could very likely prompt quite unsolicited from the user the idea that something else on the subject will be acceptable. Never use the word "substitute," because it connotes an inferior alternative, and is much more likely to be resisted as an option, especially if the person has limited knowledge of the subject.

The last phase in an interview of this type when it becomes clear that it is the specific item only that is needed and difficulty in verification persists is an inquiry, again based on probability, about the source of the person's information: course list, instructor's remark, inquirer's own reading, bookstore, talk show or friend's recommendation. The possibilities are finite and rather predictable depending on the subject and situational clues.

Here are three brief examples. A caller, a young man, requested from me a book entitled *Numerical Analysis* by a specific author. Considering the apparent age of the caller, the fact that the time of year was mid-March, and that this level of mathematical inquiry is unusual for our library, I surmised that this was a college student (he was in fact a graduate student) home for spring vacation who, it turned out, would have used any title on that subject. Again, a request for a specific book on Hitler from a high school student can almost always be satisfied with any comparable book on him that has the virtue of being on the shelf at the time. Last, I remember another occasion on which an elderly gentleman requested a specific, very old veterinary textbook, but as the search began to encounter difficulty gradually revealed that he really wanted some general information on a disease of cattle, and had requested that particular book because he remembered using it as a student many years before.

Sometimes a person requests a specific item in order to answer a factual question. Of course, this is more difficult to recognize, but the same approach as just described for revealing a masked subject request should apply.

OPENING QUESTION

The next category of opening question has received considerable attention in the literature. This type should always in EVERY SINGLE CASE be a signal that there may be an unstated need for information on a subject, or less often, some particular factual information. Further, always and immediately alert to such a possibility, the librarian's initial response to this type should always consist of (1) a brief answer to the question as stated, and (2) an almost simultaneous, pleasant, appropriate remark designed as possible opening for further exploration.

I am speaking here, of course, of the type that Teller calls "misplaced independence" which Katherine Emerson offered as the proto-type conundrum of question classification, "Where are the German dictionaries?"[52] In its other classic form, "Where is the *Readers' Guide*?" it has been discussed in detail by all three reference textbook authors,[53] who all note its significance and all propose similar solutions. It is Charles Benson, however, who has provided perhaps the most thorough analysis:

> Often the user is responsive to clarification efforts while the librarian escorts him to the materials requested. To attempt clarification while at the reference desk can suggest a lack of responsiveness to the question posed by the user. In contrast clarifying questions during the trek to the sources may often be received cordially by the user. This approach reassures the user.[54]

All commentators recognize the chief problems here as the potential inappropriateness of the source or sources requested for answering the actual question, and the potential resentment that can arise from probing.

I have nothing to add to all this but a couple of examples and few recommendations in the "comic" mode. As examples, only recently I have had a request for the *Readers' Guide* when the topic turned out to be Mark Twain, and for the encyclopedias where someone expected to find a "complete bibliography" of Ernest Hemingway for a short paper on his "The Short Happy Life of Francis Mc-Comber." People ask for the *Readers' Guide* when other indexes would be more appropriate all the time. Finally, another common situation is a request for a "computer search" when either books or a few needed articles are readily available through conventional sources.

I find that asking someone if s/he has "used it before" creates more problems than it solves. If an index or indexes are requested a good second remark is frequently a question such as, "Are you looking for periodical articles on a subject?" (there is an obvious logic to this, at least), followed quickly by the observation that you "just wanted to make sure you knew that _____ covers mainly general magazines and doesn't have many articles on, e.g., the War of 1812." In the case of encyclopedias the "hook" can often be the casual observation, "Do you want any one in particular? . . . did you know some require using the index and some do not?" The objective is to keep the person talking, but in a way that is closely and logically related to a probable question.

An illustration of the blind request for a reference source that is unique to the library where I work arises from the special circumstance that we have a book catalog supplemented with various computer printouts, so that all day long people are approaching the reference desk to ask, "Where is your catalog?" or "Where is your card catalog?" or even "Where are the drawers?" or better "Where is (are) your index(es)?" In the last case, incidentally, I always have the courtesy to ignore the person's unfamiliarity with libraryese, and simply answer as I would if s/he had used the correct term. I always first answer the question by indicating the location, but before s/he can move away I continue.

Now if someone requests the catalog, then the probability is that s/he believes that books will answer his or her question. Therefore, rather than ask an "open" question like "what information" the person is seeking, it is logical to inquire whether s/he is looking for a specific book or books on a subject. Eighty to ninety percent of the time the answer is a subject and a quick statement to the effect that, "if you would like to tell me what the subject is, perhaps I can show you where the books are" more or less concludes the interview. Once at this stage it is usually a short step or two to refine the subject, establish the context, and proceed with the search. It all takes about thirty seconds; a librarian can handle a lot of questions at that pace.

As the last type of opening question factual ones, Teller's "abstruseness," can perhaps be the most misleading. I remember being asked for the address of a small publisher by a girl who eventually revealed, as the search on her request proceeded, the need for any monolog for a forensic competition. (This question had a middle stage in which she asked for a specific play, incidentally.)

That was a rather unusual circumstance, for as Katz indicates in his discussion of question types, factual questions "such as, 'What is the population of New Jersey?' rarely need an interview,"[55] and usually involve an "automatic, or almost automatic, response . . . by matching the question to sources."[56] In keeping with a "comic" or simplified concept of the reference interview it is important to observe how very large a proportion of factual questions are straightforward and easily answered. This includes bibliographic verifications of items already used but inadequately recorded, brief biographical data, directory requests of all types for names, and/or addresses, dates, prices, and for quotations. Even statistical questions, once related to their context in the inquirer's situation, resolve themselves most of the time. Area demographics—whether needed for course assignments or market research usually present little problem related to the interview. The request for a "profile" of a town can almost immediately be placed in context according to the situational cues provided by the inquirer and verified in the first reply by the librarian to the question.

FACTUAL QUESTIONS

On the other hand there are certain types of factual questions that, if accepted at face value, can lead to interminable complications. Questions in legal matters are prone to this confusion. Again in these instances an initial surmise about what is happening can stimulate a conversation that will reveal the background of the question, and cause the librarian to revise a search in the direction of greater subject generality or to perceive some error in either the inquirer's terminology or concept of the problem. Someone's asking for the penalty or punishment for a particular crime could well be almost unconsciously disguising the need for more general information on a legal matter for an actual situation in which s/he is involved or maybe for a course assignment. Manner of speech and/or dress can be especially revealing in this situation.

It is in the domain of the factual question that I think the truly "open" question-reply has its greatest value. For those few situations in which the original question is so baffling that you can't make head or tail of it, it is often helpful simply to confess ignorance and to ask directly for background information. You can tell someone that you really do not have any idea where to begin searching for an answer, and that you really do need more information in order to proceed. "Give me some idea of how this question came up, please." Remember, the obscure or abstruse factual question constitutes only a minor fraction of all reference inquiries, and there is a kind of inverse relationship frequently at work: the more obscure the question the less significant (or more trivial) the circumstance. I have surmised on more than one occasion that a person was playing trivial pursuit, and although that remark did not answer the question, it certainly cleared the air and made the subsequent searching less pressured. Although as librarians we accord the same effort to the search for the obscure fact to settle the office argument as well as for the research worker or advertising agency, knowing the context of such a question puts the consequence of failing to find an answer after a reasonable search in proper perspective. Also, knowing the actual context can prompt alternative strategies depending on the general subject area of the question.

Having examined the major types of reference interview opening forms and suggested some practical approaches, I would now like to make some generalizations applicable to all reference interviews that I believe further substantiate the notion of simplicity in most reference situations.

The whole issue of learning "why" a question is being asked is a critical consideration. Jahoda states, "The librarian . . . must be very cautious, however, not to give the impression of prying and should NEVER ask WHY the client-patron wants the information requested."[57] Yet as Katz indicates, "The problem here is that in almost any question-negotiation situation, the librarian sooner or later must learn the 'why' of the request in order to define the parameters of the search."[58] For Katz it becomes a matter of judgment about how to proceed.

I agree with Jahoda that as a beginning this should always be avoided. I have observed younger librarians who, asking me for assistance in beginning work on difficult (often factual) questions, being told that I, too, have no idea what the person wants, and being counseled to seek further information, usually get nowhere if they immediately return to the interview by blurting out, "why do you need this?" (Of course, I have learned to mention specifically to avoid this approach, if there is time.)

This is yet another reason that I regard the logical question or educated guess, drawing upon all the factors that I have enumerated, as the most preferable response, simultaneously avoiding impertinence and demonstrating perceptive, genuine interest. It is evident that identifying the purpose of a query is important in establishing level of treatment and amount of information needed, especially for the genuine subject request, but as a device of question clarification it is perhaps even more important. In correcting an inquirer's request for the inappropriate type or wrong example of reference source(s), e.g., when encyclopedias are requested but a particular source would have the information, this approach is the most efficient. The peculiar but not necessarily obscure or trivial factual question frequently can be resolved easily in this manner.

Recently, a referral I received from a branch library for a specific legal form which no one had ever seemed to have heard of was discovered to be simply a request for general information on a perennial topic. In this example based on a reply the man made to me in answer to the question of where he learned about the existence of this legal form, I quickly tried to formulate a logical use for the material and found that he really needed general information about establishing a small business in the state. The interview consisted of two questions.

Of all the variety of library reference situations surely the most fertile soil for the employment of the "comic," simplified notion of reference interviewing is the reference interaction with students.

Given the dominance of student use of libraries noted previously along with the fact that student questions are predominantly subject requests for amounts of material that generally vary in direct proportion to educational level, it seems only reasonable that any special techniques that can be devised for interviewing will have wide applicability.

ROSTER OF COMMENTATORS

I believe that almost every writer who has dealt with the reference interview has at some point made the suggestion that the student can be asked if s/he is requesting information for an assignment. Look at the roster of commentators: Anita Schiller in her 1965 landmark article—"it is doubtful that much interrogation would have been required had the student been asked, 'What is your topic?'"[59]; Katz—"if a 12-year old boy asks . . . the purpose is probably to write a term paper, and . . . he will rarely object if you ask"[60]; Thomas et al.—"Time might be saved by a more direct approach . . . 'Is this for a course?'"[61]; Callaghan—"I have found that asking 'are you studying this on your own or is this a school assignment' works in an all purpose context"[62]; White—

> In a public library, for example, he can identify a client as a student by a combination of dress, age, demeanor, and time of day, assume the most typical problem orientation of this type of client, such as class assignment, and postpone or eliminate questions in this area until the problem assumption seems faulty or inadequate without particulars.[63]

Now *there* is consensus, but in every instance of this recommendation I have seen it is mentioned more or less in passing as an off hand comment in the context of general discussion. What I am suggesting is only that this device be made the most prominent element in reference interviewing with students. I can state unequivocally that in my experience that virtually every request from a student for a general subject in the form of a question for "your books on psychology . . . on animals . . . on business" . . . on any subject, or for "articles on . . ." can be efficiently handled by one or two well chosen questions.

In reply to these types of openers I must ask dozens of times a day, "Are you writing a report [for young children] (or a "paper" [for high school, college or mature students]) for a course?" If the answer is yes, as it almost always is, the next, obvious question becomes, "What is your topic?"

This is so much more satisfactory than asking an open question like "what aspect of psychology are you interested . . . ?" or as in one of Jahoda's examples, "what kind of information about sharks are you hoping to find?"[64] I am often reminded of Dorman Smith's interesting experiment conducted in 1972,[65] and have often thought that if a librarian had surmised that he was a student (I always thought that there were no other species of human beings in the Boston area anyway) and had simply asked him if he were writing a paper for a course, and if so, what his topic was, how different a report he would have given of his experience. Not a single librarian did use that technique.

Given the prevalence and in my opinion the high degree of predictability of student requests the more complete a description of what we can expect in our reference encounters with students the more efficient will be our interviewing technique. Let me make what I consider several key observations. Answers to the question about report or paper or assignment topic can be expected to vary in specificity on the one hand directly with educational level and on the other directly with level of student intelligence or capability.

Ordinary high school students will be writing their papers on "Hawthorne" or "Shakespeare" with the honors classes more likely to be choosing topics like "good and evil in the *Scarlet Letter*" or "appearance and reality in *Hamlet.*" Upperclassmen and majors will be approaching this same material with papers on "the symbolism of the letter 'A'" or "the imagery of light and dark in *Hamlet.*" Social science topics and science projects will show the same progression with younger project entrants looking for experiments on "light," and older students being more specific, sophisticated and advanced. Eventually, science and mathematics students will cease to use general libraries much at all except for an occasional special project, since merely learning the material in the textbooks will be keeping them busy. As the educational level rises and the curriculum broadens, requests for foreign relations, economics, and more sophisticated historical issues will begin to appear.

Also, *never* ask a student "how much information do you need?" I have observed countless times librarians encountering interviewing impediments when even small children let alone older ones will answer, "as much as I can get," "all you have," or even, "everything there is" to such a question. Simply inquire how long the paper is or how long the oral report is to be. Then you as a librarian and former student yourself will know rather definitely how much searching you are going to have to do, i.e., whether you are assisting someone with a 3-5 page, 8-10 page, or 15-20 page paper or a 2, 5, or 10 minute talk. It requires practically no time at all to obtain this information along with the due date. Obviously, there can be no photocopies from another library for a project due in three days. Also, it's just not true that most students do their work at the last minute; the better students usually give you plenty of notice.

If it is objected that every student does not have a precise topic when s/he approaches the desk, I answer that this approach is a most efficient way of ascertaining that fact. Once this is clarified, the librarian knows that s/he has now a different question, i.e., assistance in selecting a topic. Incidentally, I am very reluctant, and feel all librarians should be also, to engage students in discussions of selection of assignment topics. I consider that to be a matter between the student and instructor, even when the librarian has the necessary subject competence, but I am only too pleased to be able to provide sources and materials presenting subject surveys that will aid in topic selection.

Then, of course, there are the instances, very, very few I can say, when the person is not doing an assignment for a course. One immediately attempts to reassess the situation and begin again, often with some courteous remark indicating where books on the subject may be found along with some pleasantry about the fact that student requests are so prevalent—all conversation taking place while the person is being accompanied to the appropriate location in the library. The few times that a course assignment is not being pursued often involve adults who are working on job-related projects in which a written report is the goal anyway. A quick second guess usually reveals this, especially when the subject area is business or economics.

The evidence from not only the library literature, but from reference practice as well, it seems to me, is incontrovertible. Closely analyzed, most reference interviewing can be designed to be rapid and efficient, releasing the librarian's time to confront the genuine dilemmas of library work—not enough books and other materials on the shelves and the pressures of heavy demand for service at the reference desk. Once we have acknowledged the significant portion of questions that do not require an interview at all, have identified the easily predicted student requests, have learned to recognize and respond to all the routine subject, directory, and title requests, there is not a great deal left that is perplexing. The "tragic" yields to the "comic" sense of interviewing.

Clearly, the development of techniques that contribute to improving interviewing speed and effectiveness would be enhancements to reference performance and productivity in general. I further believe there are implications for evaluation here as well. Evaluation is becoming the key issue of the eighties in reference work; Number 11 of the *Reference Librarian* was devoted to the subject. In the first place, by releasing more of the librarian's time to devote to the search for answers and information there will be more time available for the crucial element of "follow-up" in the reference process. "Since we have been helping reference librarians . . . we have noted that the single most important behavior is asking the *follow up* question, 'Does this completely answer your question?'" (italics mine)[66] or "Have you found everything you need?" is the suggestion of Thomas et al.[67] Reference accuracy will improve. In the second place I believe that if we pay close attention to established prescriptions for responding to dominant types of questions, we will then be able to ask whether a librarian has adhered to the norms or standards for those types in evaluating his or her performance. Reference interviewing and reference work have always seemed to me less of an "art" and more like a "craft" that can be taught and learned anyway.

NOTES

1. William A. Katz. *Introduction to Reference Work*, Volume II. 3d ed. New York, McGraw-Hill, 1978, p. 70

2. Geraldine B. King. "The Reference Interview," RQ 12 (Winter 1972): 158-159; Marilyn Domas White. "The Dimensions of the Reference Interview," RQ 20 (Summer 1981): 378; Gerald Jahoda and Judith S. Braunagel. *The Librarian and Reference Queries*. New York, Academic Press, 1980, p. 139-40. Amusing parodies of the "tragic sense" are found in: Mark Plaiss, "Stupid Reference Questions . . . ," Library Journal 110 (October 15, 1985): 46; Ruth A. Pagell, "The Reference Interview," Unabashed Librarian, No. 30: 8; and D. H. Figueredo, "The Reference Interview," Unabashed Librarian, No. 33: 15

3. Thomas Lee Eichman. "The Complex Nature of Opening Reference Questions," RQ 17 (Spring 1978): 215

4. Ibid.

5. Robert S. Taylor. "Question Negotiation and Information Seeking in Libraries," College and Research Libraries 29 (May 1968): 178-94

6. Ellis Mount. "Communication Barriers and the Reference Question" Special Libraries 57 (October 1966): 575-78

7. Charles A. Bunge. "Interpersonal Dimensions of the Reference Interview: A Historical Review of the Literature," Drexel Library Quarterly 20 (Spring 1984): 9

8. Ibid., p. 19-21, mostly items 44-68

9. Gerald Jahoda and Paul E. Olson. "Analyzing the Reference Process," RQ 12 (Winter 1972): 148-156; and Jahoda and Braunagel, op. cit., Chapters 1-6

10. N. J. Crum. "The Librarian-Customer Relationship," Special Libraries 60 (May/June 1969): 269-277

11. Kathryn Sexton. "Don't Point," Texas Libraries 38 (Winter 1976): 183

12. Bunge, p. 12

13. Katz. 3d ed., p. 61

14. Michael McCoy. "Why Didn't They Teach Us That? The Credibility Gap in Library Education," Reference Librarian 11 (Spring/Summer 1985): 174

15. Diana M. Thomas, Ann T. Hinckley, and Elizabeth R. Eisenbach. *The Effective Reference Librarian*. New York, Academic Press, 1981. Chapter 5

16. Mary Jo Lynch. "Reference Interviews in Public Libraries," Library Quarterly 48

(April 1978): 119-142; Katz in his fourth ed., p. 46; Thomas et al., p. 99; and Bunge, p. 12 all draw upon her observations

17. Lynch, p. 133-34
18. Ibid., p. 137
19. Margaret A. Joseph. "Analyzing Success in Meeting Reference Department Management Objectives," Reference Librarian 11(Fall/Winter 1984): 188
20. William G. Jones. "How Many Reference Librarians Are Enough?", RQ 14 (Fall 1974): 18
21. John P. Wilkinson and William Miller. "The Step Approach to Reference Service," RQ 17 (Summer 1978): 298,299
22. Bunge, p. 10,11
23. Katz, 3rd ed., p. 65
24. William A. Katz. *Introduction to Reference Work, Volume II*. 4th ed. New York, McGraw-Hill, 1982, p. 23
25. David Isaacson. "Library Inreach," RQ 23 (Fall 1983): 65-74
26. Lynch, p. 132,133,136
27. Idem, p. 136; and Norma J. Shosid as cited in Elaine Z. Jennerich. "Before the Answer: Evaluating the Reference Process," RQ 19 (Summer 1980): 360,365
28. Lynch, p. 134
29. Ibid.
30. Marilyn Domas White. "The Reference Encounter Model," Drexel Library Quarterly 19 (Spring 1983): 38-55, see diagram on p. 45, e.g.
31. Idem. Dimensions, p. 373-381
32. Idem. "Evaluation of the Reference Interview," RQ 25(Fall 1985): 76-84
33. Idem. Encounter, p. 55
34. Ibid., p. 41
35. Ibid., p. 46, 49
36. Ibid., p. 51
37. Katz, 3d ed., p. 73
38. Bunge, p. 7
39. Linda Ward Callaghan. "Children's Questions; Reference Interviews with the Young," Reference Librarian 7 (Spring/Summer 1983): 60
40. Katz. 4th ed., p. 41
41. Idem. 3d ed., p. 9
42. Mary K. Chelton. "Young Adult Reference Services in the Public Library," Reference Librarian 7 (Spring/Summer 1983): 31
43. Lynch, p. 126-27
44. Gary E. Strong. "Evaluating the Reference Product," RQ 19(Summer 1980): 371
45. William G. Jones. "How Many Reference Librarians Are Enough?" RQ 14(Fall 1974): 17-18
46. White. Encounter, p. 46
47. Melissa Watson. "The Unresolved Conflict," Reference Librarian 4 (1982): 118
48. Thomas, p. 118
49. Richard Teller. "Ethical Considerations in the Question Negotiation Cycle," Reference Librarian 4 (1982): 135
50. White. Dimensions, p. 377-78
51. Ibid., p. 377
52. Katherine Emerson. "National Reporting on Reference Transactions 1976-1978," RQ 16 (Spring 1977): 202
53. Katz. 4th ed., p. 45; Thomas et al., p. 118; and Jahoda and Braunagel, p. 117
54. Charles Benson. "The Hidden Reference Question: Where Are the . . . ?" Southeastern Librarian 29(Summer 1979): 91
55. Katz, 4th ed., p. 41
56. Idem. 3d ed., p. 83

57. Jahoda, p. 117
58. Katz. 3d ed., p. 72-73
59. Anita R. Schiller. "Reference Service: Instruction or Information," Library Quarterly 35 (January 1965): 58
60. Katz. 3d ed., p. 73
61. Thomas, p. 120
62. Callaghan, p. 62
63. White. Dimensions, p. 379
64. Jahoda, p. 132-33
65. Dorman H. Smith. "A Matter of Confidence," Library Journal 97 (April 1, 1972): 1239-40
66. Ralph Geis and Lillie J. Seward. "Improving Reference Performance: Results of a Statewide Study," Library Journal 110 (November 1, 1985): 35
67. Thomas, p. 116

REFERENCE SERVICES WITH SPECIAL FUNCTIONS AND SUBJECTS

The Telephone Patron
and the Reference Interview:
The Public Library Experience

Rosemarie Riechel

Studies and analyses of the reference process and the elements of the reference interview abound in library literature, but the factors necessary to discover and satisfy the telephoning patron's real information needs have not been addressed. As the supervisor of a centralized telephone reference service in a large urban public library, I have experienced the evolution of telephone reference service from a switchboard-type operation to an important and unique part of public library reference service. It has expanded to meet the demands of today's information seekers, whose needs are so urgent that they have not got the time to visit the library to conduct their own research. The type of question asked has gone beyond the simple and indisputable fact to include the more complex and time consuming I&R query as well as requests for recent information not findable in print, obscure data or research material which can best be retrieved via online databases.

It follows that the collection had to expand to include more than traditional ready-reference sources as the queries received became more varied and complex. For example, the collection I maintain grew from 500 basic reference sources to over 3,000 titles plus a comprehensive newspaper clipping file, special indexes and files, a microcomputer produced in-house community information resource file and access to online databases.

READY-REFERENCE

While it is true that responses to ready-reference questions are routine and impersonal, since little effort is required to discover the

The author is Head, Information & Telephone Reference Division (Online Service), Queens Borough Public Library, 89-11 Merrick Blvd., Jamaica, NY 11432.

patron's real need, it is also true that what might seem to be a simple request for a telephone number, address, etc. might not completely fulfill the caller's need for information. The stated request might be what the patron perceives will answer his question or what he believes is the limit of what he can get over the telephone. With further interviewing, the librarian might discover the real need—perhaps the solution of a consumer problem for which a better approach exists. A person asking for library hours may in fact not have known about telephone reference until he was given the requested information as well as a brief statement of the purpose of the service. An inquiry about a particular title could lead to immediate help in clarifying a research problem or information about the library's collection. If the requested title is not held by the library, does informing the patron of this fact end the reference transaction? The personal approach on the part of the librarian might reveal that the patron's real need is for any book on a particular subject.

Some people are not comfortable talking about their problems or voicing their needs to a person they do not know and cannot see, while others find it easier because they can retain their anonymity while revealing a personal problem, asking to settle an office bet on something trivial or admitting ignorance about some subject. The telephone patron is often vague and ambiguous, perhaps because the information is second-hand or the subject is not known or understood. It is incumbent upon the librarian, as intermediary between the caller and the information, to relate positively and personally to the patron in order to determine what is really sought and to deliver accurate responses on demand or within a specified time period. Despite time limitations (usually 5-10 minutes per call), all the steps of the reference interview should be followed: 1. Determine the subject. 2. Discover the patron's real need. 3. Relate the subject and need to the appropriate source or sources. 4. Formulate the search strategy. 5. Evaluate the information in relation to the patron and his needs. The choice of a "ready-interview" or an in-depth interview is dependent upon the individual caller's request.

THE QUESTIONS

The questions received are as varied as the callers. Since the purpose of telephone reference is to provide service to a remote population, it is essential to establish rapport, to satisfy needs quickly and accurately and to encourage continued use of the service as a primary source for information. This must be accomplished via the reference interview. However, negotiation is more difficult by telephone because the advantages of non-verbal communication are lacking. The librarian must be astute and interested enough to try to "read" the caller's need by listening to the tone of voice, pauses, hesitation, nervous giggling, etc. The age level and the level of information might be suggested by the tone/pitch of the voice, the language used and the nature of the request. A librarian who is approachable, empathetic and patient should encourage the patron to talk about his request, why he needs the information and what level of information is necessary. A friendly voice, devoid of any hint that the patron is being judged in any way by the question asked, is certainly desirable. For example, the librarian's response to a gentleman asking what century this is should be straightforward. In fact, when informed that this is the 20th century, the patron stated (soberly) that he thought it was the 19th and expressed gratitude for being put in his place in time. The man was genuinely confused about the 1900s being in the 20th century but any hint of judgement on the part of the librarian might have lost the patron—with his dilemma unresolved.

"This may sound silly, but I'd like to know how many cats there are in the United States." This patron should be assured that no question is silly. A little friendly remark about the question being interesting relieves embarassment and results in a satisfied patron.

The child with a homework assignment calls the library for any of the following reasons: he is lazy, his teacher told him to, he is ill and afraid of not completing an assignment, he is genuinely confused and is seeking some guidance. The interviewer should determine the reason for calling, the level of need and without sounding judgemental, attempt to guide the child, giving brief answers and sources for further research. A homework question should be dealt with constructively so that the child's experience is a positive one.

COMMUNITY INFORMATION—INFORMATION AND REFERRAL

Establishing trust is another significant aspect of the reference interview, particularly when dealing with the I&R query. For many it takes courage to call the library to gain information or help for the resolution of a personal problem. This type of caller is usually not receptive to a request to call back, therefore it is important to quickly determine the real need and turn to the community information resource file (as the most up-to-date source) and provide a referral, assuring the patron that others have been helped in the same way. If the patron expresses concern about calling the agency, the librarian might offer to do it on his behalf or encourage the patron to call telephone reference again if the referral agency does not come through with the answer to the problem.

In my experience, the elderly are particularly anxious about events in their lives. Sometimes they call just to talk about their problems, believing that they will find a sympathetic ear at the library. They are usually uninformed about where to turn for solutions, so carefully worded questions can lead to the real need behind their chatter, i.e., a heat or rent problem, a medical concern, a consumer complaint. Assurance that the information they give is kept confidential, will often lead to disclosure of facts needed to provide the correct information or proper referral. Encouraging the patron to call again if any other problems arise reinforces trust and makes the reference interview for the repeat caller easier to conduct.

ONLINE SEARCHING

I read an editorial about a study of the ages of people who use tissues versus handkerchiefs. It said that people 35 years or older tend to use handkerchiefs.

I am looking for any reports on the structural analysis of the Hartford, Connecticut Civic Center which collapsed in 1975.

I need the date of an article on a book exchange at a garbage dump in Wellesley, Massachusetts.

I am looking for information on emotional disturbances and stress treatment of opera singers.

Most telephone requests for online searches begin as reference questions which cannot be answered fully, if at all, using the library's collection. Frequently the patron has difficulty expressing his needs, as evidenced by the ambiguity, brevity or incompleteness of the query statement. In order to determine if a question is appropriate for an online search, certain guidelines might be followed:

1. Has the patron been carefully interviewed to determine the real need, the context of the request, the specifics, whether any previous attempt was made to obtain the information, which sources the patron used, the level of need?
2. Is some or all of the information findable in hardcopy sources in the collection—books, newspaper clipping file, pamphlets, file of frequently asked questions, etc. or is it too recent or obscure to be located without using online databases?
3. Is the needed information too difficult to pull together using printed indexes? Is the patron combining several concepts into one question? Would searching an online database, using the key word approach, retrieve the information?
4. Is the most current information required? Would the available printed sources fail because they are not updated as frequently as the online sources?

Once it is determined that the best way to approach the patron's request is through the use of online databases, further interviewing must follow, using a search strategy worksheet (see Figure 1).

The patron's request should be written down as stated. Then the librarian must solicit further information in order to translate the request into searchable terms. Since the telephoning patron will not be present during the actual search, close interaction with the patron is crucial during the process of defining the search, formulating the search strategy, selecting the appropriate database(s) and retrieving the correct information. Open questions should be asked at a relaxed pace in order to gain as much information as possible about the request and closed questions should be used for further clarification of needs. The search request should be restated by the librarian to verify the accuracy of the interpretation of the request. Also, the interviewer should not hesitate to admit ignorance about a subject. Asking the patron/expert to explain the topic or define terms encourages him to elaborate, clarify and supply key words and concepts.

If problems arise during the online retrieval process, the search should be stopped and the patron contacted—this is the best alternative to having the patron present for interaction during the searching process.

It is unrealistic to demand that the telephoning patron come to the library to pick up printouts. The results of searches taken over the telephone should be reported to the patron in the same way—unless

FIGURE 1

SEARCH STRATEGY WORKSHEET

DATE: _____   TIME: _____

REQUEST STATEMENT:

****

VENDOR SERVICE: NEXIS: ____ DIALOG: ____ BRS: ____

SEARCH STRATEGY:

CONCEPT A   CONCEPT B   CONCEPT C
_____   _____   _____
****

DATABASES TO BE USED:

TYPE OF MATERIAL: ARTICLES ____ REPORTS ____ OTHER _____

MODIFIERS:

YEARS OF COVERAGE _____   LANGUAGE _____

OTHER _____
      _____

INSTRUCTIONS _____
_____
_____

****

PATRON'S NAME: MR. MRS. MISS MS. (CIRCLE ONE) _____

PATRON'S TELEPHONE NUMBER: (   ) _____ WHEN AVAILABLE _____

PATRON WILL CALL (DATE? TIME?) _____

STAFF WILL CALL PATRON (DATE? TIME?) _____

LIBRARIAN TAKING REQUEST _____

****

he expresses a desire to come to the library to continue his research. During the post-search interview, the results should be explained and the patron should be asked if his information needs have been satisfied. Approachability and an expression of genuine interest in the caller's topic is essential. A satisfied caller is often a repeat caller. A previous relationship with the patron is valuable since the interview routine is known. The patron might try to work out his own search strategy and define terminology before calling.

The proper use of interview techniques should ensure that the telephoning patrons who will benefit from an online search will have access to automated information retrieval service.

STAFF TRAINING

The successful operation of a telephone reference service is dependent upon continuous training of staff. This activity is carried out on two levels: 1. the basic training of new staff in ready-reference service, the maintenance and use of the collection, approaches to I&R work, community information service skills and the fundamentals of online searching. 2. advanced sessions with experienced librarians in order to teach further refinements of technique.

As I see it, staff training is a combination of individualized tutoring, hands-on experience and group discussion. Interview techniques and approaches to particular requests can be monitored and search strategies and results analyzed. Exercises, using actual questions, particularly unsuccessful searches, difficult requests for obscure data and failed online requests, reinforce training. The staff has the opportunity to analyze the reference process and the outcome of individual transactions while identifying methods of improving the interview or search strategy—and without pressure from callers.

To a great degree, the development of staff interview skills and rapport with patrons depends upon the ability to communicate with the supervisor without fear of being judged. The quality and quantity of telephone reference service is dependent upon successful communication. It follows then that interest and approachability must be characteristic of the supervisor if efficient staff performance is to be achieved.

In conclusion, much has been written about the reference interview but studies which statistically test the quality of telephone ref-

erence service in public libraries are rare. Thomas Childer's unobtrusive study, using a number of short-answer fact-type questions
which were telephoned to sample libraries, revealed a disappointing
level of correctness. Questions concerning the many variables
which influenced the results, i.e., the book collection, library hours,
referrals, total number of staff, the simplicity of the questions, the
handling of more complex queries, were raised and the finding suggested further inquiry. (See bibliography for citation.) Clearly, to
increase the reliability of public library telephone reference service,
the patron's real need must be understood. Therefore, further study
of the reference interview in this setting is significant.

REFERENCES

Auster, Ethel and Lawton, Stephen B. "Search Interview Techniques and Information Gain
as Antecedents of User Satisfaction With Online Bibliographic Retrieval." *Journal of the
American Society for Information Science*, 35 (March 1984), 90-103.

Auster, Ethel. "User Satisfaction with the Online Negotiation Interview: Contemporary
Concern in Traditional Perspective." *RQ*, 23 (Fall 1983), 47-59.

Childers, Thomas. *Telephone Information Service in Public Libraries*, in Crowley, Terence
and Childers, Thomas, *Information Service in Public Libraries; Two Studies*, Metuchen,
NJ: Scarecrow Press, 1971.

Dalrymple, Prudence W. "Closing the Gap: The Role of the Librarian in Online Searching."
RQ, 24 (Winter 1984), 177-185.

Gers, Ralph and Seward, Lillie J. "Improving Reference Performance: Results of a Statewide Study." *Library Journal* 110 (1 November 1985), 32-35.

Hutchins, Margaret. *Introduction to Reference Work*. Chicago, IL: American Library Association, 1944.

Jahoda, Gerald and Olson, Paul E. "Analyzing the Reference Process." *RQ*, 12 (Winter
1972), 148-156.

King, Geraldine B. "The Reference Interview." *RQ*, 12 (Winter 1972), 157-160.

Markham, Marilyn J., Stirling, Keith H. and Smith, Nathan M. "Librarian Self-Disclosure
and Patron Satisfaction in the Reference Interview." *RQ*, 22 (Summer 1983), 369-374.

White, Marilyn Domas. "Evaluation of the Reference Interview." *RQ*, 25 (Fall 1985),
76-84.

The Interlibrary Loan Interview

Virginia Boucher

Interlibrary loan has come to be regarded by the library patron as an expected part of library service. It is considered a right, just as circulation of many library materials is considered a right. From the library patron's point of view, interlibrary loan is somewhat harder to accomplish than circulation, but it should be possible to make the process relatively easy to do. The library patron generally has some idea that interlibrary loan is a way to get materials from other libraries. Explaining what it is or why it is done is not as urgent as in the past, though still necessary at times. With a brief introduction covering "what" and "why," the librarian can get down to the business of giving and finding answers to specific questions.

Such an interlibrary loan interview is a variation on the reference theme. The skills used in conducting a good reference interview, both verbal and non-verbal, must be brought into play when guiding an interlibrary loan interview. Where both activities are done at the reference desk, the interlibrary loan interview may be a continuation of a reference interview.

There are several reasons for doing an interlibrary loan interview instead of merely handing the library patron a form to complete. First of all, the interview is an opportunity to teach the library patron how to use the service, the mechanics of what must be done to get the request filled. The discussion during the interview can clear up misconceptions the library patron may have about the service. Secondly, the interview is a time to instruct the library patron in the requirements of acceptable bibliographic citations. This knowledge often can be used in other contexts. Another reason is that the interview saves searching time because omissions and illegible handwriting can be addressed. The information necessary for transmitting an interlibrary loan request to another library can be obtained by questioning. The old interlibrary loan adage, "you only get what you are

The author will be found in Interlibrary Loan Service, University Libraries, Campus Box 184, University of Colorado, Boulder, CO 80309.

wise enough to request properly,'' is still true. The omission of a series, for example, can result in a negative response, if the lending library classifies that series together so that there is no author or title access. Lastly, an interview is a chance to point out the use of reference tools and the whereabouts of other kinds of materials, such as government documents, with which the library patron may not be familiar.

The librarian's attitude is an important part of the interlibrary loan interview. The projection of a helpful attitude is necessary, though difficult at times, because of the many roadblocks which exist along the interlibrary loan path. The copyright law is an example of a possible roadblock in the case of a request for photocopy of an entire copyrighted work. Time can be another. A positive attitude is hard to maintain when the library patron is impatient and frustrated because the material is not in the library and available for use.

Another aspect of the interlibrary loan interview concerns the verbal communication between the librarian and the library patron. This exchange is characterized by very specific questions for which factual answers are sought. The library patron's questions are largely predictable, and routine answers can be prepared to satisfy most queries. As for the librarian, most of the information necessary to complete a successful interlibrary loan transaction is also known so that questions can be asked to elicit what is needed.

QUESTIONS ASKED BY THE LIBRARY PATRON

Can I Borrow This Material Using Interlibrary Loan?

The library patron often has a specific request for a monograph or a periodical article and has in hand all or part of the bibliographic elements needed for an interlibrary loan request. Assurance is sought that this is the right place and the right service.

How Long Will It Take?

This is not an idle question, for the library patron is frequently working against some kind of deadline. The probability of getting the material by the time the deadline arrives is what must be discussed. If the librarian does not know precisely how long it takes to get material using current transmission and delivery methods, then data about transit time should be gathered from completed requests.

Accuracy in answering this question is of vital importance to the library patron.

How Much Will It Cost Me?

The library patron is always interested in the condition of his or her pocketbook. In the case of graduate students on a limited budget, the answer to this question may dictate whether the request can be pursued or not. The librarian should know what the charges for medical requests are, what an average book loan from a charging lender costs, and what photocopy fees are likely to be. Of course, those libraries which absorb all charges for interlibrary loan rather than passing them on to the library patron make the answer to this question very simple.

How Will I Know When It Gets Here?

The method for notifying the library patron when the material has arrived can be explained be it telephone, mail, electronic mail, or asking in person.

How Long Can I Have It?

The usual loan period of two weeks comes as a shock to some library patrons who are accustomed to longer loan periods through circulation. Since some library patrons tend to think of books in their possession as "belonging" to them, the short loan period for interlibrary loan books must be emphasized. The possibility of a renewal can also be mentioned and clarified.

What Must I Do?

Whether this question is verbalized or not, it must be answered. Some libraries find it useful to have a brochure which tells something about the interlibrary loan service and gives instructions on how to fill out an interlibrary loan request form.

Where Can I Find a Source of Reference?

This question becomes important when the bibliographic information is insufficient, appears to be inaccurate, or is very complex. Instructing the library patron in the use of unfamiliar reference tools, referral to the correct index or abstract service, or teaching the use of an online system can often have benefit far beyond solving the immediate problem. In extreme circumstances, an appointment can be made for a complete discussion of research needs.

QUESTIONS ASKED BY THE LIBRARIAN

Is This Person Eligible to Use the Service?

The librarian must determine if the library patron belongs to the library's clientele. For interlibrary loan, it is often not possible to serve those from other jurisdictions because of funding patterns. Once the eligibility has been established, then the person's name, identification number (if needed), address, and telephone number can be requested.

Have the Holdings in This Library Been Checked?

It is not customary to request from other libraries material owned by the borrowing library. Asking the library patron if the public catalog, online catalog, or serial records have been checked is necessary as a reminder, for this simple step may have been omitted. At this time, materials which are not described in such sources can be pointed out. In some libraries, for example, some special collections are not in the public catalog, so the library patron may be unaware that the item needed can be located in the library.

Could a Substitution Be Used?

The mature researcher will not tolerate a substitution, but the more casual reader may not object. Another edition, or translation, or book on the same topic may be just as well, and these may be in the library's collection. Another kind of material, e.g., periodical articles instead of books, may meet the library patron's needs.

When Is the Material Needed?

The answer to this question is invariably "as soon as possible." Such a response tells the librarian very little that is helpful. The last use date, or need before date, or cannot-use-it-if-it-comes-the-next-day date can usually be pinpointed. Then a calculation can be made as to whether or not the material will arrive in time.

Is the Information Complete and Readable?

Here specific data elements are particularly important. The bibliographic information needed is as follows:

— Book: author, title, edition (if any), place of publication, publisher, date of publication, and series (if any).
— Periodical article: title of periodical, volume, issue number or issue date, year, author of article, title of article, and pages.
— Newspapers in microform: title of newspaper, section (if any), place of publication, date. (When asking for photocopy, the author of the article, title of the article, and pages are necessary.)
— Dissertations and masters' theses: author, title, institution, degree, year.
— Government publications: the usual information for a book or a periodical article and the issuing agency, report number, and Superintendent of Documents classification number (if known).
— Technical reports: corporate author, report number, individual author, edition, issuing agency, date, series, and contract number (or as much as possible of this information).

Does This Request Meet the Requirements of Interlibrary Loan Codes?

The policy governing interlibrary loan is contained in interlibrary loan codes. Very often there is a local or state code, a regional code, as well as the "National Interlibrary Loan Code, 1980,"[1] which must be considered. "International Lending: Principles and Guidelines for Procedure (1978; revised 1983)"[2] comes into play for overseas requests. These codes frequently specify what can and cannot be borrowed. For example the "National Interlibrary Loan Code, 1980," lists the types of materials not ordinarily loaned by most libraries:

1. Rare or valuable material, including manuscripts;
2. Bulky or fragile items that are difficult or expensive to ship;

3. Material in high demand at the lending library;
4. Material with local circulation restrictions;
5. Unique material that would be difficult or impossible to replace.[3]

It may be possible, though not likely, to borrow a best seller such as Jean M. Auel's *The Mammoth Hunters* from the public library in the next town. That is not the sort of request, however, to be made of a large research library.

How Much Can the Library Patron Pay?

If fees are passed on to the library patron for payment, then the maximum amount the library patron is willing to pay should be established. This aids in selecting a library from which to make the request.

Has the Copyright Statement Been Read and Signed?

The order warning of copyright must appear on the patron request form and must be signed in applicable cases. This requirement is necessary only in the case of requests for photocopy. It is often advisable to explain the provisions of the copyright law to the library patron. It can be helpful to have a written statement ready to hand out.

Can the Library Patron Read the Language in Which the Material is Written?

Nothing is more disconcerting than to have a library patron become angry because the periodical article came in Japanese instead of English as was expected. A librarian is more alert to the bibliographic nuances which tell whether the material will come in a language other than English. Asking if that language can be read, while insulting to a few, can only be helpful to most.

Would It Be Better to Send the Library Patron to the Material?

There are a number of cases when the library patron would be better served by going to the material rather than attempting an interlibrary loan: (1) the time frame is too short to allow for an interlibrary loan, but the material is available in a nearby library; (2) the nature of the material, e.g., manuscripts, prohibits use of interlibrary loan; (3) the quantity of material needed is excessive in interlibrary terms; or (4) the possibility of added resources, such as those of the Library of Congress, make a trip desirable. Giving information on what other libraries are like and what they require in the way of identification, fees, or the like can be most useful to the library patron.

The interlibrary loan interview can be helpful as a mechanism for determining precise bibliographic information needed to get an interlibrary loan and for teaching the library patron about the service, bibliographic citations, and other reference sources in the library. The interview is largely a matter of asking specific questions and giving factual answers. These questions and answers are largely predictable and may be prepared in advance of the interview. A successful interlibrary loan interview can be a powerful aid in obtaining material efficiently and quickly for the library patron.

NOTES

1. "National Interlibrary Loan Code, 1980." In Virginia Boucher, *Interlibrary Loan Practices Handbook* (Chicago: American Library Association, 1984), 139-141.

2. "International Lending: Principles and Guidelines for Procedure (1978; revised 1983)." In Virginia Boucher, *Interlibrary Loan Practices Handbook* (Chicago: American Library Association, 1984), 177-182.

3. "National Interlibrary Loan Code, 1980." In Virginia Boucher, *Interlibrary Loan Practices Handbook* (Chicago: American Library Association, 1984), 139-140.

Independent Scholars' Roundtable: A Pioneering Project at Nassau Library System

Dinah Lindauer

The public library's traditional role in education and research has been in support of individual rather than group learning and scholarship. Although many libraries have broadened their activities in support of continuing education, a pioneering project at the Nassau Library System has been offering a new kind of framework for working with adults who are doing serious learning or research on their own. Since April 1984, Independent Scholars' Roundtables are providing library-based encouragement and support to researchers who are self-motivated and self-directed. In this new kind of intellectual environment, librarians are exploring how to improve service to this special clientele, while participants benefit from contact with others who want to turn their interests and enthusiasms into rewarding projects. This article presents the background of the current interest in independent scholarship nationwide, the origins of the project at the Nassau Library System, the initial implementation and findings, including guidelines for other public libraries seeking to adapt the program to their needs.

INDEPENDENT SCHOLARSHIP NATIONWIDE

The term independent scholar is widely identified with Ronald Gross, director of the federally-funded Independent Scholarship National Program, which coordinates such efforts throughout the country. Gross' books in this field include *The Lifelong Learner*[1] and *Independent Scholarship: Promise, Problems and Prospects*.[2] As the leading authority in the field, Gross reminds us that independent scholarship is not a new phenomenon. An independent scholar can

The author is the former Coordinator of Programs and Services, Nassau Library System, 900 Jerusalem Ave., Uniondale, NY 11553.

be anyone who falls in love with a subject, whether he or she is entirely self-educated or a candidate for a doctoral degree.

> Emerson had prophesied for the new democracy a culture in which men and women from all walks of life would also be active in the world of ideas. For a while, it happened. During much of the 19th and early 20th centuries, lawyers, doctors, railroad conductors, school teachers, and clergymen were often involved, and some deeply involved in scholarship. But over the past three or four decades, inquiry and theorizing have become concentrated almost totally in the universities: for people with intellectual ambitions there has come to be no other choice other than the academy.[3]

Gross contends that today, however, the Emersonian ideal is reasserting itself. There is emerging an "independent sector" in the world of learning, with both individuals and organizations now engaged in scholarship outside the university.

Some 40 support groups for independent scholars have emerged throughout the country over the past five years, such as the Institute for Research in History (NY), the Princeton Research Forum (NJ), the Academy of Independent Scholars (Colorado), the Alliance of Independent Scholars (Cambridge), the Center for Independent Study (CT), the Independent Scholars Association of the North Carolina Triangle (NC), Independent Scholars of Asia (CA), the Association of Independent Historians of Art (NY), and the Minnesota Independent Scholars Forum (MN). The significance of work by researchers and writers outside of academe is recognized increasingly at the national level. For example, the Rockefeller Foundation has funded a program of annual grants for outstanding work by such investigators, awarded through the Modern Language Association, the American Historical Association, and the American Philosophical Association. Other sectors of intellectual life, such as the national network of state humanities councils, have become increasingly responsive to such work, too.

PROJECT BEGINNINGS
AT NASSAU LIBRARY SYSTEM

At the Nassau Library System, the first stirring of interest in finding an appropriate role for small to medium-sized suburban public libraries in serving independent scholars began in mid-1983 with an inquiry from a member of the Board of Trustees.

Taking advantage of the presence on Long Island of the federally-funded Independent Scholarship National Program, supported by the Fund for the Improvement of Post-secondary Education, the trustee contacted Gross, the leading authority in the field. During 1984, a major story about Gross in the *New York Times* [4] highlighted several examples of Long Islanders who had turned a devout passion for a subject into research leading to worldwide correspondence, publishing projects and national awards.

The Nassau Library System (NLS) is a cooperative system of 54 independent public libraries within commuting distance of New York City. More than 1.5 million county residents are served by generally well supported local libraries that are backed, not only by a wide range of support services from NLS but by the academic and special libraries of the Long Island Library Resources Council, and NYSILL, the New York State Interlibrary Loan network.

With support from a variety of federal, state, and foundation funding sources, primarily LSCA and New York State's Education Information Centers grant programs, libraries in Nassau County were already offering a broad range of resources and services to the adult independent learner. New York State's external degree program had been supported for some time by special collections and librarian/mentors offering assistance to students enrolled in non-traditional degree programs or preparing for advanced professional examinations.

In addition, Nassau's libraries provide a number of innovative reference services in the area of community information and referral, linked to the 85 agencies that are part of the Health and Welfare Council. Since 1976, the system's libraries also offer access to a teaching/learning network known as The Learning Connection, through which individuals register their teaching specialties and learning needs and are able to arrange and/or exchange services. Since 1984 The Learning Connection is available for computerized search on a dial-in basis in each of the 54 libraries. Missing from the eclectic mix was anything directed at the unaffiliated independent scholar who might be pursuing a single topic in-depth over a longer period of time.

With planning assistance from Gross, a proposal was developed in the System's 1984 proposal for 1985 LSCA funding. The grant was approved and the pilot began in January 1985 under the direction of Dorothy Puryear, who also administers a wide range of innovative projects as Chief of Special Library Services.

In an attempt to tie the independent scholar concept to the needs of growing numbers of older people whose earlier retirements offered them time to pursue research, the pilot designed a link to the national Elderhostel movement. During 1984, through ALA and Elderhostel cooperation, every public library had received a catalog of campus based one week Elderhostel courses around the country. These programs were already enrolling more than 80,000 people who were 60 or older. With ALA and Elderhostel help, the NLS pilot offered Nassau's former Elderhostelers the opportunity to convert new interests into serious research opportunities in the supportive setting of an Independent Scholars' Roundtable at two public library locations. Roundtable participants, however, would not be limited by age. The project called for launching the effort with a public event, followed by monthly information-sharing sessions led by a scholar-in-residence.

The Roundtables were to be a

> self-help device through which individual scholars can do more to meet their needs through mutual encouragement and support . . . sharing useful information, sustaining morale, refining ideas, making connections, launching activities, fostering interdisciplinary discussions, enlisting public awareness and support, networking with others around the country to share fundings, acting as a clearinghouse for resources, opportunities, etc.[5]

Planning sessions were held early in 1985 to ready twin opening sessions during National Library Week at two library sites. The committee includes an administrator and program support person from each site, two program representatives of NLS, the site coordinator/scholar-in-residence, and Ronald Gross who continues to act as Consultant.

Early planning sessions were devoted to sorting out relationships and responsibilities among the System, project and local library staffs and refining the concept and goals of the project with the Consultant. The pilot was viewed as an opportunity to assess the possible implications for improved reference services in the small to medium-sized public library to serve a growing number of self-motivated intellectual explorers. The Roundtables would use the library meeting spaces not merely as independent tenants, or as a library program audience. Rather, site coordinator Dr. Virginia Leipzig, herself a graduate of independent learning projects, would facilitate the self-planning process to encourage each group to set its own agenda. The reference services link was to grow out of the needs of the individuals who actually attended. After the opening sessions the lecture format was to be avoided, in favor of information sharing on a self-selection basis. The sessions were to provide ongoing opportunity for mutual encouragement, stimulation, support, and recognition for patrons interested in pursuing research. Librarians were to be alerted to the needs of such patrons and to provide occasional events addressed to issues in this field.

LAUNCHING AND DEVELOPING THE GROUPS

The twin public events held during National Library Week were titled, *Use Your Mind For All It's Worth*, featured Ronald Gross, and were intended to be a focus for publicity to attract prospective group members. A promotional flier was designed to be used both as a mailer and as a poster, and appealed specifically to those who:

— Are doing your own research in any field, topic or issue.
— Want to explore new areas of knowledge and understanding.
— Enjoy the company of other lively-minded people.
— Need to continue learning to meet your career or personal goals.
— Consider yourself a "lifelong learner."
— Are interested in opportunities to get grants, to teach your subject, to publish your writings, to find colleagues, or to access information in your field.

In addition to the mailing to all Elderhostel participants, mailings also went to the complete community mailing list at each of the two sites. The reference staffs of the 54 member public libraries were asked to help identify likely candidates who were engaged in ongoing research or sustained learning in any field. Additional suggestions included part-time or retired college professors, or adult education or high school teachers; book dealers; local or regional historians; people involved in non-traditional degree programs;

free-lance non-fiction writers; librarians who were conducting their own research; PhD's working outside academe; business entrepreneurs with research interests and retired persons with intellectual and cultural interests.

Despite bad weather, the NLW events drew sizeable enthusiastic audiences—with more than 90 coming from 35 different communities. Women outnumbered men better than two to one and despite the preponderance of seniors in the mailings, the age range in the audiences was considerably wider. In ensuing months, men proved to be the more regular participants so that the core of regular attendees is more balanced.

Participants at both sites were provided with an opportunity to indicate preferences for meeting days and time. Out of these, four groups were formed—an afternoon and an evening group at each site. After nearly a year of sessions, one site dropped the afternoon session, leaving three Roundtables by early 1986. Ad hoc subgroups occasionally formed, geared to the needs of writers or for other limited purposes.

To counteract the loss of momentum of a summer hiatus, the September 1985 sessions at each site were publicized as an Open House invitation from the participants. Particular attention was given to reaching the memberships of local organizations in fields serving the interests of serious students and scholars: astronomy, archaeology, history, and historic preservation, ethnic studies, nature conservancies, etc.

Coordinator Virginia Leipzig continues to use a variety of techniques to maintain the atmosphere of informal and supportive communication and group cohesiveness. Discussions are channeled in such a way so that each meeting can be said at the end to have afforded some particular benefit, that no one dominated the questioning, and all have a chance to speak. Some of the early meeting themes were built around issues such as: personal growth through individual research projects (the journal); joining the independent scholars national network; sharing problem-solving research techniques (what about copyrights?); using the *Independent Scholar's Handbook*[6] as a specific guide. Early meetings also utilized an activity to underline group solidarity and individuality as well as explore the theme of individual creativity. The point of emphasis was a reiteration that research in material that has been researched before is not a waste if new eyes can produce a new viewpoint.

LIBRARY/RESEARCH FOCUS

As the groups moved toward a second year of meetings, a core of regular attendees emerged, with an atmosphere where people felt secure enough to ask for help. Each meeting includes brief presentations about work in progress on a voluntary basis and whenever appropriate, a brief library or research component related to a group's current interest. These may be selected from a sample list provided by the library liaison or the planning committee, and have included the following topics for discussion:

1. How can I find special subject collections in the metropolitan area?
2. How can I gain access to special libraries?
3. How can I obtain materials not in a local library or in Nassau County?
4. Where are there specialized bookstores in my subject field?
5. What materials does the government publish in special fields?
6. What special indexes and bibliographies are there in my field?
7. What special journals and periodicals are issued in my field?
8. What special materials does a library have to help a writer in search of markets or dissemination of his/her writing?
9. How can I find out what foundations are giving grants in my field?
10. Are there any professional organizations or associations in my field?
11. What materials does the library have on tax implications for independent researchers?
12. How do I go about copyrighting my work?
13. What films and other non-print materials are in existence about my field?
14. How do I find out if PhD dissertations or other research work exists about my subject?
15. What materials does the library have on research methods? On writing a book proposal? On lesson plans for teaching my subject?
16. How can I ask my question so that I can get maximum cooperation from the reference staff?

With the renewal of the project for a second year, a new component was added—a one page insert on "Independent Scholarship in Nassau County" contracted for inclusion in the *Independent Scholarship Newsletter* produced by Gross. The first issue included anecdotes from presentations at recent meetings, and tips on upcoming events, lectures, and conferences in the Metropolitan area. Promised for a future issue was an article on finding outlets for manuscripts by surveying likely specialized periodicals in the library.

The variety and complexity of the research projects continues to generate enthusiasm. The range is impressive—from the dragon research by a retired kindergarten teacher writing a children's book; an astronomy teacher whose obsession is calculating celestial events; an auto parts dealer doing a scientific evaluation of the Bible; a marketing executive in the entertainment field tracing sources of Celtic myths; a housewife researching early women pioneer diaries as she readies her family to emigrate to Israel.

Sometimes the project has an obvious link to the researcher's professional interests—a retired physician is writing a medical history. Others may be of short duration—the reaction of an inquiring mind to a question. "What language did Abraham speak?" drew on sources in history, language, anthropology and archaeology, as well as the Bible, over a three-month period. In contrast, another's doctoral research begun 15 years earlier on "The role of civilian scouts in the Arizona Apache Wars" may end as a book without the academic degree.

GUIDELINES FOR ADAPTATION

What has the pilot taught us about improving reference services? What guidelines can be offered to others who wish to develop a special reference service sensitivity to serving the timid and tenacious individuals who are doing serious thinking, research and writing?

Clientele

Unlike many of the special audiences that libraries provide with information services—the elderly, the handicapped, business men, parents, job seekers and career changers, new Americans, and others—independent scholars are few in number. Fewer still, are those who would risk or crave the company of others in a group setting. Yet there is an obvious role that public libraries can play in providing support services to these very special people whose compelling need may grow out of intellectual curiosity or rage at injustice. If you would start a Roundtable for Independent Scholars, don't expect the attendance numbers that impress legislators. Do expect participation of those as yet undiscovered Miltons and his contemporary counterparts—the incipient I.F. Stones, Barbara Tuchmans, Ralph Naders, Betty Friedans, Erik Hoffers, Buckminster Fullers—independent scholars all.

Leadership

If you are interested in organizing a Roundtable in your locality, a starter kit of materials that shows how to create and promote such a group is available from Ronald Gross, 17 Myrtle Drive, Great Neck, NY 11021. Gross is also a spellbinding keynoter, and a resourceful and an innovative planner, who has links to every major initiative in the world of independent scholarship throughout the country. On the local level, your facilitator/scholar in residence is best chosen from among those whose own scholarly background includes off-campus experience. Although electing a leader from within the group has worked well in some places, it may be hard to get that kind of a commitment. Librarians are usually not themselves scholars, and would need to avoid at all costs the heavy handed approach of an undergraduate library orientation.

What is essential, is an individual who provides continuity and stimulation to a constantly changing group of lively minded people. Participants need to have a sense of purpose and planning without rigid formalities. Library liaison needs to be responsive to needs as they emerge—ready to postpone something prepared in advance in favor of a timely answer to a newly identified research or resource problem.

Administrative Support

A few communication support services are a must: regular notices about upcoming meetings; notices in the libraries' own calendar and newsletter, and on bulletin board postings; regular releases about special activities in the local weeklies and publicity that can generate feature stories in the dailies. Inserts inviting membership from special subject disciplines are welcomed by special interest newsletters. A clearinghouse listing of activities and opportunities that would interest scholars is especially desirable and may be possible in collaboration with a nearby university. A bimonthly or quarterly newsletter may be possible with volunteer editors from the Roundtable membership. The goal is to keep up momentum with a reasonable amount of regular communication, sensitivity to the needs of the participants, and understanding that tangible products and rewards are few and slow in coming.

Funding

An independent scholar roundtable need not be a costly project. Unless a paid consultant is used to help get the ball rolling, staff planning time is the major outlay. The facilitator/scholar in residence contract costs will vary with the expectations in each locality. Grants have been available for more ambitious programs, such as the Fall 1985 six-part lecture series at the Amarillo Public Library, funded by the Texas Committee for the Humanities. Initiatives in support of lifelong learning and adult scholarship are supported in a variety of state, federal, and foundation grant programs.

Interloan

Borrowing materials from distant sources is probably the major need of most independent scholars. Interviews conducted with a sample of members in the Nassau County Roundtables confirmed this. Yet beyond the simple interloan of monographs, the availability of more complex requests for the interloan process is less widely known and infrequently offered by reference staff. An interloan request may be the first approach made by a scholar to the reference desk at a public library. When requested materials are denied by a distant owning library, the reference librarian should be ready to suggest a variety of possible alternatives—other sources, photocopies, commercial or custom microforms. Indeed, the reference librarian must be as tenacious in support of a scholar's need, as is the scholar. Case histories of success stories are filled with kudos to the reference librarians who filled this vital intermediary role.

Access

The help of the reference librarian to arrange access privileges when on-site use is required, was the next most cited aid. In the Nassau area, members of the Roundtables were made part of the Research Loan Program of the Long Island Library Resources Council, which permits outsiders use of member academic and special libraries. Where no such formal arrangements exist, the reference staff should be ready to serve in an advocacy role on behalf of scholars.

Microforms

Frequently cited in interviews with researchers was the problem of eye-straining hours in front of microform readers. Although state-of-the-art equipment offers some flexibility, too little attention is given to the effect of light on legibility. This is one time when too much light is the culprit. Researchers would also welcome an opportunity to borrow portable microform readers. More and more public libraries have equipment loan programs for the general public. Special arrangements to lend both film and readers for home use by scholars would involve minimum risk. A number of years ago the annual report of the New York Public Library took note of the opportunity provided by public libraries for self-directed adult learners to pursue knowledge on their own. The photos and quotes were from persons who had achieved notability through study and investigation: Dewitt Wallace, Agnes DeMille, Cornelia Otis Skinner and Edwin Land. "I have a lifelong affinity for libraries," said historian Barbara Tuchman. "I find there happiness, refuge, not to mention the materials for making books of my own."

Others who have achieved distinction refer to the debt they feel to the librarians who nurtured their quests when their single-mindedness was still considered aberrant. From a recent article on Xerography and its inventor Chester F. Carlson,

> Carlson approached this task with an unrelenting single-mindedness that one would not hesitate to label lunacy had the outcome been different . . . For many months he spent spare moments at the New York Public Library, poring over fat technical volumes. He concluded early on that his copying device, whatever it turned out to be, would have to depend on a process that used light to affect matter in some way . . . One day in the course of his reading Carlson came upon a property called photoconductivity.[7]

The rest, as they say, is history. The Xerox machine has provided a means of preserving and sharing all sorts of information. It is itself one of the major components in that mysterious equation through which remarkable accomplishments may be nurtured by bringing together committed scholars and supportive reference services. That generative atmosphere of support need not be limited to the great research institutions. Systems and networks are making every public library a potential base for significant inquiry.

NOTES

1. Ronald Gross. *The Lifelong Learner*. New York: Simon & Schuster, 1977.

2. Ronald Gross. *Independent Scholarship: Promise, Problems, and Prospects*. New York: College Entrance Examination Board, 1983.

3. Ronald Gross. "Libraries lure and link learners," *Adult & Continuing Education Today*, Vol. XVI, #2 (Jan. 20, 1986).

4. Fred Bratman. "Scholars seek new horizons," *New York Times*, LI Section, July 29, 1984, p. 1+.

5. Ronald Gross. "Scholarship in the community," The Learning Connection, Vol. 2, #4 (Winter 1982).

6. Ronald Gross. *The Independent Scholar's Handbook*. Reading, Mass.: Addison-Wesley Pub., 1982.

7. David Owen. "Copies in seconds," *The Atlantic Monthly* (Feb. 1986), pp. 65-72.

Libraries, Literacy
and Lifelong Learning:
The Reference Connection

Jane C. Heiser

Today there is an abundance of material being published to support the needs of adults involved in literacy programs or learning basic skills. Are these materials available in libraries? Yes—and no, depending on the library. If asked the same question about materials to support lifelong learning activities of adults in libraries, I'm sure a majority of librarians would answer with a resounding "YES"! And they would be correct, if we view the lifelong learner as the traditional, mature, adult, independent learner who has the skills to "use" the library to gain additional knowledge. But what happens if we say lifelong learning begins with zero skills? Of course, most libraries accept the "cradle to grave" philosophy of service but it is generally reviewed in terms of physical development. Libraries have a progression of services and materials that help the preschool child with reading readiness and other developmental activities through the acquisition of skills in the childhood years, on to the strengthening of those skills in the teen years, culminating in materials to maintain those skills and support continuing education in the adult years. The same resounding "yes" cannot be said when the adult did not follow this developmental continuum and instead of needing help in maintaining skills needs to start with acquiring and developing basic skills. What does this departure from what we believe to be the normal progression mean for library service? Is reference service as we generally view it necessary for this population, or is it necessary only for the mature, independent learner?

The author is Administrator, Office of Lifelong Learning, Enoch Pratt Free Library, 400 Cathedral St., Baltimore, MD 21201.

THE PROBLEM OF ILLITERACY

The literacy problem is staggering—27 million adults in this country are functionally illiterate. That means that one out of every five adults in America is affected by this problem. The cost to society is enormous. Billions of dollars go to welfare programs and unemployment compensation directly traceable to illiteracy. Perhaps the greatest tragedy is the loss of self-respect, the frustration of constant helplessness and fear of being "found out" experienced by many adults who cannot perform the tasks necessary to have control of their lives, care for their children or experience simple human pleasures like reading a letter from a friend.

The American Library Association has a long history of involvement in the attempts made to solve this problem. With the establishment of the Coalition for Literacy in 1981, libraries, particularly public libraries, have been urged to take a more active role. Many have, and we see more and more libraries starting tutorial programs and Adult Basic Education classes, buying materials to support programs in the community, etc. Much has been written about these efforts and there is an increase in the "outreach" attitude and cooperative efforts with other service providers to establish community-based programs to serve the needs of this population.

THE ROLE OF THE LIBRARY

Serving the adult learner is not a new idea in library service. From its very beginning, the library was established to provide an educational resource for those who could not continue their schooling. In fact, libraries were started before public education in the United States.

In the past libraries have focused on the adult who had a high enough skill level to be considered an "independent learner." Librarians "feel comfortable" fulfilling the traditional educational objectives of library service: maintaining *reading* skills by developing broad based book collections; stimulating the *reader* to use print and non-print materials through programs, films, book talks, exhibits, etc.; and guiding the *reader* in the selection of materials, in any number of subject areas, to increase their knowledge.

In the Sixties libraries, as well as other social and educational agencies, started to focus on the "disadvantaged" and with funding from the Library Services and Construction Act (LSCA) many special projects were started.

In the Eighties we seem to be focusing on technology, information and access issues and there is a growing awareness that many will not be able to have access to the information they need because of their limited skills.

Libraries have a major role to play in resolving the adult illiteracy problem. They are the only agency with the responsibility to select, acquire, organize and interpret materials for the general public. The reference librarian, as an interpreter of these acquired materials, can play a key role in the progress of adult new readers.

THE ADULT NEW READER

It's impossible to profile the adult new reader without reinforcing outmoded stereotypes. In the past, those in need of literacy programs were characterized as "disadvantaged." Although many participants in literacy and adult basic education programs can be described as culturally, socially, economically, and educationally disadvantaged, there is representation from *all* walks of life, and *all* social and economic backgrounds. *All* are not from cultural minorities. In today's economic climate more and more adults in need of literacy and adult basic education programs have had skilled jobs and good incomes. They have "made it" as far as society is concerned—until they lose their jobs and have to take a written test to reenter the job market or be retrained to keep up with technological advances. Helen Lyman in her writings about libraries, literacy and the adult new reader gives in-depth perspectives on illiterate adults which are very helpful for those unfamiliar with this population.

In order to understand who the adult new reader is, in order to provide service, it is easier to think of this population in terms of skill levels. There are two major groups:

1. Those adults and out of school youth (sixteen years and older) who cannot read, write and compute on a basic survival level. This group comprises the 27 million adults we talk about as being functionally illiterate. Their skills range from zero/completely illiterate to a fourth grade level.
2. Those adults and out of school youth who have marginal skills. They have learned the basics, can survive or cope, but are not truly independent as they function with difficulty. Their skills range from the fifth to eighth grade level. This group comprises another 47 million people.

In general, limited English speakers and non-English speakers are included in these categories depending on their abilities.

The following table, taken from *Literacy Resources: An Annotated Check List for Tutors and Librarians*, was developed to aid in the selection of materials for the adult new reader (see Table 1).

Each level shows the skills that are gained by the learner in each area. Levels III and IV represent the independent learners we most often see "using" the library and are the *readers* that librarians are most "comfortable" with. Levels I and II reflect the two groups that define the adult new reader. They can't be considered in the same way as our traditional independent learner. However, their needs are very much the same.

What Material Does the Adult New Reader Need?

There are three major categories of materials that are needed by the adult new reader:

1. Study or instructional materials which include:
   a. Basic Reading—focusing on teaching and application of skills, such as learning the alphabet, phonics, and reading comprehension.
   b. Basic English and Study Skills—grammar, spelling, vocabulary, use of the dictionary and other library tools, and how to study.
   c. English As A Second Language (ESL)—oral communication, reading, and writing for the foreign born.
   d. Test Preparation Materials—high school equivalency test (GED), armed forces entrance examination, entry level civil service examinations and practice exams for entry into local job training programs.
   e. Basic Skills Texts—especially those utilizing the "life skills approach." Reading, writing and computation are taught in the context of everyday situations.
2. Informational materials which are life skill oriented and provide help in solving the problems of everyday living. These include:
   a. Basic Resources—reading instructions, filling out forms, using the telephone, reading maps, telling time, etc.
   b. Consumer Education—budgeting, taxes, wise buying, checking and savings, insurance, etc.

TABLE I

	LEVEL I (Grades 0-3) (Functionally Illiterate)	LEVEL II (Grades 4-7) ABE, Pre-GED	LEVEL III (Grades 8-12) GED, High School	LEVEL IV (Grades 12+) ESL only
Basic Reading	Alphabet, beginning phonics -- sounds of consonants and simple sound patterns. Word recognition. Basic writing -- manuscript and cursive started.	More advanced phonics patterns and word attack skills built to the point of independent reading. Reading comprehension skills start to be developed.	Assumes student knows phonics. Concentrates on reading better, comprehension, and application of reading skills to a particular subject area.	
Leisure Reading	Short simple sentences and paragraphs -- one- to two-page articles or "stories."	More complex sentences and paragraphs but with controlled vocabulary. Articles and selections three to ten pages -- beginning novels.	Complex structure -- greatly increased vocabulary. Increased length, but not too long to be intimidating. Short novels, adaptations.	
Basic English	Basic sentence construction -- nouns, simple verb tenses, adjectives, pronouns.	Introduction to concepts and rules of spelling, grammar, vocabulary, punctuation, and capitalization. Basic study skills include use of dictionary and library, how to alphabetize, interpretation of simple charts and graphs.	Grammar, spelling, and vocabulary on a high-school level. Gives concepts and rules. Includes punctuation. Drills usage. Study skills include note-taking, organization, use of reference tools, interpretation of charts and graphs.	

TABLE 1, continued

	LEVEL I (Grades 0-3)	LEVEL II (Grades 4-7)	LEVEL III (Grades 8-12)	LEVEL IV (Grades 12+) ESL only
Mathematics	Basic concepts of numbers, counting, simple addition, subtraction, multiplication, and division.	General practice and application of addition, subtraction, multiplication, and division. Assumes knowledge of basics.	Application of basic operations (addition, subtraction, multiplication, division) to decimals and fractions. Introduction to high school algebra, geometry, and trigonometry.	
Life Skills	Informational materials can be used independently if student has reading skills listed in each level of basic reading. Many materials designed to reinforce these skills.			
ESL	Student has little or no knowledge of English. Illiterate or low reading level in own language. Books have many illustrations. Focus on listening, understanding, and speaking, simple sentences and verb forms.	Student has some knowledge of English and can read and write in own language. Focus on refining pronunciation, holding conversations, more advanced structure and grammar. Note: At the point a student can communicate at this level, the tutor can use other materials in the collection, especially Basic Reading and Life Skills.	Student has good reading and writing knowledge of English and own language. Very few pictures in materials. Oral communications skills built rapidly. Focus on advanced grammar, writing, and comprehension.	College level -- advanced construction and style. Professional and technical communication.

NOTE Most materials in the collection fall into Level I or II. Once the student has mastered basic reading skills and is an independent reader, the resources of the entire library are available.

  c. Health—child care, preventive medicine, drugs, family planning, first aid, etc.
  d. Government and Law—contracts and other legal documents, legal aid, how to register to vote, applying for citizenship, etc.
  e. Community resources—how to assess services of the employment office, Social Security Administration, Recreation Department, Housing Department, etc.
  f. Occupational Information—job descriptions and qualifications, salaries and benefits, workmen's compensation, self-employment, unions, etc.
3. Leisure Reading Materials—high *adult* interest, low level so that they can practice the skills that they are learning and succeed at reading a book for fun and enjoyment. Adults who have difficulty reading don't have the same feelings toward recreational reading that the independent reader does. When reading is difficult it isn't fun or enjoyable. However, as skills improve, they need something other than instructional or informational material to practice on. Materials needed are:
  a. Fiction—easy reading novels or short stories—preferably paperback.
  b. Nonfiction—high interest/low level books of popular interest such as crafts, sports, hobbies, travel, etc.

MEETING THE NEEDS

Any library can, if it wants to, develop a full literacy program with classes, tutoring, etc. What is more prevalent, and perhaps better, is a cooperative community effort where each agency or organization plays the part it is best equipped to handle or is most comfortable with. Many library programs have demonstrated a wide range of activities and levels of involvement, however, the provision of materials to support the adult new reader is the most common. It's also the most comfortable and familiar activity for librarians to start.

Meeting these needs does not mean going to the children's department, finding easy reading materials and giving them to the adult. It means determining the particular needs in your own service area, finding out what materials already exist in the collection that are suitable, identifying the gaps, and purchasing new materials to meet the need.

COLLECTION DEVELOPMENT

In most cases librarians do not have to do an in-depth assessment of existing collections to find existing materials to meet the needs of the adult new reader. They are already aware that although there are many materials in the areas outlined above, they are not in a suitable format or at a level that is basic enough for the adult new reader. The most common response is to "start a special collection" for immediate use and draw on existing resources at a later time when the new readers' skills are improved to a level to make the transition. With the increased focus on the problem of illiteracy, publishers are seeing a "market" for these materials and are producing more titles, at appropriate reading levels, than ever before.

1. Sources

In order to build a collection to support the needs of the adult new reader, a basic knowledge of the learning activities, resources and needs of your community is necessary. Teachers and administrators of literacy and other adult related education programs, as well as the adult learners themselves, are the best resources. They can provide a wealth of background information and also help conduct an informal needs survey if necessary. However, do not limit your survey to current participants in programs. Others in need can be surveyed through cooperation with social service organizations, leaving questionnaires in clinic waiting rooms, churches and other public areas, including the library.

To find suitable materials librarians have to go beyond their usual selection tools. Today, gaining an awareness of what is available and suitable is made easier by the publication of bibliographies from established literacy programs such as *The Reader Development Bibliography* from the Free Library of Philadelphia, *Books For Adult New Readers* from Project: LEARN at the Cuyahoga County Library, and *Literacy Resources* from the Enoch Pratt Free Library in Baltimore. They offer complete annotations, materials are grouped in lifeskill areas, and skill levels are indicated. Major publishers are also listed. Some reviews can be found in "Pivot," a quarterly publication of the Free Library of Philadelphia, and in "Booklist," as well as education journals. Another good source is publishers exhibits at education conferences. Unfortunately, even those companies that publish this type of educational materials do not bring them to ALA annual or mid-winter conferences. Cambridge Books is a notable exception. Some may at state library conferences if they know that numerous libraries in the area are involved in literacy efforts or have been asked to do so.

2. Evaluation

As in other areas of book selection, it is very important to evaluate the materials you wish to purchase—even though they are recommended by reputable sources. In well-known bibliographies annotations contain evaluative information, but no one list can be transferred to another program. Publishers' catalogs often seem to contain enough of the right information to make a decision. A word of caution—DON'T. A good rule of thumb is not to purchase without seeing first.

In the evaluation process the librarian will analyze the major aspects of the work in question as they would do with any other material being considered for purchase. However, some aspects may take on a higher relevance or be viewed in a different perspective when purchasing for the adult new reader than the general library user.

The following aspects should be examined:

a. Physical appearance. How a book looks may be the determining factor in the adult new reader's decision to read a book or not. Layout and format make a difference. Is the cover visually appealing? Are these adult oriented illustrations? Larger than average type, wide margins and generous spacing between lines will be more appealing and easier to read. The length of the book is important also. The reader must feel there is a chance of finishing the book in a reasonable amount of time. If the book provides information, look for bold headings and simple indexing and arrangement that will lead the reader quickly to specific areas of interest. Fiction is a problem. Many publishers meet all the above criteria and then print it in an unusual size. The more the book—which is most often paperback—conforms to the standard size that we see everywhere, the more it will appeal to the adult new reader.

b. Content. Most adults who are motivated to acquire the skills they didn't learn as a child are not motivated to read for reading's sake, but because they want or need to read particular material. Therefore, attention should be paid to the relevance of the content to the real-life needs and experiences of the adult reader. It should not be childish or insulting to the reader's intelligence or experience. A simple way to illustrate this is to look at a biography from the Children's collection. You will find that approximately three quarters of the book will cover the individual's childhood and young adult years. In an adult biography these are covered in a chapter or two and the main focus is on adulthood.

c. *Style*. The writing style used can make a big difference in reading and understanding the content of the material. Which of the following examples is easier to understand?

1. The chief motivation for the purchase of curtains in industrial communities is practicality.

or

In factory towns housewives buy curtains that wash weil.

2. It has been recommended that vaccinations be administered every third year in order to maintain immunity.

or

You should get vaccinated every three years. Otherwise, your old vaccination may not protect you.

A clear and simple writing style uses: concrete words and phrases, avoids jargon and highly technical terminology; short sentences that express one idea per sentence and eliminate unnecessary details; simple format with short paragraphs limited to two or three sentences; an active voice and the personal I/you instead of the third person.

d. *Reading Level*. Using the information you've gained so far in this article, it is possible to "guess" at an approximate reading level of a given piece of material. However, there are formulas that determine readability more exactly. The two most commonly used in evaluating materials for the adult new reader are "The Gunning Fog Index" and "The Fry Readability Graph." Both are based on the length of sentences and difficulty of vocabulary in one hundred word samples, though these two factors are utilized differently in each method. These formulas are easy to use and can be easily programmed for use on a computer. For a complete explanation and examples of both methods consult *Using Readability* by Robert S. Laubach and Kay Koschnick.

The above evaluation guidelines are only a brief introduction to the process. Before starting out one should read Chapter 8, on the

"Evaluation of Reading Materials" in *Reading and the Adult New Reader* and *Materials Analysis Criteria (MAC Checklist)*.

3. Organization

What do you do with the materials once they've been purchased? There are many problems and considerations:

a. Format. Most materials are paperback, often come in "sets" that can include several different sized pieces (text, workbook, teacher's manual, answer key, etc.). Shelving can be difficult, workbooks can be consumable, answer sheets get lost, etc.

b. Cataloging. Is it necessary? Can the adult new reader use the card catalog, micro fiche or computer terminal? If you don't catalog, how will teachers, researchers and others find out that the library has the material?

c. Arrangement. If we don't catalog it, how do we arrange the material? According to subject areas and levels? Label the shelves/ books? Code them with those colorful dots librarians love to use? If you integrate with the rest of the collection, will the adult new reader find it? If kept as a special collection, will it make the adult new reader afraid to be seen using the collection?

There is no *one* way to make these materials available to the adult new reader. The answer is in a combination of access modes depending on the local situation. This includes using print alternatives in the collection. Films and filmstrips, video tapes, audio tapes, and computer programs are a valuable resource. The materials suggested at the end illustrate a variety of successful solutions that can be adapted to meet local use. The guiding principle is accessibility in a non-threatening environment. The most vital link between the adult new reader and the materials collection is the librarian.

THE ROLE OF THE LIBRARIAN

The librarian who can competently select, evaluate and organize a special collection for the adult new reader is in a position to know the varied resources—facts, knowledge, ideas—contained in the collection. That librarian may have organized the collection and placed it in a highly visible and inviting place in the library. But is that librarian the right person to work with the patron? To be the link between the adult new reader and the materials? The staff for this collection must be flexible, highly sensitive and develop skills in interviewing a population that is learning to read, write, compute, develop competencies and gain new knowledge. The focus is now on the librarian's ability to interpret and promote the collection. In this context, the traditional "readers advisory" concept takes on a whole new meaning. There is a greater need to assess the skill level of the reader and take on the role of learning counselor. The adult who is developing reading skills requires supportive encouragement, guidance and direction. He needs to experience success in finding what he needs in the library or his conclusion, even after one failure, will be that the library only has things for adults who are good readers. Since an adult will rarely say "I can't read," or "I read very little" or tell you a book is too hard after you've spent a good amount of time finding it, it is important that there is a range of materials from which to choose.

As the special collection is used you will quickly find that it is not capable of meeting all the needs and interests of the new adult reader, particularly in meeting the need for specific information. All the resources of the library must be used, including the reference collection.

Utilizing Reference Materials

The information needs and interests of the adult new reader are the same as any other library patron. The major difference is that the required information has to be presented in a simple, clear and non-threatening way. The information materials mentioned above tend to be general in nature and are often in an instructional work-text format. The well informed, sensitive reference librarian can help the adult new reader make the transition from the special collection to the resources in the rest of the library.

If we believe most of the literature and standard bibliographies of reference materials, there appears to be very little real-life material for the adult new reader. It is unfortunate too, that the phrase reference department brings to mind rows and rows of large thick books where people do involved research. The adult new reader doesn't always equate information with reference. Libraries themselves often add to the confusion by putting them in two separate departments. There are materials in the reference area that the adult new reader needs. However, he needs the information, not to read the book. This means that the role of the librarian as interpreter of materials must be expanded. Quite simply that means when a patron asks "what is the longest bridge in the world?" the librarian must do more than point automatically to a shelf and say "you'll find it over there in the *Guinness Book of Records.*"

Utilizing the other resources in the library to supplement the special collection means that assessing the materials in the rest of the collection is necessary. Librarians make judgments about "hard" and "easy" books everyday. It's what we're taught to do—not in those terms but in phrases such as for a lay person, technically oriented, for the student, etc. We often find easy to read books for children in adult collections. Combining those skills with the information above can facilitate the assessment process and produce quick results.

In a brief experiment, that you could easily duplicate, I examined several very common reference tooks trying to find samples of a type or subject area that would illustrate whether a book was hard or easy according to the evaluation factors above. Several were checked for readability level where appropriate.

a. Encyclopedias. Encyclopedias all tested High School level and above. For comparative purposes look at the *World Book Encyclopedia* and the New *Encyclopedia Britannica. World Book* is a childrens' set but it has an adult perspective. Readibility according to Fry and Gunning Fog was 6-7 grade level. The *Micropaedia* tested 12+ and the *Macropaedia* went right off the college scale. Since I'd used the entries on George Washington for my samples for the readability test, I looked at several books on presidents. The *Complete Book of Presidents* by William A. Degregoria scored a 12th grade level on the readability scale but the format made it much easier to locate specific facts.

b. Dictionaries. After pulling eight different volumes off the shelf, I gave up. In general, numerous columns on a page and extremely small print ruled out their use for the new adult reader. The *Random House Dictionary of the English Language* was better than most.

c. Almanacs. A wonderful resource to quickly answer many of the informational questions of the adult new reader. Bold headings help, *but* access is a problem. All had barely readable indexes.

d. Drugs. The standard *Physicians Desk Reference* can frustrate even the best reader. It's difficult to use and has a readability score well into the college level. Compare it with the *Professional Guide to Drugs* put out by Intermed Communications and the *Essential*

Guide to Prescription Drugs by James W. Long. Although it says it's for "anyone who prescribes and takes medicine," the *Professional Guide* is just what its name implies. The *Essential Guide . . .* has the same readability level (11-12 grade) but the format makes it the best choice.

In looking at random samples of other sources just to see if they might be useful with the adult new reader, I found that publishers have improved the physical appearance and format of the tools: plenty of white pages, bold headings, reasonably sized type. However, none of the materials could be used without the aid of the librarian.

My morning search leads me to three conclusions: (1) for adult new readers on the 0-4 level information was only available through a librarian and an alternative such as telephone reference service is the answer; (2) it would take a lot of research on my part to find suitable tools for samples to use on a library instruction unit for an ABE class, and (3) there has got to be a better way.

Assessing the existing collections is a difficult task. There are no notations in our guides to reference materials that tell whether or not a book is suitable for the adult new reader. No studies have been done that result in lists of suitable reference sources and general reviewing tools make no comment either. Publishers don't publish such materials.

And a brief survey of the reference collection shows that the materials must be interpreted by the librarian at least for the lowest level readers. But we still need a range of materials to help those who want to develop the skill of working on their own. The solution is in the expansion of the "reference" collection to include materials that are life related and presented in a simple, clear non-threatening way. One good resource is a book called *Reference Work in the Public Library* by Roland E. Stevens and Joan M. Walton. The materials listed in this work are based on the types of reference questions asked by patrons in an average public library and are "real life" materials. A trip to the children's department is worthwhile, as well as, to a local middle school or junior high school library. There are some reference books for children that may not talk down to the adult. A good example are those written to explain how things work. The librarian in the middle school can be an invaluable resource as students there are also in the same transitional position the adult new learner is. Perhaps the best solution or resource of all is the library that has an integrated non-fiction and/or reference collection. Having children's, young adult and adult materials side-by-side allows the librarian to have a range of levels to present to the adult new reader; and it allows the adult to choose the level best suited to his needs without embarrassment. Librarians should also expand their point of reference to include alternative materials especially in audio-visual formats and increased utilization of human resources.

Promoting Use

Creating an awareness of the resources developed for the adult new reader is important. They are traditionally non-users and much has been written about attracting the "disadvantaged," "minorities," and other non-users to the library, but very few successful methods have been developed. In promoting the library to our traditional users we have activities such as book talks, films, lectures, and other programs. In trying to attract the adult new reader or illiterate adult, the librarian must actively sell the library as a learning resource that will help improve skills and/or the quality of their lives. Traditional approaches such as newspaper articles, booklists, newsletters, etc., will not work. Television is good if it focuses on what you can get from the library rather than passively reporting on a library program after it's over. Creative use of radio time could be the most effective way to reach this population. Promotion must be concrete. For example, a series of public service announcements that say "your library has books to help you learn to read/read better so that you can read to your child, get a better job, get your GED, etc." Be Creative! Go where the potential patrons are. Visit a literacy or ABE class. Don't give a book talk, talk about books that will help them in their lives.

THE BOTTOM LINE

If the library is to maintain its traditional role as an educational resource, deliver user oriented library and information services to *all* and insure equal access to *all* citizens, major changes must be made in organizational patterns and routines, staff training, budget allocations, and attitude towards the adult who is just entering the lifelong learning continuum. Service to this population must become an integral part of what we do, rather than a "special project." The key elements required to meet the needs of this growing population have been discussed above and include: developing a special collection to meet the instructional, informational and leisure reading needs of the adult new learner/reader; insuring that staff has the knowledge and sensitivity to assess the needs of the adult and access and interpret the information that the adult cannot read himself; expanding collections to contain materials on all levels; and creating an awareness of the availability of these materials and services in the community. By definition, the reference librarian is the crucial element in providing access to the special collection for the adult new reader, answering questions, providing encouragement, guidance, and direction in the pursuit of skills, and aiding in the transition to a mature, independent user in the mainstream of lifelong learning.

REFERENCES

Bayley, Linda. *Opening Doors for Adult New Readers: How Librarians Can Select Materials and Establish Collections.* Syracuse, New York: New Readers Press, 1980.

Buckingham, Melissa R. Forinash. *Reader Development Bibliography: Books Recommended for Adult New Readers.* Syracuse, New York: New Readers Press, 1982. (Currently available from Bowker.)

Establishing Library Learning Centers for Adult Basic Education. Austin: University of Texas, Division of Extension, 1975.

Heiser, Jane-Carol. *Literacy Resources: An Annotated Check List for Tutors and Librarians.* Baltimore, Maryland: Enoch Pratt Free Library, 1983.

Laubach, Robert S. and Koschnick, Kay. *Using Readability: Formulas for Easy Adult Materials.* Syracuse, New York: New Readers Press, 1977.

Lyman, Helen Huguenor. *Literacy and the Nation's Libraries.* Chicago: American Library Association, 1977.

_____ *Reading and the Adult New Reader.* Chicago: American Library Association, 1976.

_____ *Reading Instruction for the Adult Illiterate.* Chicago: American Library Association, 1981.

Materials Analysis Criteria: Standards of Measurement (MAC Checklist). (Found in "Library Materials in Service to the Adult New Reader" by Helen Huguenor Lyman). Chicago: American Library Association, 1973.

Printed as a separate by Dome Press, Inc., Elgin, Illinois, 1979.

O'Brien, Roberta Luther. *Books for Adult New Readers.* 2nd rev. ed. Cleveland, Ohio: Project: LEARN, 1984.

Stevens, Rolland E. and Walton, Joan M. *Reference Work in the Public Library.* Littleton, Colorado: Libraries Unlimited, Inc., 1983.

"The Public Library in The Coalition Against Illiteracy." Special Feature. *Public Libraries* 23, No. 4 (Winter 1984): 107-123.

Information Services
to the Academic Scientific Community
in the 1980s

Arleen N. Somerville

Information needs of scientists differ considerably from those of social scientists and humanists. Science librarians and academic library administrators who understand these unique needs and recognize that they are legitimate can establish effective information service programs for the scientific community.

While some differences exist between scientific disciplines, laboratory experiments are common for all researchers, except theoreticians. They, in turn, conduct research utilizing numeric calculations and computer modelling of physical phenomena. Every research project requires extensive library work before, during, and after the laboratory work. Each scientist and engineer needs full access to information while the work is proceeding. For example, if an experiment takes an unexpected turn, the experiment cannot be halted while the researcher waits 2-6 weeks for an article to arrive. Rapid delivery of information and documents is essential. A laboratory decision must be reached on the basis of quickly available information. Such decisions typically require that the researcher check one or several specific articles rather than complete an extensive search. Making the right decisions is crucial in any experiment, but especially so at a research university, where researchers compete against their counterparts in other institutions and in industry. Even a few weeks' delay can cause a researcher to be "scooped," and thus lose credit for years of effort.

Laboratory experiments necessarily continue seven days a week and all months of the year. Researchers work in laboratories evenings and weekends during the semester, as well as days and eve-

Arleen N. Somerville is Head, Science and Engineering Libraries, University of Rochester, Rochester, NY 14627. She received the BS and MLS degrees from the University of Wisconsin—Madison.

nings during school vacations and summer months. As a result, services must continue at the same levels during these periods and access to the collections must be maintained.

Scientists frequently have other tight deadlines. Thoroughly documented grant proposals must be completed on a regular basis, especially in research institutions, to pay the cost of supplies, equipment, and stipends. Because most scientific research is a group effort, professors' success is often linked to the quality and number of graduate students, post-doctoral fellows, or research associates they can support financially. Even the youngest professor is obliged to seek external funding to support his research group. Preparation of successful proposals requires a thorough and up-to-date review of the literature, with rapid access to references. In other grant-related activities, scientists review and evaluate articles and grant proposals from fellow researchers. Again, prompt access to diverse and often very recent books, journals, and reports is essential to meet tight deadlines.

Scientific information is growing rapidly and is often highly intricate. A look at abstract journals in two disciplines confirms the rapid increase. The 1965 *Engineering Index* included approximately 45,000 abstracts; by 1984 the number had grown to 140,030—a 211% increase in 20 years. During that same time period *Chemical Abstracts* grew from 35,926 to 560,569 abstracts—a 1460% increase in 20 years. *Chemical Abstracts* also demonstrates the increased complexity of sources. While readers only need to consult 23 volumes of the Subject Index, arranged in one alphabet, for the 1962-66 Collective Index, the same search in the 1977-81 Collective Index requires consulting 78 volumes divided into three parts. Other growing and complex reference sets include Beilstein's *Handbuch der Organischen Chemie* (Springer-Verlag) and Landolt-Bornstein's *Zahlenwerte und Funktionen aus Naturwissenschaften und Technik* (Springer-Verlag). Scientific literature comprises not only bibliographic, but also numeric information, such as spectroscopic and toxicity data. Spectroscopic data are found in texts, indexes and tables of spectra, and online sources. Some online sources of data have no printed counterpart, such as x-ray crystallographic,[1] infrared spectra,[1] c-13 nmr spectra,[1] or semi-conductor properties.[2] Scientific and technical literature can be located in specialized sources, e.g., *Pollution Abstracts, Metals Abstracts,* or *High Energy Physics Index. Science Citation Index* (Institute for Scientific Information) is unique in that it covers the major journals and selected books from all areas of science, engineering, and medicine.

However, several abstract journals cover scientific and technical fields in an extremely comprehensive way. These titles include *Bibliography and Index of Geology*, *Biological Abstracts*, *Chemical Abstracts*, *Current Abstracts of Chemistry and Index Chemicus*, *Engineering Index*, *Science Abstracts* (*Physics Abstracts*, *Electrical and Electronics Abstracts*, *Computer and Control Abstracts*, *IT Focus*). These abstract and index titles may cover as many as 30,000 journals and most also cover technical reports, patents, conference proceedings and selected books. This comprehensive coverage often produces articles of interest in obscure journals that are difficult to locate.

PARTNERSHIP WITH FACULTY

Establishing Credibility

The importance of developing a partnership with faculty was affirmed by ACRL in its symposium at the 1981 ALA Conference, entitled "Scholars and Librarians: Partners in Learning and Research." During the session, faculty and librarians described three examples of successful cooperative programs between the two groups. Recently in its "recommended actions for the 1985-95 decade," ACRL reaffirmed "the academic librarian's key role as a proactive analyst, subject expert, counselor, consultant, linker, and intermediary in the cycle of scholarly endeavor and scholarly communication."[3] Achievement of these capabilities would accomplish the desired partnership with faculty.

The science librarian must possess subject knowledge to fulfill such ACRL roles as counselor, consultant, and intermediary. In contrast to some subject areas, it is unrealistic to expect science librarians to hold advanced subject degrees, especially PhDs. Job opportunities for science graduates abound and library degrees increase their options. Industrial positions pay higher salaries, and this strong competition often means that potential academic librarians may opt for industrial positions. Nevertheless, a scientific background is essential, because the academic science librarian must develop subject expertise to understand clientele information needs, complete highly technical computer searches, answer scientific reference questions, and conduct information instruction for extremely complex and technical sources. Only with a science background can librarians discuss teaching and research topics with faculty in a knowledgeable way. Sitting in on courses is a useful way to extend your knowledge into related subjects or become familiar with new trends within a subject area. Faculty are often pleased to see such interest.

Other activities lend credibility to science librarians and can strengthen the partnership with faculty. The librarian should demonstrate interest in and ability to aid the faculty in their teaching and research, as well as support the department. You can inquire how a research program is progressing and how recruitment of graduate students or undergraduate majors is proceeding. The librarian can provide information, such as background information about potential faculty or visiting lecturers, to support department administration. The librarian can also participate in recruitment activities, such as conducting library tours and attending receptions for prospective students and faculty.

Participation in subject-related professional associations increases credibility with faculty. Although not all societies have information sections, several offer excellent opportunities. These include the American Chemical Society's Division of Chemical Information; the Geoscience Information Society, which meets annually with other American Geological Institute societies; and the American Society for Engineering Education's section for engineering libraries. Attendance at the same conferences as faculty is useful in itself because faculty see you at their meetings. Increased credibility arises when librarians present papers at such meetings and when they hold offices and committee assignments in these organizations.

Communication

The librarian can establish the partnership early by sending a welcoming letter to newly appointed faculty two-to-four months *before* they arrive. Such letters can describe the quality of the collection in their subject specialties, indicate an interest in discussing their teaching and research topics after they arrive, emphasize your services orientation, and invite them to tour the library. Such letters can also ask them to specify books and journals crucial to their specialties, so these can be ordered and can perhaps be on the shelf when the faculty arrive. After new faculty have had time to settle into their office, visit them in their offices to describe library services and explain how to order books and journals. These meetings offer opportunities to determine their expectations of libraries, to learn about special services of their previous librarians, and to ask about their initial experiences in your library. This is the time for the first discussions of their teaching and research topics. Explaining your various roles—reference librarian, information instructor, computer searcher, collection developer if appropriate—and how each activity reinforces the other, helps faculty see you as an information counselor and consultant. Relevant flyers and brochures can be distributed, if the faculty member has not received them earlier.

Communication should continue with faculty so you can remain current with changing research topics, remind faculty of current services, update them on library activities, and listen to their experiences in using your library. Ideally, visits in offices should occur at regular intervals, possibly every 2-3 years. It is wise to ask questions specifically about turnaround time for their requests, responsiveness of staff to their questions and those of their students, and availability of needed books and journals. Stressing your interest in their satisfaction will reinforce your partnership role and encourage them to mention both good and unsatisfactory experiences throughout the year.

Regular meetings with chairs of relevant departmental committees, such as undergraduate and graduate curricula as well as faculty and graduate recruitment, will help you stay current on changing curricula and new faculty research interests. Annual discussions with department chairs are useful for learning of long- and short-term changes in department programs and in updating them on library activities. Newly appointed department chairs and library liaison representatives appreciate a visit from you, because it is an opportunity for you to update their knowledge of library procedures and the acquisitions budgeting process and to discuss their roles and yours in their new assignment. It is important to mention your role of interpreting the library to the department and the department to the library. This helps faculty understand your need to stay current with anticipated new programs and changes in enrollment levels. At this time you can stress the importance of evaluating library collections and staffing when the department plans potential new teaching and research programs. Ask to receive departmental mailings, such as teaching and committee listings, colloquia announcements, newsletters, receptions, etc. Express an interest in attending department meetings and a willingness to participate on committees. More frequent meetings with liaison representatives or library committees may be necessary.

Informal, on-going communication with all faculty can be very effective in learning about changing research interests, graduate student recruitment and retention, and departmental activities. Lunch and such social gatherings as colloquia receptions can be settings for brief but often productive conversations. An occasional short conversation in the library is another option. Even walks between buildings can be opportunities for unexpected chats.

Library newsletters can update faculty on library programs and professional activities of librarians. Contributions to departmental newsletters are an attractive alternative for transmitting such information. Other library publications can provide basic information about library services and policies. Brochures can advertise specific activities, such as computer searching.

All this activity requires a great deal of time, so it is wise initially to identify the most receptive and influential faculty—the gatekeepers.[4] As highly attractive and dynamic individuals, these faculty will provide the greatest word-of-mouth publicity for the library's good work and your credibility will therefore increase greatly among other faculty and students. Closer interaction can be extended to other faculty as time and resources permit.

INFORMATION SERVICES

A user-oriented information program strengthens the partnership between librarians and faculty by continually reinforcing librarians' contributions to institutional teaching and research functions. Once a partnership link has been established with faculty members, it is easier to maintain that relationship, because they will treat you as a professional peer. However, with new faculty, one must often start at the beginning to develop the partnership. Successful partnerships with current faculty influence new faculty perceptions of the library and make your job easier.

All staff should be approachable and service-oriented. Training programs for full time assistants and student workers should focus on acquiring a service orientation as well as learning clerical duties and, if appropriate, how to answer basic reference questions. This is especially important for library assistants who often work directly with faculty and students. Approachability is essential for encouraging questions from users. However, even the friendliest atmosphere will not prompt all users to ask questions. Staff should watch for users who seem to be uncertain and take the initiative to ask, in a non-threatening way, if they would like some help. Some users, especially at the research level, are reluctant to admit they could use help. It is more effective to ask them if they have found *all* the information they need. In this way, you avoid implying that they were unable to find information on their own. It can be beneficial to ask users who are walking away from indexes what subject they are working on and if they found what they needed. Their responses can prompt you to affirm the value of the index for that question, suggest additional sources, or recommend ways to locate references.

At all times library staff must make users' questions *their* questions. This attitude requires that staff consider each question as if it is their personal question, for which it is important to get the best possible answer. Such a personal interest in a question will provide incentive to conduct an effective reference interview. The librarian should use recommended interview techniques to clarify and analyze the question, in order to identify exactly what information is needed.[5] Following a question through to completion is necessary for developing and maintaining credibility.

Only a *comprehensive* information service will help achieve the desired partnership. An active outreach effort is necessary to promote a service that includes answering a wide range of reference questions, providing current awareness services, mounting extensive and practical information instruction programs including computer sources, conducting computer searches, and facilitating the rapid receipt of documents. Success will be assured when such a comprehensive information program is provided effectively and in a timely manner by service-oriented staff.

Reference Questions

A strong reference service answers a wide range of questions and provides rapid turnaround, as needed. Quick reference questions, such as decoding incomplete or erroneous references, providing addresses of organizations, acquiring biographies and bibliographies of individuals, and identifying conference locations, are common in all libraries. Non-science questions often arise in support of scientific administrative and research projects. When faculty give talks to non-science groups, meet with state and national legislators, and visit potential funding organizations, they may need economic data, biographic information about these individuals, and information about the organizations. Frequent research questions from science users are for properties of compounds or materials, such as toxicity, viscosity, electrical resistance, or infrared spectra. Short specific questions are also common, such as the ground level elevation of a geographic location or the production rate and cost of a commercial chemical. Other questions, such as binding of ethidium bromide to DNA or mating behavior of ducks may require more extensive checking of books and indexes. A challenge in directing users to relevant books is to understand the subject area well enough to know what books will include the needed information. For example, information about the extinction coefficient of a chemical compound will be found in ultraviolet and visible spectra sources. Often the extended questions need to be searched in relevant indexes and abstracts. In-depth knowledge and understanding of scientific indexes are crucial for selecting optimum sources and for locating relevant information in print and online. This requires understanding indexing policies of the database producer and changes made by vendors to permit online searching, as well as staying current with changes in the database and changes made by vendors for both the system and specific databases.

Computer Searching

Computer searching is an integral part of reference service. It is used routinely for answering quick reference questions to save staff and user time. Access to a variety of systems is necessary to meet information needs of scientific clientele. Systems with the broadest scope of databases include BRS, DIALOG, and SDC. Wilsonline, with access to Wilson Company databases, provides references for students taking introductory science courses or writing papers on science topics for other courses. Other systems required for specialized scientific needs include Chemical Information System, DARC, and STN International (for chemistry); DOE or NASA Recon (for contractors of those agencies); SPIRES (for high energy physics); Pergamon Infoline (for chemical engineering, plastics, paper, patents); and ESA-IRS European Space Agency (for semiconductor properties, robotics, and European science/technology). Although multiple systems require significant investments in on-going training and documentation maintenance, the wide range of information needs of scientists necessitates such efforts.

Subject knowledge is crucial for conducting effective computer searches. Constructing effective search strategies and evaluating relevancy of retrieved references require this knowledge. The reference interview for a computer search incorporates additional information about the online process, but like any such effective discussion it requires understanding of the question.[6] Encouraging users to be present for the search facilitates making decisions while online, not all of which can be anticipated, and gives users a better understanding of the search process in general and how their question can be searched in particular.[7] Productive searches mean satisfied customers which will bring users back again and will spread the word to other potential users.

Computer searches reinforce one's knowledge of the clientele's course and research interest. This in turn aids collection development decisions, reinforces understanding of the subject, and facilitates answering reference questions.

With the availability of microcomputers, downloading of search results is possible. Downloading provides a database that can be edited with word processing software to produce a tailor-made, error-free product. Some searchers may find their users interested in receiving search results on a disk, which they can manipulate as needed.

Current Awareness Services

Because scientists must stay current with research in their areas, especially with competing research groups, library services that facilitate their efforts are greatly appreciated by busy faculty.

Providing quick access to newly published materials can be accomplished in a variety of ways. Displays of newly received journal issues and books are extremely popular. *Current Contents*,[8] available in several scientific areas, offers convenient access to the table-of-contents of a wide subject scope of journals and selected books. Laboratory subscriptions to *Current Contents* might be useful for some researchers. A library service that supplies tables-of-contents to faculty of journal issues newly received in the library is greatly appreciated. This is especially helpful to research groups with interdisciplinary interests or with laboratories located some distance from the library. Faculty welcome information about commercial current awareness services, such as ASCA, ASCATOPICS, *CA Selects,* and *BIOSIS/CAS Selects*.[9,9,10,11] The opportunities for SDI computer searches should be explained and SDI searches maintained when needed. Informal forwarding of information to faculty on subjects known to interest them is welcomed, especially if such information is contained in publications, not generally seen by them.

Provision of Documents

Scientists' need for rapid location of references also requires fast delivery of documents. To fill this need, science librarians should work closely with interlibrary loan staff to provide documents quickly. Rapid verification by science staff when reference sources are located only in branch libraries facilitates processing of requests. In addition to using the interlibrary loan system, scientific researchers welcome the option of paying for documents when speed is especially crucial. These document delivery options are offered by database producers (e.g., American Geological Institute, Chemical Abstracts Service, and Institute for Scientific Information), information brokers, and other commercial organizations such as Research Publications, Inc. for patents. Online ordering facilitates use of many of these services, although phone and mail requests are also accepted.

Information Instruction Programs

Instructional programs which emphasize efficient use of information sources, search strategies relevant for the discipline, and the active role of librarians are effective means of raising library consciousness of students and faculty.

Instruction plans for each discipline should be based on the unique information needs and use patterns of the subject area, and need to consider the department's teaching objectives. Extensive discussions with a variety of faculty, research staff, and students are necessary in order for the librarian to understand what information is needed in each discipline and how knowledgeable researchers seek answers to typical questions. Sitting in on courses provides the librarian with additional opportunities to understand the kinds of questions asked in the subject area and to see how information sources help answer them. Monitoring reference questions and computer search topics also contribute to such an understanding. Library use patterns vary significantly between subject areas and the types of sources vary, so search strategies should match the needs. Seeking information on the properties of chemical compounds requires significantly different search strategies than tracing a theme in literature.

A comprehensive, coordinated information program is a long-term goal that may take many years to achieve. Such a program aims at transforming students into effective information users who recognize the librarian as a knowledgeable information counselor and consultant. One way to accomplish this objective is to teach a course, such as the long-standing chemical information course at Purdue University. More often, information instruction in scientific disciplines is integrated into courses. This approach requires that librarians work closely with and have the cooperation of faculty who teach the courses.[12] This close working relationship takes time to develop, so it is wise to begin with receptive faculty. Effective instruction will increase credibility among faculty and bolster your confidence. Each year's work builds on the previous year's efforts. Gradually an overall program is built.

Teaching Printed Sources

Integrated information instruction is most successful if it is linked to course content or preferably to a particular assignment. Handouts and lecture material should match the level of student needs. Because scientific reference sources are often complex, such material should provide in-depth instruction for using them. A presentation about *Chemical Abstracts* is not complete without clearly describing how to locate the systematic index name for a chemical compound. Even sophomores require this information and advanced students need to understand even more about index nomenclature and index policies. Noting what sources will answer general questions typical of that subject is a good way to catch students' attention. For example, specifying sources that answer questions about the chemistry of functional groups is a practical approach, because it addresses a specific need of organic chemists. Students welcome and respect such hints. Technical reports, patents, standards, and specifications are important types of scientific literature and especially important for students who enter industry. Students should learn how these types of literature differ from books and journals and how to identify and acquire copies of them. In addition, students need to understand the patent process and how to read and interpret patents. An effective information program also instructs students in how to do library work for a new research project, how to stay current on a topic, and how to locate review articles.

Assignments that enable students to use sources described in the lecture provide important reinforcement. Mentioning the specific library requirements early in the lecture may increase students' attention. Papers assigned by faculty as part of course requirements serve this purpose very well. Instruction as part of laboratory courses helps students see information gathering as an expected and integral part of the design and execution of all laboratory projects. Student maintenance of a literature searching log for experiments is an excellent way to have students apply their new knowledge in the laboratory. Evaluation of such a log can be based on the following criteria: were the most useful sources checked first, was a thoughtful pattern used to search, and were the sources used effectively. Assigned questions developed by librarians or faculty can also be used, but should reflect the level of the course, department or course orientation, and the typical information needs of the subject. For example, an applied question such as "analysis of nicotine" is not appropriate for chemistry majors in a department that emphasizes research even in baccalaureate courses. In such an institution the librarian gains credibility if research-type questions are asked, such as locating articles about the antitumor activity of adriamycin. In addition, assigned questions should be realistic, individualized, reflect up-to-date format and indexing, be revised occasionally to avoid overuse, and not require excessive time of students to complete or instructor to correct.[12] Library questions on exams are additional options, as are library skills tests. Librarians are the logical individuals to correct the assigned questions. Such work reinforces the educational role and provides excellent opportunities to identify aspects of information searching that were not clear to all students. In this way instruction content can be improved.

Teaching Computerized Sources

Teaching use of computer databases is an important part of an up-to-date and relevant information instruction program. The instruction can be incorporated into appropriate courses or treated as a special topic outside of class. Online instruction occurs at two levels: lecturing about searching, and teaching students to conduct their own searches. The latter approach involves detailed lectures and online practice time for students. While this method requires considerably more time of both instructor and students, hands-on practice is a more effective way for students to become familiar with the search process and to recognize the benefits and limitations of computer searching. Implementing online instruction requires additional consultation with faculty to identify time available and to determine how the searching costs will be financed. Online costs can be shared with academic departments. Less costly searching provided by BRS (After Dark and BRKTHRU), Dialog (Ontap files and Knowledge Index), and STN International (CAS Academic Plan and Chemical Abstracts Learning Files) offer more affordable teaching opportunities. As is true for teaching use of printed sources, the information should be presented from students' perspectives: how do I search to locate information needed for my paper or my laboratory work? Some vendors and database producers have prepared manuals specifically attuned to the needs of users,[13] while individual librarians have often found it necessary to develop their own teaching materials. Locally-developed materials that utilize topics and faculty names from your own school can create greater interest in the lecture and practice questions.

Extension of computer searching instruction to researchers (faculty, research associates, and graduate students) follows naturally. The objective for this group is to teach them to become effective searchers, because research decisions require full information. Instruction should also stress more sophisticated ways to develop and refine search strategy, which in turn requires that the librarian possess an in-depth knowledge of the database organization, its indexing policies, and system implementation of the database. Online practice is equally important for this group. Librarians may want to encourage researchers to bring their own laboratory questions to online practice sessions. Effective teaching of computer searching, especially to researchers, greatly enhances librarians' credibility and increases respect.

End user and librarian searches are often completed on microcomputers, which permit downloading references to disks. End users are beginning to manage their personal bibliographic files on microcomputers. This interest offers an opportunity to teach them to use bibliographic file management software packages as a natural extension of teaching them how to search computer databases and to download.[14] Librarians' use of microcomputers also provides the expertise for serving as hardware and software consultants, as users move into these computer applications. Thus, the consultant and instructor roles are natural extensions of increased use of microcomputers.

Regardless of instruction technique used—course or integrated—consciousness-raising is equally important for research staff, including faculty, post-doctoral fellows, and research associates. Faculty who attend information instruction sessions with their classes update their knowledge of new sources and techniques. Students exposed to new sources or techniques often stimulate faculty awareness. Ways of reaching other researchers include presentations to regular department seminars or to research group meetings. For example, a talk on how computer searching can aid research in a discipline is an effective presentation, especially when sample searches are aimed at the audience. Informal, one-to-one conversations often account for a large percentage of instruction for researchers.

All the above actions—communicating with faculty, presenting effective lectures, providing relevant handouts, participating in development and grading of assignments, and extending instruction to researchers—contribute to increased credibility of librarians and reinforce their role as partners in the educational and research processes.

CONCLUSION

All activities of a dynamic science librarian reinforce and support each other, contribute to increased credibility with faculty, and establish and maintain a partnership with faculty in scholarly endeavors. An effective librarian possesses a scientific background and understands the information needs unique to the scientific community. Strong communication skills promote regular and varied interactions with faculty, so the librarian can stay abreast of academic activities and update faculty on library matters. A wide-ranging information services program tailored to the clientele's needs includes answering technical questions; conducting in-depth scientific computer searches; providing current awareness services; implementing user-oriented instructional programs for print and computerized sources, and facilitating rapid delivery of documents.

Implementation of such a service program for the scientific community cannot be provided without encouragement and commitment of resources from the library administration. A librarian can gain such support not only by being an articulate spokesperson for these priorities within the library, but by establishing a level of rapport and demand from faculty that will reinforce these needs with the library administration. Faculty, with whom credibility has been achieved, can help you acquire resources which will enable you to continue extending the partnership relationship to other faculty.

NOTES

1. Chemical Information System, Inc., a subsidiary of Fein-Marquart, Associates.

2. EMIS (Electronic Materials Information Service) from Inspec and available on the ESA-IRS (European Space Agency, Information Retrieval Service) System.

3. *College and Research Libraries*, 46:4 (July 1985) 307.

4. Thomas J. Allen, "Organizational Aspects of Information Flow in Technology," *Association of Special Libraries and Information Bureaux Proceedings*, 20:11 (November 1968), 433-454.

5. William A. Katz, *Introduction to Reference Work*, Vol II: *Reference Services and Reference Processes*, 4th edition. (McGraw-Hill Book Co., N.Y., 1982), 41-52. Marilyn Domas White, "Evaluation of the Reference Interview," *RQ*, 25:1 (Fall 1985), 77-78. David Isaacson, "Library Inreach," *RQ*, 23:1 (Fall 1983), 65-74.

6. Arleen N. Somerville, "The Place of the Reference Interview in Computer Searching: the Academic Setting," *Online*, 1:4 (October 1977), 14-23.

7. Kristine Salomon, and Curt Burgess, "Patron Presence During the Online Search: Attitudes of University Librarians," *Online Review*, 8:6 (1984), 549-558.

8. For example, *Current Contents: Agriculture, Biology, & Environmental Sciences*; *Current Contents: Engineering, Technology, & Applied Sciences*; *Current Contents: Life Sciences*; and *Current Contents: Physical, Chemical, and Earth Sciences*.

9. From Institute for Scientific Information, Philadelphia.

10. From Chemical Abstracts Service, Columbus, Ohio.

11. From Biosciences Information Service, Philadelphia, or Chemical Abstracts Service.

12. Arleen N. Somerville, Chemical Information Instruction of the Undergraduate: A Review and Analysis. *Journal of Chemical Information and Computer Science*, 25: p.320; 1985.

13. Mary Ann Palma and Charles Sullivan, "Searching Chemistry on DIALOG," DIALOG Information Retrieval Service: Palo Alto, CA, 1984. "Chemical Abstracts Online At Your Desk; CA File for Chemists," Chemical Abstracts Service: Columbus, OH, 1984.

14. Howard, Curtis, "The Mann Library Microcomputer Center," *Small Computers in Libraries*, (December 1984), p.8-9.

Health Information Services
for Lay People:
A Review of the Literature
With Recommendations

Ellen R. Paterson

Having reviewed the last ten years of literature on health information services for lay people, I urge librarians to assume a more active role in providing health information to the public. Librarians and health professionals can also facilitate the medical self-care movement. After a brief review of the topic, I propose ideas for librarians to make health information available to the public. Though consumer health is presently a very popular issue, acceptance of the medical self-care movement is not as widespread as it might first appear. There are still conflicts of interest among several parties: the consumer, the physician, the social worker, hospital administrator and insurance salesperson.[1] Society is still disease- and crisis-directed rather than health-promoting. While health promotion is widely discussed, many libraries are not active co-partners with government and private agencies who do make health information available to the public. There is endorsement of informed patient choice, health promotion, medical self-care and self-help because of the ever-increasing, chronically ill elderly population, but the ways to access health information have been developed for the professional and not the consumer.[2,3]

Let me review some of the proponents of informed patient choice, health promotion, medical self-care and self-help. Etzweiler warns that informed patient participation is a must and failure to provide health information to the patient may constitute malpractice.[4] Hacker advises against the big brother approach to consumer health education but supports informed personal choice.[5] Johnson includes

The author is Reference Bibliographer for the Sciences and Health, State University of New York College at Cortland, Memorial Library, P.O. Box 2000, Cortland, NY 13045.

self-care and informed decisions as main objectives for the national center for health education.[6] Levin has written many articles in re-sounding support of the lay person as primary care practitioner.[7] Lewis reports success with a child initiated visit to the school nurse as well as the child's continued participation in the decisions regarding his or her care.[8] Lunin comments on the growing force of con-sumerism in health care and estimates that up to 75% of all health care is provided by lay people to themselves.[9] Maina discusses social, political and ethical implications of providing health and medical information to the public. Maina and Groen reassure librar-ians that there is nothing to fear legally if they supply information from a printed source and do not mingle printed information with their own personal opinion or interpretations.[10,11] Somers promotes the transfer of personnel and resources from the disease industry to health information.[12] Milio has written extensively on promoting health and preventing illness through changes in public policy.[13]

WHY FAILURE TO RESPOND

If everyone is writing in favor of health promotion and self-care, why is not every library responding with programs and services? Public libraries instead have been very selective and conservative in the acquisition and provision of health information. Medical li-braries do not encourage public use of their collections and usually refer questions to the public library.[14]

One far-reaching and heavily used example of the way public and hospital libraries have responded to consumer requests for health in-formation is Healthline or Tel-Med.[15,16,17] The vast number of ar-ticles on Tel-Med positively evaluate this telephone answering ser-vice consisting of some 300 audio cassettes on varied health topics. Each tape runs about 3 to 5 minutes. Libraries report several thou-sand calls per month. A clerk can answer a call a minute and run the appropriate tape. This has satisfied an information need where con-fidentiality is required in such areas as sexual behavior or mental health.

Hospital and public libraries have joined forces in health consor-tiums to share information resources and provide referral to physi-cians, pharmacists, and other health professionals in local private and public health agencies,[18,19] but these networks remain scattered around the country.

What are some possible reasons both for and against the provision of health information to the general public by libraries? Listed here are ten reasons for each side of the argument. Librarians should provide health information to lay people because (1) Consumers are demanding more health information, questioning their doctors and suing hospitals for malpractice; (2) The cost of health care is too high compared with other services and that cost could be reduced with health education; (3) Improved patient compliance reduces unnecessary visits to the doctor or emergency room; (4) The fear of cancer can be reduced and hope provided so people will seek early treatment; (5) Mass media education may be effective in reducing the prevalence of risk factors for cardiovascular disease;[20] (5) Self-medication is common practice and the trend is toward self-administration of medication in hospitals;[21,22] (7) Doctors, nurses, and other health professionals make mistakes and with increased malpractice insurance costs, people must put a knowledgeable check on medical care; (8) The change from disease-oriented medical care to disease-preventing health care is demonstrated by the great interest in diet, exercise and environmental health; (9) Segments of the population do not receive any medical care, for example, runaways, homeless, poor, rural dwellers, middle income and middle aged;[23] and (10) The best medical care is not readily available to everyone in every community nor is it likely to be.

Librarians should not provide health information because: (1) Not everyone can nor should they be able to handle health information and such knowledge can frighten; (2) People want advice rather than just information and are often unable to reconcile several possible medical solutions;[24] (3) Lay people need non-technical information with interpretation by a doctor; (4) People do not want to change lifestyles or behaviors and health education has been pretty ineffective in reducing obesity or smoking;[25] (5) Self-diagnosis may mean that a person will delay seeking medical care when needed; (6) No one pays for the prevention of illness or health teaching; (7) Society is still disease-oriented and hospitals do not make money on empty beds or home care; (8) Librarians and other non-medical people have no background for answering medical information questions and would not be up to date on the latest treatments; (9) Beliefs and values are impossible to alter even when knowledge is gained; and (10) One cannot appeal to all people with different educational backgrounds, beliefs and traditions. Though I find some truths in the negative arguments, I believe the positive reasons outweigh the negative. Each person is responsible for his or her own health and librarians can help individuals decide more intelligently about their own health care and lifestyle. Physicians, nurses and other health professionals may participate in a patient's care, but should not take over for the person. I am not fearful of self-care, self-diagnosis or self-help groups though I am mindful of some limitations.[26,27] Milio and the Sidels are skeptical of the long term benefits of self-help. Let me review the self-help literature very briefly.

SELF-HELP EXPLOSION

Though self-help is not new, there has been an explosion in the literature to match the tremendous growth in activity in recent years. Peer referral and peer teaching by lay volunteers is one definition of self-help. Self-help groups are usually started by non-professional people who share a common problem with which professionals have had little success such as: chronic illness, addiction, child abuse, slow learning, handicap, and being an ex-prisoner or former mental patient. The goals of self-help groups are to cope with daily living, promote individual self-fulfillment and to provide health education. Women's self-help groups have provided members with the knowledge of their bodies and helped build self-reliance.

These grass roots networks are sometimes begun by a physician or social worker, but most are separate from larger organizations like the American Cancer Society or the American Heart Association. In terms of rehabilitation, self-development, mutual support, self-actualization and health education, these efforts are applauded and encouraged. There are warnings from careful observers. Local self-help groups have such a narrow focus that they can hamper the development of rehabilitative service by larger organizations or government. These groups may also discourage family and friends from providing mutual aid. Medical self-help or self-care groups tend to focus in on only one type of chronic illness or addiction, for example, Alzheimer's disease,[28] heart surgery, stroke or alcoholism. Groups usually meet near large medical centers and can alienate rural dwellers. Self-help groups tend to be white, middle to upper class and well educated. Poor, minorities and less well educated are not served.

There is the tendency to blame the victim so well described by

Ryan.[29] Rather than pointing the finger at society's failures, clients are convinced of their own uniqueness and inevitable responsibility for their problems. There is also political strength in organizing rather than fragmenting people into groups with different problems. The future existence of self-help groups rests on their ability and willingness to cooperate with doctors, social workers and others who offer present services. These professionals must be sensitized to human concerns and reminded that the disabled elderly are on the rise. Society must make a basic commitment to the equitable redistribution of resources and the improvement in the quality of life for those with lesser economic and social power. Not all problems are solvable through local action, but self-help groups can make people more aware of needed services that they have had to provide for themselves.

There is a message here for librarians concerning the equitable redistribution of resources which have largely been provided to health professionals and not made readily available to the lay public. What can librarians do to raise the health knowledge level of the lay public and encourage self-help or self-care groups to change the present health care system? Pelletier might call librarians medical self-care consultants.[30] Kay proposes "the librarian as (health) educator-catalyst."[31] Rubin discusses "counselor librarians" and the practice of bibliotherapy.[32] Here are some possible suggestions for librarians to aid the lay person and enlist the cooperation of the health professionals in the community. (A) Loan blood pressure cuffs from the library. Ferguson reported that consumers spent $60 billion on them in 1979![33] (B) Promote and sponsor a health fair in the library. They have been very successful and well attended at local shopping malls![34] (C) Co-offer *Tel-Med* with the local public or hospital library. (D) Have the library subscribe to a journal called, *Medical Self-Care*,[35] as well as a selection of lay health and general medical journals. (E) Publish a newsletter with book reviews and other evaluations of new health resources. Enlist the help of health professionals as there is criticism of self-care books in that they do not reduce physician visits.[36,37] (F) Serve on a local health planning board and offer a library conference room for a regular meeting place. (G) Purchase the most current medical and nursing textbooks, diagnosis and therapy manuals, and guidebooks like James Long's, *Essential Guide to Prescription Drugs*.[38] (H) Print book reviews of a variety of self-help books in the local paper. (I) Offer display areas in the library to local private and public health agencies as well as self-help groups. (J) Distribute self-help book-marks[39] and other flyers on library holdings as well as materials and services available to the community. (K) Start a health information consortium with much advice from the existing ones in the country. Get on all appropriate mailing lists.[40] Maybe some grant money is available from the Council on Library Resources or elsewhere. (L) Organize and advertize a self-help minicourse or short workshop on health information for the lay person. (M) Show health-related films in the library. (N) Have speakers provide information on nutrition, exercise and specific health concerns. (O) Provide bibliographies on specific health topics. (P) Ask other librarians what they have done or might do in the future to provide health information for the lay person. Librarians have a responsibility to make health information available to all people not just the professional.

NOTES

1. Walter J. McNerney, "The Missing Link in Health Services," *Journal of Medical Education*, 59:11-23 (January 1975).

2. Marta Dosa, "Development and Evaluation of a Health Information Sharing Network," *ASIS Proceedings*, 15:102-104 (1978).

3. Lois F. Lunin, "Information for Health is an Issue," *ASIS Bulletin*, 4:11-19 (April 1978). Comment 5:18-19 (February 1979).

4. D. Etzweiler, "The Contract for Health Care," *JAMA*, 224:1034 (May 1, 1973).

5. S.S. Hacker, "Can Some Approaches to Health Education Become Hazardous to Health?" *Journal of the American College Health Association*, 26:121-123 (December 1977).

6. R.L. Johnson, "The National Center for Health Education in the U.S.: A Role of Major Significance," *International Journal of Health Education*, 19:170-173 (1976).

7. L.S. Levin, "The Lay Person as the Primary Care Practitioner," *Public Health Reports*, 91:206-210 (1976).

8. M.A. Lewis, "Child Initiated Care," *American Journal of Nursing*, 74:652-655 (April 1974).

9. Lunin, "Information for Health is an Issue."

10. W. Maina, "Health Information for All," *Library Journal*, 102:1552-1553 (August 1977).

11. Frances Groen, "Provision of Health Information Has Legal and Ethical Aspects," *Canadian Library Journal*, 40:359-362 (December 1983).

12. A.R. Somers, "Priorities in Educating the Public about Health," *New York Academy of Medicine Bulletin*, 54:37-41 (January 1978).

13. Nancy Milio, *Primary Care and the Public's Health.* Lexington, Massachusetts: D.C. Heath, 1983. *Promoting Health Through Public Policy.* Philadelphia: F.A. Davis, 1981.

14. Cathy Schell, "Preventive Medicine: The Library Prescription," *Library Journal*, 105:929-931 (April 15, 1980).

15. Susan Branch, "Healthline: A New Reference Service," *RQ*, 18:327-330 (Summer 1979).

16. A. Diseker, "Use and Reported Effectiveness of TEL-MED: A Telephone Health Information System," *American Journal of Public Health*, 70:229-234 (March 1980).

17. D.J. Sager, "Answering the Call for Health Information," *American Libraries*, 9: 480-482 (September 1978).

18. Lynn Yellott, Interview in Syracuse, N.Y. at the Onondaga Public Library on CHIC. (July 31, 1980).

19. Eleanor Y. Goodchild, "The Chips Project," *Bulletin of the Medical Library Association*, 66:432-436 (October 1978).

20. R.B. Shekelle, "Public Beliefs about Causes and Prevention of Heart Attacks," *JAMA*, 240:756-758 (August 25, 1978).

21. Deborah J. Williams, "Push Button Pain Relief Puts the Patient in Control," *American Journal of Nursing*, 84:1458 (December 1984).

22. "Patient-controlled Analgesia," *American Family Physician*, 29:126,128 (March 1984).

23. Nancy Milio, "Self-Care in Urban Setting," *Health Education Monographs*, 5:136-144 (Summer 1977).

24. Yellott, Interview on CHIC.

25. Somers, "Priorities in Educating the Public About Health."

26. Milio, "Self-Care in Urban Setting."

27. Ruth and Victor Sidel, "Toward the Twenty-first Century," *Reforming Medicine*, pp. 272-273, edited by the Sidels, New York: Pantheon Books, 1984.

28. Miriam K. Aronson, "Coping with Alzheimer's Disease Through Support Groups," *Aging*, 347:3-9 (1984).

29. William Ryan, *Blaming the Victim*. (NY: Pantheon, 1971).

30. Kenneth R. Pelletier, "In Search of Optimal Health," *Medical Self-Care*, pp. 48-50 (Winter 1980).

31. Paul Kay, "Public Access to Health Information: A Psychoanalyst's View," *RQ*, 22:406 (Summer 1983).

32. Rhea Joyce Rubin, "Public Access to Health Information: A Librarian's Response," *RQ*, 22:409-410 (Summer 1983).

33. Tom Ferguson, "MSC and Advertising," *Medical Self-Care*, (Winter 1980).

34. "Good Health Roundups Attract Older Ohioans," and "Nationwide Health Fair Projects to Mark Older Americans Months," *Aging*, 293:2-7 (1979).

35. *Medical Self-Care*, Box 717, Inverness, California 94937.

36. Alfred O. Berg and James P. LoGerfo, "Potential Effects of Self-Care Algorithms on the Number of Physician Visits," *New England Journal of Medicine*, 300:535-537 (1979).

37. S.H. Moore, "Effect of Self-Care Book on Physician Visits," *JAMA*, 243:2317-2320 (June 13, 1980).

38. James W. Long, *The Essential Guide to Prescription Drugs: What You Need to Know for Safe Drug Use*. (NY: Harper & Row, 3rd ed., 1982).

39. Grant Miller, Joan Cirone and Mike Looney, "Self-Help Bookmarks for Common Emotional Problems of College Students," *Journal of the American College Health Association*, 28:174-175 (1979).

40. National Health Information Clearinghouse, P.O. Box 1133, Washington, D.C. 20013.

REFERENCES

Alloway, Catherine, "Adult Services: Issues in Consumer Health Information Services," *RQ*, 23:143-149, Winter 1983.

Averill, M.S., "The Library: Passport to Health Information," *Medical Self-Care* 38-39, Summer 1980.

Beatty, W.K., "A Medical Collection," *American Libraries* 5: 250-253, May 1974.

Brandon, Alfred N. and Dorothy R. Hill, "Selected List of Nursing Books and Journals," *Nursing Outlook* 32: 92-101, March/April 1984.

Charney, Norman, "Ethical and Legal Questions in Providing Health Information," *California Librarian* 39: 23-33, January 1978.

"Consumer Health Information Project," *Interface* 2: 9, Summer 1980.

Consumer Self-Care in Health. Edited by J. Gallicchio. Washington, DC: National Center for Health Sciences Research, August 1977.

Coppernoll-Black, Penny, "Presenting a Workshop on Drug Information for Public Librarians," *Illinois Libraries* 62: 293-295, 1980.

Dalton, Leslie and Ellen Gartenfeld, "Evaluating Printed Health Information for Consumers," *Bulletin for the Medical Library Association* 69: 322-4, July 1981.

Dosa, Marta L. et al., "Development and Evaluation of a Health Information Sharing Network," *The Information Age in Perspective; Proceedings of the ASIS Annual Meeting*, 41st, 15: 102-104, November 1978.

Drake, Robert F., "Information for Mental Health," *Library Association Record* 82: 587, December 1980.

Drazba, Mary T., "The Blue Cross Association and Blue Shield Association Library," *Illinois Libraries* 62: 237-239, 1980.

Eakin, Dottie, "Consumer Health Information: Libraries as Partners," *Bulletin of the Medical Library Association* 68: 220-228, April 1980.

Ellsworth, Susan Marsh, "Crisis Center Librarian? You Gotta Be Weird . . . ," *Top of the News* 32: 67-72, November 1975.

"Evaluating Medical Information," *Harvard Medical School Letter* n.p., February 18, 1982.

Fecher, Ellen, "Consumer Health Information: A Prognosis," *Wilson Library Bulletin* 59: 389-391, February 1985.

Ferguson, Tom, "The Self-Care Revolution," *American Pharmacy* NS 20: 12-15, June 1980.

Gardner, Trudy A., "Consumer Health Information Needs and Access Through Existing Indexes," *RQ*, 20: 366-372, Summer 1981.

Gartenfeld, Ellen, "The Community Health Information Network; a Model for Hospital and Public Library Cooperation," *Library Journal* 103: 1911-1914, October 1, 1978.

Goodchild, Eleanor, "The CHIPS Project: a Health Information Network to Serve the Consumer," *Bulletin of the Medical Library Association* 66: 432-6, October 1978.

Green, Lawrence. *The Professional and Scientific Literature on Patient Education: A Guide to Information Sources*. Detroit, Michigan: Gale, 1980.

Help = Health Education Library Project, Nioga Library System, 6575 Wheeler Road, Lockport, NY 14094, brochure, no date, 4 p.

Help Yourself; Blue Print for Health. Blue Cross Association, Chicago, Illinois: pamphlet, 92 p., 1978.

Hudnall, Marsha, "ACSH Survey: How Popular Magazines Rate on Nutrition," *ACSH News & Views* 3: 1-3, Jan/Feb 1982.

Ittner, Dwight, "The Medical Reference Question in the Small Library," *Sourdough* 17: 12-13, May/June 1980.

Jennings, Kelly. *Consumer Health Information: The Public Librarian's Role*. Tulsa City-County Library, 1980.

Kabler, Anne W., "Delivery of Health-Related Information to Rural Practitioners, *Bulletin of the Medical Library Association* 69: 382-386, October 1981.

Kay, Paul, "Public Access to Health Information: A Psychoanalyst's View," *RQ*, 22: 400-408, Summer 1983.

Kolner, Stuart J., "A Regional Union List as an Online Catalog for Consumer Health Information," *Bulletin of the Medical Library Association* 72: 29-30, January 1984.

Larson, Miriam T. *Patient/Health Education—The Librarian's Role; Proceedings of an Invitational Institute* (February 5-9, 1979). Detroit, Michigan: Division of Library Science, College of Education, Wayne State University, 1979.

Moeller, Kathleen A. and Kathleen E. Deeney, "Documenting the Need for Consumer

Health Information: Results of a Community Survey," *Bulletin of the Medical Library Association* 70: 236-9, April 1982.

Napoli, Maryann. *Health Facts; A Critical Evaluation of the Major Problems, Treatments, and Alternatives Facing Medical Consumers.* Woodstock, NY: Overlook Press, 1982.

Pender, Nola J., "Patient Identification of Health Information Received During Hospitalization," *Nursing Research* 23: 262-269, 1974.

Rees, Alan M. and Jodith Janes. *Consumer Health Information Source Book.* NY: Bowker, 1984.

Rees, Alan M. *Developing Consumer Health Information Services.* NY: Bowker, 1982.

Roose, Tina, "Who are the Consumers? What are the Questions?," *Library Journal* 109: 154-155, February 1, 1984.

Rowley, Jennifer, "Consumer Information and Advice: the Role of Public Libraries," *AsLib Proceedings* 32: 417-424, November/December 1980.

Self-Care: An Annotated Bibliography. Division of Health Education, Center for Health Promotion and Education, Department of Health & Human Services, October 1982.

Self-Medication in Health Care: An International Perspective. World Federation of Proprietary Medicine Manufacturers, April 1985.

Tabor, Roy, "Information for Health: Informing Patients and Public," chapter 4, *Medical Librarianship* pp. 52-66. Edited by Michael Carmel. Library Association, England, Phoenix, Arizona: Oryx Press, 1982.

Ulene, Art. *Help Yourself to Health: A Health Information and Services Directory.* NY: Putnam, 1980.

Vaillancourt, Pauline M., "The Librarian and Patient's Information," *Catholic Library World* 50: 393-396, April 1979.

Vaillancourt, Pauline and Marlene Bobka, "The Public Library's Role in Providing Consumer Health Information," *Public Library Quarterly* 3: 41-49, Fall 1982.

"Where Californians Get Information," *Unabashed Librarian* 37: 18, 1980.

Wood, M. Sandra, "Ethical Aspects of Medical Reference," *The Reference Librarian* 4: 75-87, Summer 1982.

Yellott, Lynn. *The Onondaga County Public Library's Consumer Health Information Services and the Consumer Health Information Consortium.* Prepared for Raven Systems & Research, Inc. under contract with US Department of Health & Human Services, Public Health Service, Center for Disease Control, Center for Health Promotion and Education, Community Program Development Division, Atlanta, Georgia, August 1981.

Yellott, Lynn and Robert Barrier, "Evaluation of a Public Library's Health Information Service," *Medical Reference Services Quarterly* 2: 31-51 Summer 1983.

REFERENCE SERVICES AND STAGES OF AUTOMATION

Self-Service
at the Information Supermarket:
Report on an Enduser's
Online Shopping Trip

Justine Roberts
Lydia Jensen

The first author of this report is smart, stubborn, curious, impatient, sometimes arrogant, and perennially harassed for time—in short, the very model of a potential enduser of online literature databases. These traits, combined with her minimal experience at the reference desk and as a searcher, offered us an opportunity to explore the enduser's online literature search experience with a fresher perspective than one can usually bring to a professional realm. It seemed to us that it might be worthwhile to record and examine a novice's encounters with three of the major services now being actively marketed to library users: DIALOG's Knowledge Index (KI), BRS' BRKTHRU (BRKTHRU), and the National Library of Medicine's MEDLARS system (NLM).

Reports evaluating various enduser systems and discussing enduser searching are not scarce.[1,2,3,4,5,6] Eisenberg in 1983,[7] Janke and Lyon, in 1984/85[8,9,10] provide extensive bibliography. Recently, Haynes et al. provided an especially thorough report on the costs of searching Medline using 14 different systems[11] and intermediary software, and several reports surveying costs and users of BRS/AFTER DARK are cited above. User perceptions have ranged from hosannas[12] to thumbs down,[13] after the use of one or two systems. However most of the surveys report on fully- or partly-subsidized use, or, in the case of Haynes, the systems have been tested with

---

Ms. Roberts is at the Library Systems Office, University of California, San Francisco, CA 94143. Ms. Jensen is at the same address, but in the Reference Division.

professionally-formulated searches. We felt unsure of what enduser searching meant for the ordinary practitioner, whom, we are convinced, follows Mooers' Law: "An information retrieval system will tend not to be used whenever it is more painful and troublesome for a customer to have information than for him not to have it".[14]

NOVICE QUALIFICATIONS

The "novice" enduser's previous experience (additional to the free practice time offered on all systems) included an 18-months-old KI subscription used for several personal searches, a 3-months-old NLM password, used for a couple of personal searches, and a 1-month-old BRKTHRU subscription, used for one personal search. As a systems librarian, she is knowledgeable about computers in general, and frequently accesses a computer online to accomplish various parts of her work. (Faculty members and other potential endusers also often use computers in their work.) However, in the preceding 10 years, her "professional" literature searching had included no work on DIALOG, and fewer than 5 BRS and MEDLARS searches. She had attended NLM's compulsory enduser/librarian Medline training class in mid-1984 when it was still a 3-day course, but had heeded the advertising that implied that no introductory KI or BRKTHRU training was expected or needed. The report's second author is an experienced reference librarian and online searcher who regularly attends training updates for the systems she uses. She is experienced on both the NLM and daytime BRS systems, and occasionally searches on DIALOG. She took no part in and was not consulted with respect to any searches carried out during the searching period.

HEALTH SCIENCE ENVIRONMENT

The authors' normal user population and potential online endusers come from the medical, dental, nursing, pharmacy and graduate science departments of the University of California, San Francisco (UCSF), a campus solely devoted to the health sciences. The novice's subject background and supplementary education, together with information on the search form, seemed to allow at least a rough approximation of the subject knowledge which would be brought to a search session by potential campus endusers.

METHOD

Before starting the trial searching period, the novice collected and made a log entry for all of the (63) questions from approximately one month's searches completed by Reference librarians at the UCSF Health Sciences Library. The Library's "Computer Search Request" form shows the user's response to the question "What do you want these references to be about", as well as the user's occasional response to a request for up to 3 current "relevant papers". The Reference librarian's notes, trial searches, and results were copied and attached to the form, but not inspected. If the searcher had spoken to a user and annotated the face of the form with additional interpretation, this was heeded, but the Reference librarian's own research and amplification of the question were not. All collected materials were then put aside, and the log (only) was used as the source of questions for the trial searches.

SEARCH SETS

Each question became the source of one search "set": a search to be conducted via the novice's IBM-PC/XT microcomputer on MEDLARS, KI, and BRKTHRU databases, when suitable ones existed. All searches were carried out in an "after dark mode", that is, during NLM's nonprime hours, during BRKTHRU's "Reduced Rates" time (6 pm - 4 am and weekends, local time), and during KI's regular times (6 pm - 5 am and weekends, local time).

Most, but not all, of the questions proved to be most appropriately searched on the Medline files available from all three vendors. Each search session was ended when the novice felt that the best search strategy had been entered, and the costs of downloading the search results, at 1200 baud, could be estimated. The Actual online time and costs of each session were recorded, added to the estimated cost for downloading the results, and totaled to give an estimated user search cost for each session. Finally, a printout of the search session was "re-joined" to the Reference librarian's record, so that comparisons could be made where possible. The professional search record always included choice of vendor, database, and charges. It also usually included the search formulation and dates covered, and sometimes included a record of the online time, in minutes, and the number of retrievals.

SEARCH RULES

The following "rules" were followed for each novice search:

— the order in which the three systems were searched was rotated, so that each of the systems could be the first, second, or third one searched approximately one-third of the time.
— each system was searched on its own terms. That is, NLM was searched using MeSH[15] and the tree structures, as taught in the introductory class which is required in order to get a password. Other search aids, including the looseleaf manuals, user support phone lines, and user newsletters from all three systems were consulted as seemed useful and convenient for particular searches.
— Search strategies were reformulated for each search on each database, except that purely natural language statements, using the actual requester's own terms, were normally used on both KI and BRKTHRU, and also on NLM (as textwords) when MeSH didn't provide a direct bridge from the user's vocabulary to the MeSH term(s).
— Search "hits" were considered "relevant" to the search question based on the novice searcher's opinion. This obviously could be different than a real user's own ratings, but was consistent throughout the trial period in terms of the novice's satisfaction, and with her idea of what the searches were about. (Notice was taken in the later comparisons where the Reference librarian's vocabulary and formulation were notably different, possibly stemming from unnoted question negotiation with the user.)
— No reference was made to the original search records until after each search was completed on all three systems. A cursory check was made at that time, for each search, to ensure that no gross, unintended, difference existed between the two question-answering attempts. The acquisition of a "learning"

effect from these inspections was consciously (and seemed all too easily) avoided. But it may in fact not have been totally avoided because it was always possible that the novice might spot, and thus be reminded of, useful commands and checktags for use in the next search.

SEARCH TRIAL END POINT

It was decided that the search trial would be stopped either when all logged searches were used up, or when the novice began to *feel* comfortable and knowledgeable about searching all of the systems, whichever occurred first. The latter occurred after 41 of the 63 logged questions had been searched over a period of 11 weeks. However, comparison of the novice's final searches with their Reference counterparts showed that large differences in search skills remained.

Twenty seven search requests were logged-in *and* carried out in the order received. However the first 14 questions were purposely selected with the perception that they were "easy" searches. Thus the first 4 searches included all of the author searches, and the only Registry Number search. The remaining ten out-of-order search requests all involved simple concepts, though not, to the searcher's rue, simple searching. One additional medical research question was added to the original group of 63, and carried out at the time of receipt. (This search was a useful addition to the group because of the questioner's willingness to formulate the search strategy and to react to online clues for each system.)

TYPES OF USERS AND QUESTIONS

Table 1 shows the user status and broad subject area of the search requests, and confirms their health sciences orientation. The source of 14 (34%) of the questions were people in other professions or disciplines or whose status was unknown. These users included several nurses, one clinical psychologist, a librarian, at least two attorneys, and a social worker. Non-MEDLARS databases, listed in Table 2, were used entirely or in part during 12 of the total 121 search sessions. (Suitable databases proved unavailable on NLM or KI for 2 author searches, both searchable on CA Search on BRKTHRU.)

TABLE 1

Topic and Source of Search Requests

Topic	Students	UCSF Faculty, Practitioners	Outside User or Unknown	% of Searches
Medicine	2	15	6	56
Nursing	1	2	5	20
Pharmacy & Pharm. Chem.	1	3	-	10
Other health science	-	3	1	10
Other	-	2	-	5
Total				101*

*-rounding error

TABLE 2

Databases Used

Medline and other Medlars databases
PsycINFO
Biosis
International Pharmaceutical Abstracts
CA Search
Eric

MICROCOMPUTER SUPPORT FACILITIES

Certain microcomputer capabilities, described in Appendix A, were used during most sessions. The need for them wasn't anticipated at the start, but they proved to be important aids to the novice.

RESULTS

At the start of this trip, the first author expected to defend her claim of "novice enduser" results against her 21 years of experience as a librarian, extensive theoretical knowledge of information retrieval and 20 years of computer experience. If the challenge is valid, the evidence—in these 41 searches—is hard to find. As indicated in Table 3, we found that user errors and system "hassles" were the major and normal accompaniment to the discovery of relevant information.

On NLM, 1 out of 9 typed-in statements were wrong, had to be corrected, or resulted in unexpected and/or unwelcome messages. It was worse on BRKTHRU and KI: 1 out of 4 BRKTHRU, and 1 out 2 KI entries were accompanied by the need to re-enter or correct entries, and/or to cope with system "hassles".

The monthly per-search costs reported in Table 4 suggest little if any downslope to the learning curve for any of the systems, including KI, the one on which the novice had most prior experience. Total recorded online costs for search formulation and review of hits are shown in Table 5, Column (7), and indicate that exploration and learning on NLM was considerably cheaper than on either BRKTHRU or KI, but also that much of this "savings" would be spent on higher downloading costs, included in the "Cost per search" figures given in Column 9.

USER ERRORS

There were few, if any, error messages that the novice did not receive. Some were unavoidable, through no system fault, and, in

TABLE 3

Error/Problem Incidence

# of Sess.	No. Syst.	No. stmts	No. user errors	No. of averted errs.	No. of system hassles[1]	Total prob. stmts	Problem rate
40	NLM	1623	67	73	42	182	1 out of 8.9
39	BRKT	964	93	106	31	230	1 out of 4.2
40	KI	882	139	162	68	369	1 out of 2.4
Totals:		3469	299	341	141	781	1 out of 4

1 - See text for "novice´s" definition of system "hassles".

Errors: a statement to which the system responds with an error message or a statement which produces an immediately obvious erroneous response.

Averted Errors: typing or statement formulation errors corrected prior to issuing a carriage return.

TABLE 4

Average Cost Per Session - Search Entry and Review

	NLM		BRKTHRU		KI	
Month	# of sess.	Avg. cost	# of sess.	Avg. cost	# of sess.	Avg. cost
OCT	6	$1.23	7	$4.69	6	$2.37
NOV	16	$2.61	16	$7.68	16	$3.26
DEC	12	$3.79	14	$5.72	14	$4.62
JAN	4	$4.49	3	$7.47	3	$4.91
OCT-JAN	38	$2.96	40	$6.45	39	$3.74

TABLE 5

Non Prime Time Costs for Novice Usage
(all downloads with abstracts)

(1) # of sess.	(2) System	(3) # of "hits"	(4) Avg. size "hit" (n)	(5) Download cost per "hit"*	(6) Estimated download costs (3)x(5)	(7) Recorded online costs	(8) Estimated total costs (6)+(7)	(9) Cost per search (8)/(1)
38	NLM	3542	1236 char. (98)	$.1223	$433.19	$109.55	$542.74	$14.28
40	BRKTHRU	4221	1227 char. (41)	$.0803	$338.95	$258.13	$597.08	$14.93
39	KI	4004	1277 char. (73)	$.0717	$287.09	$145.72	$432.81	$11.10

* - For BRKTHRU and KI, this is: average char.per citation with abstract/120
char. per second (cps) = no. of seconds downloading time x cost per second
= download cost per hit.

For NLM, this is: as above, plus $.01 per citation + (avg. char. per citation
with abstract/1000 x $.08) = total download cost per hit. For the "average"
hit, this was (10.3 seconds/abstract x $.0013) = $.0134 download
cost + $.01 + $.0989 online character charges = $.1223 total download
cost. Two additional charges may be incurred during downloading, but
could not be accurately estimated, for "continue printing" carriage returns
and for extra disk accesses. With the page length profile set at its maximum
100 lines, it was assumed that these additional charges ($.01 per CR,
$.06/100 disk accesses) were minimal for each abstract. NLM billing for 16
sessions during November showed an average interaction charge of $.37 per
session (included in the recorded online costs shown above) with no separate-
ly billed access charges.

All costs are based on nonprime or discounted time usage of the Medline
database as of December 1985: NLM: $15/hr; BRKTHRU: $28/hr; KI: $24/hr.

the case of KI, might be said to unfairly skew results. KI's signoff command is "logoff". The signoff command from the E-Mail system which the novice uses to write to her daughter is "logout". This fact-of-life resulted in a large number of KI "error" and "averted error" occurrences.

One common and annoying source of typing error occurred when it was necessary to reenter long search statements for searching multiple files. This could usually be avoided on NLM by use of the savesearch facility, and was eventually manageable for searching Medline on BRKTHRU when the combined MESZ file became available mid-search period. For KI's tripartite Medline, one solution would be the use of a file upload to resend selected search statements. However, this solution is more theoretical than real, given the almost invariant finding that the citations resulting from the first set of carefully developed and typed-out search statements were rarely what was expected or desired.

AVERTED ERRORS

"Averted errors" do not usually enter into system monitoring, but loomed large in this novice experience. These are the about-to-be-committed errors that one corrects by backspacing and re-typing (and are easily spotted on literal session printouts because of their apparent, but harmless, error display). For these beginning sessions, they reflected the fairly pervasive state of feeling flustered, and constituted nagging uncertainty flags, hoisted in inverse proportion to confidence level. One may correct only so many errors per statement and retain any sense of control, even when the entry is apparently successful.

SYSTEM HASSLES

"System hassles" might be summed up as all of things that occur that make you want to throw the terminal out the window. They are probably familiar to all searchers who remember their online learning experience and are inescapably subjective. They *didn't* include, for this novice, such minor and/or ameliorable nuisances as NLM's "Time ovflw: cont? (Y/N)" or BRKTHRU's interminable, but avoidable, menus and prompts. They did include, for KI, the inescapable "Find term generates too many items" and the unanticipated need to re-enter commands that apparently exceeded a predetermined length. The novice was always disturbed by "xxx items to go", which irregularly and unpredictably signalled the fatal "too many items". For BRKTHRU, system hassles included the disconcerting and never explained "Overflowed after xxx words". "No documents found", when it occurred following a prior retrieval (e.g., "ribavirin.mj . . . 52 documents found . . . ribavirin . . . search term not found") was another confusion-generating hassle, and "Possible data loss", never explained, added to the discomfort.

For NLM, "hassles" included running out of savesearch space ("No room to save current search . . ."), since it was rarely anticipated and never possible to remember what to do about it. Other hassles were empty "Prog:"'s, where the system responded to an earnestly typed search statement only with another user prompt, and "Procpstg ovflw" and "storpstg ovflw", which were particularly disconcerting as output from a savesearch. Repetitive and mindless "NP (Y)" messages, as the result of attempts to circumvent the interminable input of "Y"'s to Time Overflow, Continue and/or Continue Printing messages, caused much irritation, if not confusion. "NP"'s, in response to perfectly good (as shown) terms (e.g., "NP (RABBITS)", were infrequent but always disturbing.

Phone line troubles were a minor, but unescaped, portion of system hassles for this trip, with both visible and invisible garbage characters occasionally causing unwelcome (zero) results. "System down" messages, in their several varieties, were definitely seen as hassles, but were happily infrequent. Invariably, they seemed to be received at the moment of truth when *the* definitive search statement was about to be entered.

SYSTEM QUEUING METHODS

One pervasive if uncounted "system hassle" was that of being SLOW! KI handles this condition with a series of civilized, and easiest-to-bear "Processing" messages. NLM handles it with barely bearable "Time Ovflow. Cont?" demands, but BRKTHRU handles it most objectionably of all: the system water-torture-slowly *erases* the initial characters of your search formulation whilst your request is processed. It is sheer chance if any part of your statement remains for inspection by the time the system's response to it is visible!

UNEXPECTED OCCURRENCES

Many online happenings and initial search results were just unexpected, and kept the uncertainty flag flying through 41 sessions, a series which might easily constitute one to two year's experience for an enduser. Too few, but more often, too many "hits" were of course the major unexpected and persistent happening. The novice *knew* the search statement was correct and precise, but "overflows" and unwieldy hit counts kept happening nonetheless. A response of 642,937 documents to the concept "Measure$ or therap$ or treat$" is hard to deal with effectively in a natural language search system, especially in combination with common disease terms. When "anaesthesia" overflows, what do you use instead? It often seemed impossible to heed the instruction manuals' injunctions to "narrow" the search statement. A search for "*all* references" on "malignant hyperthermia" back to 1966, for example, yielded 1160 hits. The only practical means of limiting such results, and many others, seemed to be by date, not a very satisfactory means of ensuring quality. Here, at least, NLM offers the offline print, not available on KI or BRKTHRU. NLMs and BRKTHRUs ability to limit searching to specific fields seemed useful less often than expected, but, when it was needed, proved essential, as did their greater capacity to handle highly posted terms.

CONTROLLED VOCABULARY VS NATURAL LANGUAGE SEARCHING

The MeSH list prescribed by NLM for NLM users turned out to be the single best security blanket for relevant retrieval for most searches, despite the volume's unwelcome bulk and frequent puzzling small-print annotations. It was rarely possible, without it, to get really good retrieval simply by use of the "obvious" natural language terms with which one would otherwise search. Although the obvious term was often, in fact, the MeSH term, it was surprising for the novice to see how often it was not. Thus the MeSH term was often omitted from the initial list of terms entered for KI or BRKTHRU searches, although it was usually *added* to the search after inspection of the initial displays from these systems. Any user could, of course, purchase and use the MeSH list with any Medline vendor, but there is no suggestion that it is needed, and little help in using MeSH subdivisions or trees is offered in either the KI or BRKTHRU documentation.*

The number of commands needed in order to carry out most searches was unexpectedly and blessedly small. "Blessedly", because the number of times a needed command was forgotten was embarrasingly high. BRKTHRU displays an abbreviated command list after every response (and will print a longer one if desired), but even with this display, continuous reference was needed on all systems to the system "pocket card". BRKTHRU has the right idea for this aid: it is laminated cardboard. NLM's pocket card, received a few weeks into the trial period, proved to be invaluable, and sufficed for providing almost all needed online cribs.

DOCUMENTATION AND SUPPORT

All three systems offer phone support, but despite extended hours, these hours rarely coincided with searching times. In California, the BRKTHRU hotline closes down on weekdays three hours before the computer goes down. KI's California switchboard closes two hours after the system goes up. NLM's service desk is open only on weekdays, and closes at 2 pm Pacific time. Practically speaking, this meant that phone line use was limited to persisting, and/or particularly troublesome, problems, and the system advisors were rarely the source of learning better search techniques or coping with apparent but easily circumvented system limitations.

Hotline respondents were always courteous, and gave an impression of trying to be helpful, but one can only hope that the novice's twice repeated experience of receiving incorrect information from BRKTHRU was not typical. The most troubling of these encounters was expensive: a correctly executed attempt to use MESZ (Medline and all backfiles) was made in early November after seeing this file listed on a price change sheet. The phone desk said, "no, MESZ is not available on BRKTHRU, that was an error on the pricelist". Thus, no further attempt was made to use this time- and cost- saving file until its availability was accidentally discovered in late Decem-

---

*—The BRKTHRU manual lists MeSH as a "search aid", and cites it as "Medical Subject Headings, Annotated Alphabetic List of Serials Indexed for Online Users." No citation was found in the KI manual.

ber. In response to a second query, the answer was, "why, it's been available for a long time . . ."

BRKTHRU's instruction manual is the slickest and was discovered to be the worst of the three available. Six months after the first searching bill was received, 4 of its 9 sections remain empty, including "sample sessions", and the manual's 1-1/4 page index remains unimproved and mostly useless. The system newsletter, confined to BRKTHRU for a couple of issues, was later buried in the middle of general *BRS Bulletin*, and became all-too-discardable from the day's usual heavy mail pile.

NLM's huge *Online Services Reference Manual* defied finding an adequate desk location and, despite an excellent index, was quite forbidding and would certainly have been little used. Fortunately, it was supplanted early in the search period by NLM's slim *Basics of Searching Medline: A Guide for the Health Professional*, July 1985. This text, with a couple of clipped pages, and the system's pocket card, proved easy and useful to consult on all but one or two occasions. The system newsletter, *The NLM Technical Bulletin*, seemed clearly intended for librarians rather than (other) endusers, and joined the appropriate, if not optimal, reading pile.

KI's bright orange binder was the most usefully organized of the system manuals, and was also easy and profitable to use. Its quarterly newsletter, *Knowledge Index News*, was the most readable and helpful of any of the supplemental publications.

NOVICE MEETS PROFESSIONAL

One cake recipe, baked in the same oven, may rise or fall depending on how the baker uses the ingredients. Most of the Medline searches done by the "novice" on all three systems have the same ingredients: MeSH, tree structure explosions, subheadings, text words, age groups, and languages. Table 6 shows how very different the search outcomes often were, despite availability of the same elements. Figure 1 shows the novice search strategies and Reference staff formulation for the same question, an example of one such different mixing.

Throughout most of the novice's searches, the ingredients were used inconsistently or inappropriately, and she failed to take advantage of knowledgeable support personnel at the time the (unanticipated) need for them occurred.

TABLE 6

Novice / Professional Search Retrieval Counts

SEARCH NUMBER	SEARCH DATE	DBASE ORDER	NLMRET# NLM	BRSRET# BRKTHRU	KIRET# KI	REF-RET# UCSF
AF169	10/20	BKM	0	30	0	41
AF176	10/21	BKM	7	4	7	19
EAJ152	10/23	MKB	0	2	0	??
IG204	10/23	MBK	91	115	102	135
JB159	10/27	KBM	188	188	279	85
DIS143	10/28	BMK	1075	1075	1160	1093
ECR153	10/28	BMK	39	637	10	217
BP158	11/03	MKB	31	33	45	241
MGS200	11/03	BKM	20	30	52	??
RJE185	11/03	MKB	131	99	188	57+
RZS216	11/07	KMB	136	54	194	31
HH174	11/10	MBK	48	168	53	24+
JD166	11/10	KBM	60	39	23	26
NA199	11/10	BKM	4	33	3	13
JLS162	11/12	BMK	10	22	11	37+
MJ180	11/17	MKB	22	20	4	??
KD150	11/18	KMB	105	168	51	6?
JK156	11/26	KBM	13	13	7	84
KD151	11/26	MBK	14	10	11	??
RC154	11/27	BMK	2	3	0	49
HM155	11/28	MKB	15	54	14	77
SR100	11/28	BKM	8	15	54	—
RC157	11/29	KMB	61	56	94	150E
CA0149	12/01	KBM	27	30	30	??
JTR146	12/01	MBK	28	29	33	271
KME142	12/02	MKB	9	23	5	??
KMK144	12/02	BMK	10	33	33	??
PT161	12/04	BKM	19	38	118	??
SK164	12/08	KMB	21	8	19	85
LS170A	12/09	MBK	190	287	502	269
LS170B	12/11	KBM	97	55	12	200
KE163	12/17	BMK	30	9	118	21
KD165	12/18	MKB	46	37	40	112
AST160	12/19	BKM	67	25	61	387
CL177	12/23	KMB	85	141	63	30
JC167	12/28	MBK	202	284	300	204
MAD99	12/29	MBK	36	55	67	??
KK182	13/02	KBM	2	10	9	11
RF172	13/02	MKB	554	22	214	321
MT15X	13/05	BMK	186	266	444	167
RG191	13/09	BKM	6	11	18	27
TOTALS			3695	4231	4448	

FIGURE 1

```
User search statement:    All anesthetic considerations in patients with sickle cell
                          disease


Novice search formulations (Medline):

            for NLM    (1) exp *anemia, sickle cell
                       (2) exp *anaesthesia
                       (3) 1 and 2      (Final Result: 46)+

            for KI     (1) f sickle cell anemia or sickle cell disease
                       (2) f anesthes? or anaesthes?
                       (3) f s1 or s2 and human    (Final Result: 40)

         for BRKTHRU   (1) sickle cell anemia or sickle cell disease
                       (2) anesthes$ or anaesthes$
                       (3) 1 and 2      (Final Result: 37)


Reference search formulation (Medline):

                       (1) exp c15.378.420.155 or sickle (tw)

                       (2) 1 and exp d14.166 or 1 and exp e3.155 or 1 and exp
                           d14.211

                       (3) (tw) 1 and all anesth: or 1 and all anaesth: or 1 and
                           all preanesth: or 2

                       (4) 3 and human    (Final Result: 112)
```

+ - "human" checktag unintentionally omitted from Medline search.

SUBHEADINGS

Her subheading usage exemplifies a number of problems. Her correct entry of MeSH subject heading terms on NLM indicates that she knew the commands which affect their use. However, she was apparently unaware of their scope and use by Medline indexers. Thus she often used them incorrectly or unnecessarily, or not at all (though needed).

Searching on MeSH subheadings is provided "by default" on KI, but how to use them to narrow searches is not obvious. They are shown on KI in both abbreviated and spelled-out forms, and there is a list of a few of them and brief discussion about their use in the manual. But the novice had not found this section helpful when it was first consulted, because the desired subheading wasn't listed, and had forgotten it by the time later, unsuccessful, subdivision attempts were made. On BRKTHRU, subheadings are shown in displays only as unexpanded initials, and cannot be retrieved by entering them in the same way that they are shown on the screen. The novice did not discover how to enter them correctly, and thus failed to use them at all.

COMPLEX SEARCHES

Even though the novice searcher had three days of NLM enduser training, she had trouble with the more complex searches whichever database system she used. She did very well in searches where only natural language words could be used (because there were no appropriate controlled vocabulary terms). Synonyms were not too much of a problem because she added terms which she saw in the display to her original search statement, but it seems likely that here, at least, her librarian's inspect-the-tracings training may have served to modify her novice status.

With more understanding of MeSH and the tree structures, she might have used appropriate terms from several categories instead of one, e.g., "leukocytes" (All) and also "leukocyte disorders" (C15). She rarely exploded or used MeSH tree terms. When questioned about this, she said "it was one more thing to look up" and that they hadn't "seemed all that useful". Explosion of trees may in fact not be as important in BRKTHRU or KI as it on NLM because the defaults are different, and the MeSH terms are unbound, but the inherent retrieval cutback may easily be missed by the NLM novice. (For example, that "urinary incontinence" will not retrieve articles indexed under "urinary incontinence, stress" on NLM, although it would on BRKTHRU or KI).

This novice searcher did no pre-searching, and waited until she was online to look at the indexing on KI and BRKTHRU, and, to some extent on NLM. She did pay attention to the subheadings used and sometimes incorporated them in her search strategy. Sometimes she also used some of the main headings which she saw in the indexing, but often she seemed to ignore them and lost the opportunity to broaden or narrow her search results.

Restriction to major subject headings (*, on NLM, and .MJ. on BRKTHRU) would also have improved retrieval when there were too many citations, but instead of using this option where available, she gave up the search several times. She didn't have problems with the boolean connectors OR and AND, but she seldom used the boolean NOT to delete previous search statements and, consequently, viewed the same titles repeatedly.

Selection of publication years to match the search request involved a noticeable amount of online time in earlier searches, and was frequently a source of error messages or zero hits.

The Reference librarian envied the novice her freedom to use (and pay for) more than one database per search, since *her* search requesters are usually reluctant to pay for searching in more than one database when they can't be assured in advance that they will get unique citations and not have to pay for many duplicates. "After dark" endusers may well be more likely than library search requesters to obtain the benefit of cross database searching because of the lower online and print charges they pay. The chosen databases were appropriate, but some of the searching was inherently limited without benefit of the search guides and thesauri issued by the database producers.

The first novice searches were author searches, and she had trouble with them. Author searches are simple, in that an author's name is specific, but difficult, in that each database may enter an author name differently. Search aids from NLM and KI, but not from BRKTHRU, make explicit the resulting need for the NBR, EXPAND, and STEM commands. This novice searcher was able to discover and correct several misspelled author names (either through stemming, truncating, or by seeing the correct version in the display for another sought author); librarian training may again have modified the experience.

DISCUSSION

There was rarely an outcome during this 121-search shopping trip which prompted the thought that the novice ought simply to cease wasting time and "see the Reference Librarian" instead. Even severe cumulations of "overflows", garbage retrievals, excessive hits, and error messages did not seem to outweigh the steady production of useful references, relatively easily achieved, and scheduled (usually) at the time and place of choice. Can we project this perspective—and improve on it—for our real endusers? Librarians and others have not been remiss in testing and reporting on ways to help the enduser searcher, both with the major systems and major databases. *Online* and *Database* are particularly rich as sources of methods for libraries to use in serving the enduser.

Our experience strongly supports the need for such services. Not one of the three systems we inspected was even relatively trouble free for the novice. Surprisingly, NLM came closest, in terms of the ratio of problems to statements, if only because it invoked or required more statements. However, for this novice, its clear, if inelegant, displays, its well-behaved vocabulary, its well done enduser support documentation, and, perhaps in large measure, its relatively cheap online learning and interaction costs served to make it the system of "choice" for almost all of the searches. This was a surprising result to the first author because, prior to this exposure, the system had always *seemed* rather overwhelming, rigid, fussy and demanding. Actual experience as a novice user provided a welcome contradiction.

Unfortunately, for this small subset of topical searching, KI, with its simple command vocabulary, clear displays, good manual, and relatively low costs often seemed unequal to the search task because of insufficient limiting capacity. That is, it retrieved the most "hits", but too many of them were unwanted. It might well be the system of choice for endusers whose "normal" databases do not otherwise offer a controlled vocabulary, and where normal use would be occasionally to collect some good references, rather than to monitor a field or to do comprehensive searching.

BRKTHRU

BRKTHRU, despite unfortunate encounters, a poor manual, and the most unreadable displays, clearly demonstrated the power and topical range needed to allow its use by a wide range of endusers. Although it's most likely to be the service on which a user might conclude that "it's more expensive than it's worth", it's currently (together with other BRS systems) also the only game in town for many kinds of searching. Whether we can provide adequate support for such searching is more problematic, since the very broad scope of BRS' topical coverage suggests the need for very multifaceted aid. Database aids tailored for specific user groups such as those developed by Bodtke-Roberts at Genentech[16] may make the user's search time more rewarding. BRS' own invitations to search support training seminars were quite uninviting, given their time consumption, cost and apparent "professional searcher" orientation. Changes in price and orientation may make this picture more hopeful.

FRONT ENDS

"Front end" search programs and "gateways", widely marketed as enduser solutions to many kinds of problems and system hassles, at first appeared promising as possible error preventatives. But, as the searches progressed, their prospect for offering significant help diminished: unexpected search results, rather than simple command errors, remained the most persistent continuing problem. Front end programs that allow for online intervention could have been used successfully, if available, for the systems explored here, but it seems less likely that they would have effected great improvement in results. Except for PaperChase, available directly, or via CompuServe, none of the known front end software would have helped much with MeSH, trees, or subheadings. Sci-Mate, Pro-Search, PC/Net-Link, Searchmaster, Easynet and similar systems do aid searchers with system mechanics (logon, commands, database selection), but do not help with database characteristics (indexing policies, conversion to controlled vocabulary).

Until early 1986, when the National Library of Medicine introduced GRATEFUL MED, PaperChase (at $23 an hour + $.10/hit) may have been the only "user-friendly" interface to Medline that was widely available outside of NLM itself. It seems to have many of the components which Lancaster[17] and others have long proposed as necessary for enduser searching: It is accessible and easy to use. The user doesn't need to consult manuals or go to classes. All of the instructions are online. A single word entry starts a series of questions, leading the user to MeSH and subheadings and online instructions on how to narrow or broaden the retrieval. Unfortunately, PaperChase only searches Medline. Some of its features, e.g., online help, may conceivably be added for databases in other enduser systems, but the potential cost for even that one enhancement—on a large number of databases—is sobering, and the probability of early achievement seems small.

SOME CONCERNS

On the whole, the novice in this trial did very well, and did what one might expect from a novice. She learned how to log on, searched interactively using boolean terms, with both controlled and natural language terms, used printed aids, and sometimes called system support personnel for help. That is, she did at least as well as many of our traditional users do when they use our reference stacks. The convenience and power of online bibliographic searching attracts many microcomputer users, and there are many reasons why they may get more satisfactory results than in the stacks, or via a search intermediary. The enduser knows the subject, and there is no opportunity for misinterpretation of the request. And online interaction helps the enduser reformulate the query and improve the outcome.

Nonetheless, the paternalistic concern of the librarian is invoked by the fact that the marketing of enduser searching is strongly influenced by its economic roots, and the message is that—for a price—information is accessible easily, by anyone, anywhere, and at any time. The buyer may be unaware that the most relevant material was not retrieved, and that the effort of consulting system support staff is a necessary investment, regardless of occasional failures. (A list of 800 numbers of the database producers may be as important as pocket guide cards in terms of promoting useful consultation).

CONCLUSION

Despite all concerns, our trial experience at today's self-service information market indicates that—when there is money to pay the piper—an enduser may sometimes enjoy the shopping trip and often may find the merchandise. We hope that the continued application of marketing (rather than merely selling) prowess, information science research, and librarian support systems, can serve to make trip more affordable, and easier.

Acknowledgments: It was hoped, but not assured, that support for this enduser searching trial could be obtained from librarian research funds provided by the citizens of California in the university's budget, and administered by the Librarians' Association, University of California. The possibility that all of the searching bills might indeed be personal added some measure of reality, and sometimes real panic, to each search session. Research grant awards have not been announced as of this writing, but the authors' do not underestimate the role of this support in providing courage to undertake the trial. Thus, we are grateful to colleagues who engage in the necessary critical reviews, even though it may transpire that their judgment as to quality and need differs from ours. We also gratefully acknowledge the important help of other UCSF Reference division staff members, Maria Abundo, Elisabeth Bell, James Mackie, and Carol Yates-Imah, both in assisting with mechanics, and, for the novice, in providing so much concrete evidence of "how to do it right", even if only for future reference. Marilyn A. Jensen's help was also much appreciated.

NOTES

1. Janke RV. Online after six: end user searching comes of age. *Online* 1984 Nov;8(6): 15-29.
2. Culnan MJ. The Dimensions of accessibility to online information: implications for implementing office information systems. *ACM Transactions on Office Information Systems* 1984 Apr;2(2):141-50.
3. Dodd J et al. *A comparison of two end user operated search systems; one of a series of self-studies and research projects*. College Station, TX: Texas A & M University Library, 1985. (ED255224).
4. Feinglos SJ. Medline at BRS, Dialog, and NLM: is there a choice? *Bulletin of the Medical Library Association* 1983 Jan;71(1):6-12.
5. Halperin M, Pagell RA. Free "do-it-yourself" online searching: what to expect. Online 1985 Mar;9(2):82-4.
6. Trzebiatowski E. End user study on BRS/After Dark. *RQ* 1984;23(4):446-50.
7. Eisenberg M. *The direct use of online bibliographic information systems by un-trained end users: a review of research*. Washington, DC: National Institute of Education, 1983. (ED238440).
8. Lyon S. End-user searching of online databases: a selected annotated bibliography. *Library Hi Tech* 1984 Sep;2(2):47-50.
9. Janke. *op. cit.*, pp 26-9.
10. Janke RV. Presearch counseling for client searchers (end-users). *Online* 1985 Sep; 9(5):13-26.
11. Haynes RB et al. Computer searching of the medical literature: an evaluation of Medline searching systems. *Annals of Internal Medicine* 1985 Nov;103(5):812-16.
12. Christie LG. Brkthru: research with ease. *PC World* 1986 Jan;4(1):306-8.
13. Kenward M. A library at the end of the telephone. *New Scientist* 1985 Nov;108 (1842):59-60.
14. Mooers CN. Mooers' law or why some retrieval systems are used and others are not (Editorial). *American Documentation* 1960 Jul;11(3):ii.
15. *Medical Subject Headings, Annotated Alphabetic List, 1985*. Bethesda: National Library of Medicine, 1984. 769p.
16. Bodtke-Roberts A. Personal communication, Nov 18, 1984.
17. Lancaster FW. Evaluation of On-Line Searching in Medlars (AIM-TWX) by Bio-medical Practitioners. University of Illinois Graduate School of Library Science. *Occasional Papers* 1972 Feb; (101).

APPENDIX A

Microcomputer Support Facilities

Given the novice's many initial experiences of unexpected re-sults, discussed above, it was soon felt necessary to take advantage of the scrolling capacity available on the novice's microcomputer. This feature, which allows you to "recapture" lines that have rolled off the screen, proved to be almost a *sine qua non*. The various system "Review", "Display", and "Recap" commands simply proved ineffective as counter to the frequent cases of "losing track" of what commands had previously been entered. A microcomputer scrolling facility is available in several varieties, a few of which are noted in Appendix B.

Communication Procedures

A second very important facility, included in some, but not all microcomputer communication programs, proved to be the variously-named means of "automating" the logon procedure. With this feature, it takes only one command, or keystroke, to dial a network phone number, respond to the network logon questions, request connection to a particular vendor, give the vendor password, pass through the initial vendor questions, and stop at the first search prompt. The singular contribution of this feature, sometimes called "communication procedures", was to allow the searcher to concentrate on the search formulation and on the database vendor's requirements without the distraction of irrelevant phoneline, modem and network demands. Although the very first terminal connection to a particular service is certainly the hardest, we found that the many required pre-search steps continued to be more distracting than expected. We believe that the error rates reported in this paper would have been considerably higher if it hadn't been possible to avoid them.

Uploading search questions

The facility which allows an automated logon may also be used to send (upload) pre-typed search questions. This capacity was tried in a somewhat modified form with the popular "shareware" program PC-Talk. This program allows assignment of strings of characters to a microcomputer's function and/or number keys, so that logon responses and/or pre-typed search questions may be sent with one keystroke. Use of this feature may lighten the logon typing load, but does not eliminate the need for question-by-question attention to the logon sequence. Its trial use for sending a few "obvious" and "straightforward" search formulations did not invite repetition. Only the first few letters of a pre-typed request can be seen, and, due to the abbreviated display, the searcher completely lost track of which statement was attached to which key. When sent, the statements proved to collect results which were entirely unexpected, so that all of the planned search statements had to be reformulated on the spot despite the time and attention devoted to the pre-typing and pre-programming.

One additional capacity which was not used during this trial is simply to print out searches while they are going on, a capacity which can be used with a printer capable of 120 cps or more (when transmission is at 1200 baud). It wasn't obvious at any time that this would have ameliorated novice problems, although, assuming convenient placement of the printer, it could perhaps have substituted for a scroll facility.

APPENDIX B

Scroll Facility

— For IBM-PC:	SmartcomII (communication program)*
	Backscrl (public domain utility)
	FansiConsole (resident utility)
— For Macintosh:	RedRyder ("shareware" communication program)*

The utility programs can probably be used in conjunction with most communication programs, and provide scroll recall buffers independent of communication buffers. Some communication programs provide scrolling and downloading facilities that are linked in undesirable ways. One widely advertised program for the IBM-PC allows you to scroll *or* download, but not to do both during the same session. The most widely distributed Macintosh communications program provides scrolling only if you are *also* downloading, so that it's not possible to download selectively while the scroll feature is active.

---

*—also provides for automated logons

Online Searching and the Patron: Some Communication Challenges

Sandra J. Lamprecht

INTRODUCTION

Subtle and overt communication problems can arise between the librarian-searcher and the patron during the computer search interview. For a successful search and a satisfied patron these problems must first be recognized by the searcher and resolved. Many initial problems revolve around the patron's misconceptions of the capabilities of the computer in a bibliographic retrieval situation. Unrealistic expectations of results especially on the part of new users is a common occurrence. Other challenges include two-way communication difficulties which can arise during any part of the interview. In this article I will seek to identify some of these difficulties in the hopes that new insights and an increased awareness of the complex nature of the interview process will prove useful to searchers.

Each online search interview is usually regarded by a conscientious searcher as a challenge. Reference interviews in general have been described as "one of the most complex acts of human communication [because] in this act, one person tries to describe for another person not something he knows, but rather something he does not know."[1] A search interview does differ somewhat from the general reference situation in that the patron is more likely to know what topic he would like searched. He does not know, however, how to access the information needed for his topic utilizing the computer and, in many cases, he is also unfamiliar with the complexity and constraints of the "searching universe." He requires a searcher to assist him.

In the interview setting the searcher is called upon to perform several roles—a substantial part is to instruct users on the capabilities and constraints of computer searching and to aid in the selection

Ms. Lamprecht is Coordinator of Online Searching, Humanities/Social Sciences Dept., The University Library, University of California, Davis, CA 95616.

177

of databases and vocabulary terms. He must also accurately ascertain the patron's information needs. At the termination of the pre-search interview, the searcher will have to know exactly what the patron would and would not like; i.e., the searcher must "enter into the mind" of the patron with regard to the search topic and its various levels. In order to do this, the searcher must first put the patron at ease and allow a feeling of trust to grow during the interview. This can be accomplished through various means of verbal and nonverbal communication.

PUTTING THE PATRON AT EASE

When the patron enters the search environment, many times he is initially tense or at least uneasy. This is especially applicable to new users of online services; they can be nervous for several reasons, among them being unfamiliarity with the search process and the fact that the search will cost them money. Therefore the first challenge of the searcher is to make the patron feel comfortable enough to communicate effectively.

A first positive step in this ongoing process is to provide a pleasant search environment. An area that is quiet with all of the needed computer equipment and search tools readily at hand is very desirable. In searching, the length of an interview is usually determined by the complexity of the search topic—the average time ranges between twenty and forty minutes. However, if an interview is conducted at a reference desk, it has been found that it tends to be shorter due to other distractions.[2] In this type of environment the patron will probably infer that his search is not the most important activity being conducted at that moment in time by the librarian-searcher and this impression will be validated the minute the librarian-searcher is interrupted by another patron seeking reference or directional assistance. It has also been found that, as a rule, the more time spent off the terminal interviewing the patron, the less time will be spent at the terminal itself.[3] Also the influence of the interview on the patron's satisfaction with online services in general cannot be overemphasized.[4]

VERBAL AND NONVERBAL COMMUNICATION

Once the patron enters the search environment, it is the searcher's responsibility to establish successful contact on two levels: verbally and nonverbally. Positive verbal communication can include a pleasant greeting and an introduction. Initial nonverbal communication may include eye contact, a smile indicating interest and approachability and a hand gesture inviting the patron to take a seat.[5] It should be mentioned at this point that throughout the entire interview process the searcher should pay careful attention to the types of communication the patron is sending. For example, is the patron becoming restless or impatient? Bossy? Inattentive? Is he beginning to ask too many of the wrong questions or is his conversation deviating to a marked degree from the search topic? Also be attuned to the communication you are transmitting. Are you listening attentively and asking open-ended questions in a non-threatening, non-judgemental and empathetic manner? Empathy on the part of the searcher is invaluable in opening communication channels for it enables the session to become a cooperative interaction between two people rather than a confrontational situation.[6] Are you fidgeting with pencils or materials? This can create an atmosphere of tension whereas refraining from hand or other movements can add to the feeling of relaxation. Nodding the head in affirmation can encourage the patron to continue communicating when this is needed for clarification.[7] Once the patron is at ease, the next challenge is to ascertain his level of online searching sophistication and then to handle the many online searching misconceptions that may exist. However, before discussion of this topic, I would like to mention some characteristics that have been found to be desirable ones with regard to searchers.

DESIRABLE SEARCHER CHARACTERISTICS

There is no consensus as to what constitutes a "good searcher." However, cultivation of many of the following ten characteristics enumerated by Borgman, Moghdam and Corbett can certainly prove to be useful to the searcher. The characteristics are: (1) self-confidence (which can be gained by experience and study); (2) good communication skills and "people orientation"; (3) patience and perseverance—for online searching can indeed be frustrating and tedious on occasion!; (4) a logical and flexible approach to problem solving; (5) a good memory for details; (6) typing skills; (7) a good knowledge of the subject areas being searched; (8) good organization and efficient work habits; (9) the motivation for acquiring additional information and (10) a willingness to share knowledge with others.[8] Luckily most of these characteristics can be acquired with patience and determination.

MISCONCEPTIONS OF USERS

Many misconceptions can abound in the mind of the patron and it is advantageous to both searcher and patron to confront these myths before presenting the patron with the many choices that will arise later—e.g., selecting databases, the cost factor, highly relevant versus comprehensive searching, selection of thesaurus terms, etc. Many patrons simply have unrealistic expectation levels. Some of the more popular misconceptions include: (1) The computer can "think" like a human and therefore it will automatically understand his topic. It will know just what he needs. (2) The computer has access to all of the written material in the world going back for many years and all of this information is stored in one large database. (3) The computer contains the library call numbers for the journals cited in the search results for whatever library the patron wishes to use, or, the computer will provide a full text access automatically to all articles and at no additional cost. (4) All databases selected provide excellent book as well as journal coverage. (5) There is a database for every area of research and the computer will be able to "save the day" and provide a lot of relevant citations on topics that are extremely esoteric. (6) Little effort is required to retrieve what one needs with no in-depth thinking required. (7) There is no need to investigate a topic further once the computer search has been completed. Should one or more of these misconceptions come to light, the searcher should immediately deal with them in a gentle but firm manner.

DISCUSSING THE SEARCH TOPIC

After the searcher has put the patron at ease and assessed the patron's experience with and knowledge of online searching in general, it is time to start delving into the nature of the specific search topic. Does the patron desire a comprehensive search or will ten to twenty highly relevant citations suffice? Other questions to be answered include: From what subject fields does the patron need to find literature? Psychology? Social Sciences in general? Law? Education? Popular literature? Science? One or more of the above? (Many searches, especially those in the social science fields, are indeed interdisciplinary in nature with the patron desiring five or six different database access points.) What document types does the patron require? Journal articles? Technical Reports? Dissertations? Newspaper articles? Government documents? Books? All of the above?

An equally important consideration at this time is finding out how much the patron is willing to pay for the search. If there are six databases that interest the patron in a multi-disciplinary topic and the maximum amount he is willing to spend on the search thirty dollars, then it would be wise to have the patron prioritize the databases in order of preference. Sometimes the patron does not know in what order he wants the databases searched and the searcher will need to counsel him. This is where specific knowledge of the individual characteristics of various databases is essential.

Throughout this portion of the interview it is very helpful for the searcher to "echo" the request to the patron for clarification and to continue to do so until they both agree that the searcher understands the request.[9] This is a very good way to insure that the searcher has not misinterpreted the patron. Asking open-ended questions is also an important interviewing technique that should be utilized here. In addition, enough time should be allocated for discussion of the topic before the search strategy formulation and online work begin for, as previously mentioned, it has been found that if more time is spent off the terminal interviewing the patron, less time will be spent online with more satisfactory results.[10]

The searcher also needs to know something about the topic so that he is able to conduct a reasonable discussion with the patron and ask relevant questions for it is important to establish credibility with the patron. The more the searcher knows, the better it is, of course, but he does not have to be an "expert" to be highly successful.[11] Once the discussion of the topic has taken place, the searcher is now ready for the task of search strategy formulation and for the challenge of communicating requirements and constraints to the patron.

SEARCH STRATEGY FORMULATION

A computer search needs to be structured more precisely than a manual search. Information needs to be imparted to the patron and specific decisions need to be made. For example, does the patron know how boolean logic operates? Are the terms to be developed for each of the sets in the search going to be thesaurus descriptors? Free-text terms? A combination of both? Does a patron need all of the years available on a particular database or only the most recent five years? Does he want only English language references? Does he want abstracts? Does he want the results printed online or off-line?

In formulating search strategy the searcher should generally assume a strong role.[12] In addition, anticipating potential problems before going to the terminal aids immeasurably in the success of the search. Two problems common to many searches are too many or too few references retrieved. Developing alternative search strategies can aid in the solution. Be sure to find out exactly what the patron will and will not accept. Will opening up a set or a search to "free-text" be acceptable in the event few citations are retrieved via descriptor and/or title searching? Are there terms that can be removed from a strategy when too many citations are retrieved? If a search produces 200 citations, is that acceptable? If not, what is the maximum number of acceptable citations? Does the patron know that some citations may be "false drops"? etc. With good communication during this phase of the interview both the patron and the searcher will be able to proceed with confidence to the terminal for the online session.

ONLINE

Once the topic has been thoroughly discussed and the search strategy formulated to the satisfaction of both searcher and patron, the next challenge is to instruct the patron briefly on the mechanics of the search process and to inform him of the various options available during any stage of the search whenever decisions are required. The challenge is to "equip" the patron in a short period of time so that he will be able to help evaluate the results of a search as it progresses thereby allowing him to be in a position to assist the searcher whenever a decision has to be made whether to continue a search strategy or to alter it.[13] In this manner, the patron will be able to participate in the interaction and in the final results of the online search.

CONCLUSION

The influence of the search interview on the patron's overall satisfaction with online services cannot be overemphasized. Patron satisfaction is a hard concept to define and therefore extremely hard to measure, but perhaps it could be summed up briefly as "a state of mind experienced (or not experienced) by the user."[14] By continuously communicating with the patron and requiring him to actively participate in the search process and decision-making, the searcher will involve the patron to the benefit of both. Cooperation will be established, maximum results will be obtained, and a sense of accomplishment will be present at the end of the session for both patron and searcher. The patron will also leave with a more intimate understanding of online information retrieval, its results and its capabilities.

NOTES

1. Robert S. Taylor, "Question-Negotiation and Information Seeking in Libraries," *College and Research Libraries* vol. 29 (May 1968): p. 178.
2. Eben L. Kent, "The Search Interview," in *Online Searching: the Basics, Settings and Management*, edited by Joann H. Lee, (Littleton, Colo.: Libraries Unlimited, 1984): p. 35.
3. Kent, p. 39.
4. Susan E. Hilchey and Jitka M. Hurych, "User Satisfaction or User Acceptance? Statistical Evaluation of an Online Reference Service," *RQ* vol. 24 (Summer 1985): p. 452.
5. Virginia Boucher, "Nonverbal Communication and the Library Reference Interview," *RQ* vol. 16 (Fall 1976): p. 29.
6. Roger C. Palmer, *Online Reference and Information Retrieval*, (Littleton, Colo: Libraries Unlimited, 1983): p. 134.
7. Boucher, p. 29.
8. Christine L. Borgman, Dineh Moghdam and Patti K. Corbett, *Effective Online Searching: A Basic Text*, (New York: Marcel Dekker, 1984): p. 13.
9. Lawrence R. Maxted, "The Interview Process in Online Searching," in *Online Searching Technique and Management*, ed. by James J. Maloney, (Chicago: American Library Association, 1983): p. 51.
10. Kent, p. 39.
11. Arleen N. Somerville, "The Place of the Reference Interview in Computer Searching: The Academic Setting," *Online* vol. 1 (October 1977): p. 17.
12. Arleen N. Somerville, "The Pre-Search Reference Interview—a Step by Step Guide," *Database* vol. 5 (February 1982): p. 35.
13. Maxted, p. 54.
14. Hilchey, p. 452.

REFERENCES

Auster, Ethel. "User Satisfaction with the Online Negotiation Interview: Contemporary Concern in Traditional Perspective." *RQ* vol. 23 (Fall 1983): 47-59.
Auster, Ethel and Stephen B. Lawton. "Search Interview Techniques and Information Gain as Antecedents of User Satisfaction with Online Bibliographic Retrieval." *Journal of the American Society for Information Science* vol. 35 (March 1984): 90-103.
Bates, Marcia J. "The Fallacy of the Perfect Thirty-item Online Search." *RQ* vol. 24 (Fall 1984): 43-50.
Bellardo, Trudi. "What do we really know about Online Searchers?" *Online Review* vol. 9 (June 1985): 223-239.

Borgman, Christine L., Dineh Moghdam and Patti K. Corbett. *Effective Online Searching: A Basic Text.* New York: Marcel Dekker, 1984. 201p.

Boucher, Virginia. "Nonverbal Communication and the Library Reference Interview." *RQ* vol. 16 (Fall 1976): 27-32.

Dalrymple, Prudence. "Closing the Gap: The Role of the Librarian in Online Searching." *RQ* vol. 24 (Winter 1984): 177-185.

Dommer, Janet M. and M. Dawn McCaghy. "Techniques for Conducting Effective Search Interviews with Thesis and Dissertation Candidates." *Online* vol. 6 (March 1982): 44-47.

Fenichel, Carol Hansen. "Online Searching: Measures that Discriminate among Users with Different Types of Experience." *Journal of the American Society for Information Science* vol. 32 (January 1981): 23-32.

Gavryck, Jacquelyn A. "Teaching Concept Identification Through the Use of the Thesaurus of ERIC Descriptors." *Online* vol. 4 (January 1980): 31-34.

Hammer, Mary M. "Search Analysts as Successful Reference Librarians." *Behavioral and Social Sciences Librarian* vol. 2 (Winter 1981/Spring 1982): 21-30.

Hilchey, Susan E. and Jitka M. Hurych. "User Satisfaction or User Acceptance? Statistical Evaluation of an Online Reference Service." *RQ* vol. 24 (Summer 1985): 452-459.

Hurych, Jitka. "The Professional and the Client: the Reference Interview Revisited." *The Reference Librarian* vol. 5/6 (Fall/Winter 1982): 199-205.

Jackson, William J. "Staff Selection and Training for Quality Online Searching." *RQ* vol. 22 (Fall 1982): 48-54.

Kent, Eben L. "The Search Interview." in *Online Searching: The Basics, Settings and Management* ed. by Joann H. Lee. Littleton, Colo.: Libraries Unlimited, 1984. pp. 34-40.

Knapp, Sara D. "The Reference Interview in the Computer-Based Setting." *RQ* vol. 17 (Summer 1978): 320-324.

Kolner, Stuart J. "Improving the MEDLARS Search Interview: A Checklist Approach." *Bulletin of the Medical Library Association* vol. 69 (January 1981): 26-33.

Maxted, Lawrence R. "The Interview Process in Online Searching." in *Online Searching Technique and Management* ed. by James J. Maloney. Chicago: American Libraries Association, 1983. pp. 50-56.

Munoz, Joanna Lopez. "The Significance of Nonverbal Communication in the Reference Interview." *RQ* vol. 16 (Summer 1977): 220-224.

Nichol, Kathleen M. "Database Proliferation: Implications for Librarians." *Special Libraries* vol. 74 (April 1983): 110-118.

Palmer, Roger C. *Online Reference and Information Retrieval.* Littleton, Colo.: Libraries Unlimited, 1983. 149p.

Peck, Theodore P. "Counseling Skills Applied to Reference Services." *RQ* vol. 14 (Spring 1975): 233-235.

Pilachowski, David M., R. Patricia Riesenman and Patricia Tegler. "Online Search Analyst and Search-Service Manager Tasks." *RQ* vol. 24 (Summer 1985): 403-410.

Shaver, Donna B., Nancy S. Hewison and Leslie W. Wykoff. "Ethics for Online Intermediaries." *Special Libraries* vol. 76 (Fall 1985): 238-245.

Somerville, Arleen N. "The Place of the Reference Interview in Computer Searching: The Academic Setting." *Online* vol. 1 (October 1977): 14-23.

Somerville, Arleen N. "The Pre-Search Reference Interview—A Step by Step Guide." *Database* vol. 5 (February 1982): 32-38.

Taylor, Robert S. "Question-negotiation and Information Seeking in Libraries." *College and Research Libraries* vol. 29 (May 1968): 178-194.

Tessier, Judith A., Wayne W. Crouch and Pauline Atherton. "New Measures of User Satisfaction with Computer-Based Literature Searches." *Special Libraries* vol. 68 (November 1977): 383-389.

Van Camp, Ann. "Effective Search Analysts." *Online* vol. 3 (April 1979): 10-13.

Implementation and Expansion
of On-Line Service
in a Liberal Arts College

John C. Stachacz

Database searching was first introduced to the Dickinson College Library with the establishment of the On-Line Services Department in the fall of 1978. At that time only one librarian was trained to access the databases of DIALOG Information Services, Inc., with the service available only to faculty. Today, each of the eight professional librarians is trained to perform this vital reference function, generally in any given subject area. The evolution and growth of this service was and is contingent upon establishing and maintaining good communication among librarians, students and faculty. In these six years user statistics have risen from 25 searches, performed in 1978-79, to 278 searches in 1984-85, a phenomenal increase of 1012% (see Figure 1). The service is now available to all students and faculty, and, at our current rate of growth the library anticipates to perform over 300 searches during the present year. This paper will outline the steps taken to expand the service, both in terms of statistics and staff development.

Communication was extremely important on several levels: first, all librarians had to agree on the need and importance of integrating this service into the regular reference routine; faculty had to become aware of the service; students had to be instructed in the importance of this service in their coursework; and, finally, the work flow of the entire library had to be assessed since the addition of this service created stresses and strains in other Departments.

Dickinson College is a liberal arts college of approximately 1,800 students. The Library is collegially organized, rotating a chairperson every three years from among the eight librarians.[1] As such, it was desired that all librarians have a working knowledge of several

Mr. Stachacz is Librarian, Dickinson College, Carlisle, PA 17013.

FIGURE 1

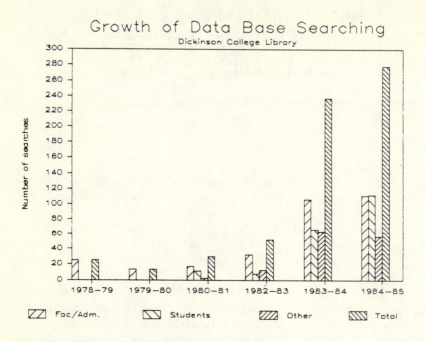

Graph provided by Doris Mumper

different positions, in order that the rotation of all professionals can occur whenever the chairperson changes. This rotating structure was also a factor which prompted the need for all librarians to become familiar with database searching.

Although the organizational structure of the library was a contributing factor to the expansion of the On-Line Services Department, the major reason was to expand the service; as such, it was essential that all librarians appreciate the power of the service and be able to incorporate its use in the general routine of the Reference Department. As is standard for most small and mid-sized libraries, all librarians participate in the Reference schedule, if nothing more than to work evening and weekend reference hours. In addition, each librarian acts as a liaison to four or five academic departments; responsible for collection development and bibliographic instruction. Each librarian is then responsible for communicating new procedures and developments to their academic departments.

HISTORY OF ON-LINE SERVICES
AT DICKINSON COLLEGE

Originally, all searches were performed on a 300 baud, Digital Decwriter II printer, connected to the DIALOG computers via a modem. Since this system was rather cumbersome, and noisy, it was placed in the technical service area. As mentioned above, only one librarian performed the searches. Given this scenario it is easy to see the limited effect of the service. During the first years, the searches performed were predominately experimental in nature. Literature searches were generally done for targeted faculty members, who were thought most likely to profit from the service. Although the library encountered initial success, the total number of searches performed plateaued at a low level. It soon became obvious that if the service were to expand both the staff and the department's visibility had to be increased. A second searcher was trained in 1980, and a third in 1982; all training for the new searchers was done through regular sponsored DIALOG training sessions. Public relations were intensified, using letters to department chairpersons explaining on-line searching, suggesting that they encourage their colleagues to use the service. Notices were also placed in the daily faculty newsletter, circulated to all college personnel, encouraging them to try the service to help their research. The pool of those who could be subsidized by the service was also increased to include students working on independent study projects. By sending additional memos, chairpersons were asked to encourage these students to inquire about database searching. After this intense publicity bombardment, user statistics began to increase.

Initially, the On-Line Services budget was a line item in the overall library budget, and thereby was set by the college administration. During the first four years of operation the funding was held to a meager $2,000 per year. With this small budget, guidelines had to be developed and made known to all faculty members telling of potential costs. Although user statistics continued to increase during this time period, the library was unable to convince the College Administration to increase the funds beyond the original $2000 level. The Librarians suggested the elimination of the line item for Data Base Searching, and attaching this service to the general book budget. In that way the department could set the apportionment as needed. Until then, expansion beyond the original guidelines of one search per year, up to $25, for faculty and independent study students was impossible.

During 1983, the picture changed dramatically for the department. The college computer center, after having discussed equipment needs with the library, supplied a 1200 baud Digital VT 102 terminal, complete with a modem and high speed printer. It was also at this time that the library's continued communications with the College administration began to bear fruit. They agreed to make the budget for database searching part of the library book budget, rather than a separate line item. The On-Line Services group in consultation with the entire professional staff, decided to increase the budget, dramatically, to $8,000. Although this figure was comparatively high considering past achievements, it was judged important to guarantee that enough money be made available to increase the availability of this service to the college community.

The number of searchers had now risen to four, or, half of the professional staff. The department staff decided that with the new equipment, and an increased budget, an excellent opportunity had arisen to relocate the department into the reference area. It was also decided that we would expand the service and do quick, ready reference searches for faculty and students, along with the traditional literature searches. For this to succeed, it was essential to have the full backing of the professional staff. This backing would have to consist of both the knowledge of, and the skill to do the database searching.

A plan of action was devised, by the On-Line Group, and brought to one of the weekly staff meetings. The staff was in full agreement that the new equipment should be placed out in the Reference area. Although there was some concern on the part of some of the non-searchers, it was agreed that in order for our plan to succeed, all members of the staff would have to participate in on-line searching for ready reference questions. Training then became the responsibility of the head of the On-Line Services Group, who compiled a training manual describing boolean operators, system commands, and the varieties of databases. A training seminar was conducted during a special workshop for the professional staff.

Since all the librarians had, at one time or another, been exposed to database searching, the training was not as difficult as might be imagined. Great attention was given to boolean operators and the various conventions of searching. Emphasis was placed on continued practice through hands on use of the system. Through continued practice, each librarian would better familiarize themselves with the system. It was stressed that the database searching budget had been increased to allow time for practice searching. For the most part, however, the unfamiliarity of the system, coupled with the fear of spending money, caused great anxiety to the newly trained searchers. Consequently, they seldom turned out to use the system for reference. Although a dramatic increase in searching occurred during this time, it was primarily on the part of the original search team expanding into the area of conducting ready reference questions.

DEPARTMENT REORGANIZATION

During the 1983-84 school year, the original group of four searchers continued doing the standard, more complex literature searches. However, a dramatic increase in searches placed a burden on these searchers, making it apparent that a reorganization of the department was needed to incorporate all staff members into the general procedure. Again, an operational plan was devised and brought to a staff meeting. The plan called for one person to continue acting as head of the On-Line Services Department, but that the department would be expanded to include the entire professional staff. A decision was needed on how to handle the work load of literature searches and how to distribute them.

The librarians divided along these lines of thought: first, dividing the responsibilities by subject, or, second, by creating a rotation, based on alphabetic sequence. The original searchers thought that the second option was the more desirable. As expected, this plan was greeted with hesitation by the newly trained staff members, thinking that the subject related approach, along the lines of liaison duties, might be a better approach. It was clearly understood by all, however, that each librarian had to have a working knowledge of those databases that would be appropriate for conducting ready reference questions. It was also pointed out that by dividing the databases along liaison lines would create an imbalance in the work load since not all departments were adequately covered by the databases available from DIALOG, nor were all departments interested in the use of the service. By rotating the searches among the whole staff, guaranteeing that each member would have an equal opportunity to do a variety of searches, the integrity of the Ready Reference Service could be maintained. The department head then scanned the user logs, kept to record all searches performed, determining which databases were the more heavily used and needing expertise by all Reference Librarians. The list of the remaining DIALOG databases were then routed to all librarians so that they could indicate in which databases they would be most interested in gaining expertise. The rotation of complex searches would be retained.

The aforementioned division of databases would make each librarian a subject specialist in a particular area, such as chemistry, life sciences, humanities, current events, business, or, government documents. Although those librarians may, or may not, be conducting literature searches in those subject areas, they would be responsible for giving advice and instruction to those who would be doing the search. The responsibility of the resource person would also extend to workshops conducted for the benefit of the entire staff. In this way, overall knowledge of the various databases would filter through the staff increasing the confidence and awareness levels of the staff.

The keystone of this reorganization was, and must be, based on continuing education and communication. A portion of each weekly staff meeting may be reserved for a continuing education seminar. Reference sources may be discussed, new items in Special Collections mentioned, or, new Government Documents tools described. Once the initial workshops on training were completed, including several follow-up refreshers sessions, the department decided to set time aside for database training seminars in which a newly designated resource person could explain the nuances and peculiarities of a particular database, or introduce a new concept in searching. The introduction of DIALOG 2, alone, generated several workshops on the new enhancements to the system. Other workshops have concentrated on topics such as: searching in Historical Abstracts and Biosis Previews, citation searching, and using Dialindex. To date, the reorganization has proven successful. The total number of searches has risen dramatically as well as building the confidence of all searchers. The more confidence each librarian develops in wrestling to construct search strategies and using them successfully on the system, the greater the success rate.

As the proficiency level of each librarian increased, so did the public relations efforts. Although the increased budget allowed great leeway in the operations, the department decided to retain the guidelines. They were rewritten to indicate that all members of the collegiate community could be subsidized up to a higher level each semester. However, the department decided that as long as the budget allowed, we would ignore the guidelines. By using this strategy, we anticipated expanding our service and meeting the rising expectations of our students and faculty. If, for whatever reasons, funding became a problem, we could return to the guidelines to protect the budget. This, so far, has not been a problem; although there are repeat users, flagrant violations of overuse have not yet occurred.

Also, to date, the budget of $8,000 has been quite adequate for our needs, adjustable at any time if needed. The Reference Librarians also keep alert to the fact that database searches are conducted for students on a need basis only. Narrowness of the research topic, lack of appropriate indexing in the library, or, inability of the student to find any information in the Library's indexes provide some of the reasons for a student search. Ready reference questions are performed at the discretion of the librarian.

BIBLIOGRAPHIC INSTRUCTION AND ON-LINE SERVICES

The best way to disseminate the information about our expanded service was through the already established bibliographic instruction programs. These instructions take three separate paths: course related bibliographic instruction, specialized instruction in which students are taught the basics of database searching, and Freshman Seminars. Librarians began mentioning the service to their academic departments in their bibliographic instruction sessions to upper division courses and seminars. Searches are then conducted on a need basis. There are certain courses, however, where there is a clear need for the service. In these classes we have developed pilot projects, designed to teach students the rudimentary basics of on-line searching.

The first pilot project was in an advanced Chemistry class on laboratory techniques. The faculty member involved had previously incorporated an instruction on the use of Chemical Abstracts and was very interested in having the students learn how to use the on-line version. This instruction included: discussion of on-line searching and what it can and cannot do; boolean logic, how to formulate search strategies; and finally, how to determine the appropriate database. The final project for this session, was for the students to select and critically think about a topic for their major paper, devising a search strategy by which they can utilize for searching the online databases. The librarian conducting the instruction, then goes over the strategy with the student, and performs the search. To date, these pilot projects have been done for classes in Chemistry, Geology, Fine Arts, and Psychology. Courses in the History and Biology departments have been targeted for future instructions. Generally, the library subsidizes half the cost of these instructions, with the department underwriting the rest. The library will, occasionally, waive the billing of the department if total costs prove to be relatively inexpensive. As yet, we do not have end-user searching available to students and faculty. We hope to be able to do so in the near future, making this initial training in preparing our patrons for this type of information retrieval more valuable.

Although the librarians average over 30 bibliographic instructions for departments in a year, we cannot guarantee that each student will receive some experience in the use of the library. However, all incoming freshman are exposed to library instruction via the College's Freshman Seminar Program. Beginning in the fall of 1981, all incoming freshman are required to take a seminar designed to emphasize library instruction, critical thinking, and writing, oral, and computer skills. Each department including the Library, offers a seminar, taught by one of the department members. The subject matter of the seminar is determined by the interests of the instructor and have varied from, Science and Moral Values to the Arthurian Legends or Humor in Comparative Context or Business Ethics. Since the topics vary so widely, the instructions the librarians conduct also must vary to fit into the context of the course. Each instruction attempts to fit into the design of the course, rather than act as a component plugged into the session at the leisure of the instructor. At the minimum, each librarian attempts to introduce the students to on-line bibliographic retrieval whether by a quick mention of the service, a short demonstration, or a complete instruction. That is determined by the need and desire of the instructor and the sources needed by the students to complete their assignments.

As could be expected, this increased activity has made an impact on both the Inter-Library Loan and Circulation departments with heightened expectation levels of information retrieval. Patience on the part of all, along with increased cooperation between the departments, has helped decrease any tensions that have occurred. All searchers have spent a great deal more time explaining the search results and interpreting the bibliographic citations to the patrons, so that all Inter-Library Loan forms could be completed in the proper way, with less burden on the part of the Inter-Library Loan staff.

CONCLUSION

As the experience of the Dickinson College Library has shown, proper equipment coupled with continued communication and enthusiasm, will ensure that an On-Line Services Department can be established in any library, and nurtured to become an essential part of the Reference Department.

NOTE

1. For additional information on the Dickinson College organizational model for librarians see Dorothy H. Cieslicki, "A New Status Model for Academic Librarians," *Journal of Academic Librarianship* 8(May, 1982): 76-81; Joan M. Bechtel, "Rotation Day Reflections," *College and Research Libraries News.* 26(November, 1985): 551-555; and "Academic Professional Status: An Alternative for Librarians," *Journal of Academic Librarianship* 11(November, 1985): 289-292.

Builders of the Future: Reference Influence on Library Automation

Jack King

Libraries are at the beginning of a lengthy automation process. Library automation will affect jobs, budgets, and services to the library users. Before the automation process is finished, automation will likely be widespread among all libraries. Certainly the vendors of automated library systems believe there is a market among all sizes and types of libraries for their products.

If reference librarians are interested in this process, they have left little trace of their interest. Through 1985 the professional literature reflects next to nothing in articles relating reference to library automation.[1] Professional meetings reflect a similar lack of interest.

There are two fundamental reasons why reference librarians should be attempting to influence library automation. First, probably most important, is the ability of the reference librarians to represent the library user. While representation of the library user by reference librarians may seem to lack the objective research results of scholarly study, the reference librarian is the best representative around of the library user. The library profession has demonstrated little interest in the study of the library user, and the reference librarian is the best representative of the user by default. Daily contact, observation, and answering reference questions, all bring expertise on library users to the reference librarian, which colleagues in other branches of library work may well lack. If library automation is to result in better basic service to the user, it will be the result of reference librarians' participation in the automation process.

Second, automation costs a great deal of money to implement and operate. Since many library budgets are stable or growing at a rate

Mr. King will be found at the Bush Library, Hamline University, St. Paul MN, 55104— when not at his word processor.

195

much below that of the demand for library services, reference librarians should express more curiosity about the effect of automation on all aspects of the library budget, including the reference budget.

At this point only speculation is possible about adverse effects on library reference service. Professional meetings do create some suspicions. Is it simply unhappy coincidence that reference library services seem to be diminishing at the very moment automation is beginning to occur in libraries on a significant scale? Is it simply an overworked imagination which wonders if automated systems are creating some odd services, such as great improvements in the internal routing of periodicals for staff, at the expense of reference budgets?

Of course, if the above suspicions seem to verge on paranoia, take the high road. See that reference librarians are involved in automation projects, so that the library user will receive the best representation in the planning, implementation, and operation of the automated system.

UNDERSTANDING THE PROCESS OF AUTOMATION

Before reference librarians can have significant influence on library automation, they must have some understanding of that process. Some general principles of automation can be derived from the experience of non-library institutions.

First, institutions automate for two reasons. The institution either wants to perform tasks which cannot be performed manually and/or wants to reduce costs, almost always labor costs.[2] In 1961 the King Report of the Library of Congress pointed out that the *National Union Catalog* information could be stored in a computer and called up by computer terminals placed in the reading rooms. The terminals would eliminate the need for the card catalogs in the Library of Congress. The elimination of the card catalogs would also eliminate the time when a book was waiting on a cataloging shelf while printed cards were prepared. As the manual catalog card production system became increasingly cumbersome and inadequate to cope with the flood of publications, the computer system would thus replace a task which was not being performed successfully manually. The King Report also pointed out that a library in Phoenix, by attaching its library symbol to the Library of Congress record, could use the same record for its local catalog. The cost of the telephone line to connect the Phoenix library to the Library of Congress would be less than the salaries of the catalogers which could be eliminated.[3] While the King Report underestimated the problems associated with establishing an on-line catalog, it demonstrated the two reasons why institutions automate.

Second, the automation of an institution ebbs and flows over the years and is particularly sensitive to labor costs. Since World War II librarians have seen steadily rising labor costs without a commensurate increase in individual productivity. There are signs today that labor costs may begin to fall before the end of the century. Traditionally automation expands when labor costs are high. When labor costs fall automation tends to stabilize or retreat.

Third, automation takes many years to accomplish. The textile industry, one of the most automated industries in existence, took over a hundred years to reach complete automation.

Fourth, tasks which can be performed either by a machine or by a person will, ultimately, sometimes after much travail, be performed by machines. Sixty years ago a telephone call was placed by lifting the handset and speaking to an operator. The system was more convenient to the user than even the most "user friendly" telephone system available today. The system handled emergencies as well as the modern "911" system. Yet today the telephone user is seldom in touch with a human when making telephone calls. The machine was more economical and efficient than the human operator. In the telephone industry the transition from human to machine was peaceful. Sometimes there is labor resistance to the introduction of machines.

Fifth, the total effect of automation can never be predicted. Automation affects too many aspects of institutional operation to predict what the final result will be. Early textile manufacturers began to install increasingly sophisticated looms, which required less and less human intervention. These early manufacturers saw reduced labor costs but did not consider that their productive, new looms would flood the market with textiles. Suddenly textile manufacturers discovered they had to develop vast new markets for their products.

These general principles serve to explain a great deal about the automation process.

Automation and Reference Librarians

But some understanding of the process of automation is not enough. The reference librarian must be able to deal with the process of automation in specific libraries at specific times. Certainly automation should not push the library into situations which worsen service to the users.

One of the principles of automation that was noted above was that the total effect of automation can never be predicted. Yet library automation has some formidible problems to resolve before reference service will be meaningfully automated. Reference service remains an art rather than a science.

One basic problem limiting the usefulness of automation in reference service is the psychology of the user. The bashful male mechanic, hanging back, while his female companion makes an inquiry on his behalf about the location of a repair manual for a Ford truck, is commonplace in a public library. Similar examples could be drawn from every station of life, from fledgling mechanics to Presidents of the United States. Human beings seem to have a reluctance to formally outline their information problems and seek help from a reference service. The research done by the library profession is miniscule in this area. Without better understanding of the human search for information, the probability is high that reference service, with its human contacts, will be a part of library service for the foreseeable future.

A second basic problem is that of language. Even the relatively precise language of science does not overcome the problem. A scientific problem may be described differently at different times, because the language of science changes over time. A scientific problem may be described differently in different locations. It is not uncommon for a scientific problem to be described in a mixture of scientific terminology and everyday English. The indexer of the scientific literature may also choose a variety of indexing terms, sometimes terms different from those of the scientific community. The user may use a completely different terminology to make the inquiry of the reference librarian. Again the lack of theory makes it likely that reference librarians will be needed for the foreseeable future to help their clients travel through a linguistic wilderness to the needed information.

BECOMING INVOLVED

Global Issues

Reference librarians must be a vital part of the automation process for the sake of the library. They are the best representatives of the library users on the staff. They can speak with an objective viewpoint, because the reference positions are relatively stable in the conventional and automated libraries. Finally, they need to monitor the automation process and operation, so that library resources go to support the goals and objectives of the library, rather than being diverted to some possible, but low priority, improvement of library operation.

It is not easy for reference librarians to become involved. Within the profession reference librarians seem to dislike administrative duties more than their colleagues in other areas. A first step toward becoming involved is asking one global question at all times.

Why is the library automating?

This question is appropriate at the beginning, middle, and end of the initial automation process. With a change of verb tense, it is appropriate at all times during the operation of the automated system.

Automation has a tendency to develop goals and objectives which differ from the institutional goals and objectives. Unless automation is monitored continuously, the independently developed automation goals and objectives will divert scarce library resources from their authorized purposes, to unauthorized purposes. There are good reasons for this.

— Automation affects all library jobs. A clerk who liked typing overdue notices, a procedure now performed by the computer, may be quite unhappy with a new job assignment, which requires staffing a circulation desk. The clerk may discover that it is possible to enter hair color of library users into the computer patron file. Suddenly hair color may begin to appear in patron records, because the clerk likes to type in the data. Clerical time will be diverted to the project, all without any authorization from the library administrators.

— Administrators have a tendency to avoid unpleasant situations. Budget and staffing problems created by automation may be deferred. The problems may become a crisis before administrators take action. Meantime library resources have been used for tasks which have little or no priority in the library operation.

— Human beings, despite the trauma which technology creates, have a tendency to use every feature of technology available.

If the automated system has an optional feature which will make the circulation terminal chime after the first thousand transactions each day, it is a feature which someone will think is useful and try to obtain scarce library resources to make operational.

Automation then requires continual monitoring at all stages—planning, implementation, and operation. Reference librarians must be prepared to ask the global question again and again—Why is the library automating?

Detailed Questions

Becoming involved in the automation process also means becoming involved in the specifics of the process. Technical jargon and level of detail may make this seem a daunting task. Yet it is in the detail that the battle for an effective and economical automated system can be won or lost.

As professionals who listen to questions for a good part of their careers, reference librarians should be able to develop questions quite easily. There are three rules to asking detailed questions.

1. If you do not understand the jargon, ask for an explanation. To some of your colleagues saying, "The 300 field must be included" may mean something. If it means nothing to you, ask for an explanation.
2. If you do not understand the issue under discussion, ask why it is being discussed. A good question to ask, if nothing else occurs, may be "Why is this significant to the user?"
3. If you still do not understand, ask until you do. Some of your colleagues may enjoy demonstrating their knowledge of computer jargon, or some other specialized terminology, but the point of discussion is to communicate ideas.

If this sounds somewhat similar to conducting a reference interview, there is a similarity. You are trying to extract information from people, and this is very similar to trying to discover the information needs of a reference client.

The questions which have been developed for this list are not expected to be definitive. The list is one which can be edited to fit local conditions, if the reference librarian so desires. The list can also serve as a guide to developing a completely different list of questions. The list gives the reference librarian a general idea of the level of detail required.

This list of questions has been compiled from a variety of documents outlining the automation specifications for academic and public libraries. The questions were developed first, then grouped into the following categories.

1. Library budget questions.
2. Library personnel questions.
3. Operation of the automated system questions.
4. Library user related questions.
5. Reference service related questions.
6. Vendor related questions.

The questions are all based on the standard interrogatories: who, what, why, when, where, and how. This was done to make formulating questions a procedure easily followed.

The categories of questions vary considerably in length. Like all classification systems, the placement of the questions in the various categories is arbitrary in many cases.

Library Budget Questions

Libraries may not have long range plans, short range plans, or annual reports. It is a very rare library that does not have a budget. The budget will never win a literary prize, but it is a statement of library goals, objectives, and policy. Unfortunately, it is largely numbers, and many reference librarians think of it as another hurdle placed in the path of good reference work by fiendish administrators.

Budgets are not always what they seem, and they can be quite complicated documents. In some libraries the budget is a matter of public record, but questions should still be asked.

The first question in the list has the most implications. If automation does not reduce personnel costs, the reference librarian needs to learn why. In many cases the answer will be that the library is expanding rapidly enough that automation means a slower expansion of the staff than would otherwise be possible, rather than laying off staff members. If the personnel budget is increasing, the reference librarian might well return to the global question, ''Why is the library automating?'' Remember that automation theory indicates that labor costs frequently drop as the result of automation.

1. How will automation affect the library personnel budget?
2. How will automation affect the reference materials budget?
3. How will automation affect reference staffing?

Library Personnel Questions

Automation affects every job in the library. Personnel problems and changes can be expected.

1. What staff members will be involved in hardware maintenance of the on-line catalog and circulation system?
3. What staff members will be reassigned because of the automation?
4. Where will staff members, made redundant by automation of their original positions, be assigned?
5. How will reassigned staff members be trained for their new positions?
6. How will automation change library staff requirements?

Operation of the Automated System Questions

These questions should be specific. The objective is to think of as many questions about the operation of the system as possible. The compiling of a list of such questions can be onerous. Yet the more details which can be learned about the automated system, before it ever becomes operational, the better will be the final system. The better the automated system, the better the service to the users.

1. How much expansion should the system be able to accommodate?
2. What type of loans will the circulation system support?
3. How will the circulation system handle overdue, hold, recall, and fine procedures?
4. How will the circulation system handle records for user fees?
5. What bibliographic forms will be maintained in the database?
6. What files will the acquisitions module handle?

7. What procedures will the serials control module handle?
8. How will the system be maintained?
9. What space and power facilities are required for the system?
10. What special staffing will be required by the system?
11. How will the database be maintained?
12. What authority controls will be used to maintain the database?
13. How many bibliographic records must the system accommodate?
14. How many bibliographic formats will the system accommodate?
15. How many copy/item records will the system store?
16. How many copy/item records does the library anticipate in 5 years?
17. How will the authority controls be maintained over the names in the public catalog?
18. How will authority control be maintained over subject headings?
19. How will authority problems be dealt with in the on-line catalog?
20. How will discarded headings be dealt with in the on-line catalog?
21. What back-up records (i.e., magnetic tapes) will the system provide for the on-line catalog?
22. How will the on-line system record payment of fees?
23. How will the on-line circulation system handle varying circulation periods?
24. How will the circulation periods be changed on the on-line circulation system?
25. What circulation statistics will be produced by the on-line circulation system?
26. How will the on-line system provide for interlibrary loans?
27. Who will be able to initiate interlibrary loans in the on-line system?
28. Where will the central processing unit be located for the on-line catalog and circulation system?

Some questions may seem obscure. For example, question seven, "What procedures will the serials control module handle?" is relevant to the reference librarian. The periodical check-in records will probably be on the system. If they are, an immediate question for the reference librarian is access. Will the reference librarian be able to call up the check-in records on a terminal at the reference desk? If the terminal is not at the reference desk, where is it? Will the reference librarian be able to call up the check-in records on weekends and evenings? Some systems permit the check-in records to be viewed from any terminal, while other systems confine such information to one or two terminals in the library.

Library User Related Questions

These are questions which reference librarians can best develop. Because of the necessity of keeping the system compatible with the best interests of the library user, these questions are particularly important.

1. What user related modules are desired in the automated system?
2. How many dial-up ports will the system have?
3. How will dial-up statistics be kept by the system?
4. What information will the public online catalog provide?
5. What kinds of search keys will the system provide (i.e., term, keyword, etc.)?
6. What Boolean searching will be available in the system?
7. How will the system indicate availability of materials in the online catalog?
8. What order records will appear in the on-line catalog?
9. What serials information will be available in the on-line catalog?
10. How will the on-line catalog differentiate between circulating and non-circulating copy/items?
11. How will the on-line catalog identify copy/items that are circulating?
12. How will the on-line catalog identify missing copy/items?
13. How will the on-line catalog identify temporary locations for copy/items?
14. What types of names (i.e., personal, corporate, conference, series) can be searched in the online catalog?
15. What titles (i.e., parallel, uniform, variant, and series) can be searched in the on-line catalog?
16. What subject headings can be searched in the on-line catalog?

17. What subject cross references can be searched in the online catalog?
18. How will key word searches be accomplished in the public online catalog?
19. How will "see" references be dealt with in the online catalog?
20. How will commands be given to the system (i.e., natural language, abbreviations, or mnemonics)?
21. How will truncation be used in online catalog searches?
22. How can searches be qualified (i.e., dates of publication, language, place of publication, type of material)?
23. How will the online catalog defend itself against unnecessarily long searches?
24. What options will be given the user when the online catalog identifies an unnecessarily long search?
25. How will the user stop an unnecessary search?
26. How will the online catalog react when a user makes an error?
27. How will the online catalog provide prompts to inexperienced users?
28. How will the online catalog permit experienced users to skip prompts and go directly to command modes?
29. How will users ask for help when using the online catalog?
30. How will Boolean searching be incorporated in the online catalog?
31. How will a user save an online catalog search?
32. What bibliographic information will be displayed to the user by the online catalog?
33. How will the online catalog display the due date for items in circulation?
34. How will a user obtain a print out of a search from the online catalog?
35. How will the user know how many records were retrieved by a search in the online catalog?
36. How will a user select one record when several have been retrieved by a search?
37. How will the sort order of a search print out be determined?
38. How will the online circulation preserve the privacy of borrower information?
39. How will user access to the catalog be maintained when the online catalog is down?

40. How will items be renewed in the online circulation system?
41. How will the online circulation system differentiate between categories of users with different privileges?
42. How will the online circulation system display a hold queue for a book?
43. How will the online circulation system provide a recall for a book?
44. How will the online catalog display titles of materials on order and in process?
45. How will the online catalog display periodical holdings?
46. How will the online catalog display continuations?
47. How will periodical holdings of branch libraries be displayed in the online catalog?
48. How will the catalog be made available when the online catalog is temporarily down?
49. How will the library materials be circulated when the online circulation system is temporarily down?
50. How quickly will the online catalog display search results under normal and peak load conditions?
51. What services will be available to users outside the library through dial up ports?

Reference Service Related Questions

These questions are more related to the reference service than to users. Nonetheless users will benefit from services related to the reference service.

1. What reference modules are desired in the automated system?
2. What field tags and subfield codes of the MARC II format can be stored and retrieved?
3. What diacritical marks will the system accept, store, and display?
4. What on order and in process records will be displayed by the on-line catalog?
5. How many branch libraries can the on-line catalog differentiate between?
6. What classification numbers can be searched in the on-line catalog?

7. What bibliographic control numbers can be searched in the on-line catalog?
8. What bar code numbers can be searched?
9. What ISBN and ISSN can be searched in the public online catalog?
10. How will Library of Congress card numbers be searched in the public online catalog?
11. How will SuDoc numbers for government documents be searched in the public online catalog?
12. How will local notes be changed in the online catalog?
13. How will reference librarians search a bibliographic utility when the online catalog is installed?
14. How will the online catalog interface with bibliographic databases?
15. How will stop words be added or deleted from the online catalog?
16. How will the reference librarians know which help screens and indexes are being most and least used?
17. How readily can the system be changed to produce various statistical reports?
18. How will online circulation records be made available to reference librarians?
19. How will standing order information be displayed?
20. What statistics will be compiled by the system relating to online catalog use?
21. How will reference librarians have access to the information in the serials control module?
22. What serials bibliographic information can be searched (i.e., variant title, key title, title statement, ISSN, LCCN)?
23. How will circulating issues be indicated to librarians?
24. How will reference librarians know if a serial issue has been claimed?
25. How will the reference librarian know if a serial issue is at the bindery?
26. How will professional literature be routed by the system to reference librarians?
27. What documentation will be provided for reference staff by the vendor of the online catalog and circulation systems?
28. What reference staff training will be provied by the vendor of the online catalog and circulation systems?

29. How will automation affect the quantity and/or quality of reference services?

Vendor Related Questions

1. What implementation schedule will the vendor follow?
2. What qualifications must the vendor have?
3. How will the proposals be evaluated?
4. What custom bar coding services are available from the vendor?
5. What training support is available from the vendor?
6. How will the system be maintained?
7. What space and power facilities will be required by the system?
8. What is the schedule of system enhancements?
9. What is the performance record of the vendor in similar installations?
10. What warranties are offered by the vendor?
11. What FTE systems staff does the vendor maintain for libraries?
12. What will be the criteria which must be met before the library will accept the system?
13. How will the database be developed for the online catalog?
14. When will the software for the online catalog and circulation system be upgraded?
15. What performance evaluations are required for the online catalog and circulation system before acceptance?
16. What is the average repair time for the online catalog and circulation systems?

STAYING INVOLVED

When the automated system is operational, reference librarians must remain involved in monitoring and modifying system operation. The principles of automation outlined earlier suggests years will pass before the library is making the most economical and effective use of the automated system. In the process the automated system will undergo many changes structurally and in the way it is used in the library.

Reference librarians will immediately discover they have a powerful bibliographic tool in the on-line catalog. They will have to learn exactly what that tool can do for them and the users. Users will have to be trained. New concepts of catalog use, such as Boolean searching and term searching, will have to be mastered and used. Reference librarians will also have to learn how to use the acquisitions and serials control systems with the user. The circulation system will also have features which will assist the reference librarian and the user.

The automated system will change. Some of these changes will be caused by software enhancements; others will be caused by modifications in the database. The way people use the system in the library will change. Reference librarians might find it is most efficient to submit requests for materials to the ordering office through the system rather than through some paper medium. The reference librarians may even directly order materials. Reference librarians may find that it is most efficient for them to enter notes about the updating of reference serials directly into the system, rather than going through an intermediary. Other members of the library will experience similar changes in their relationships to the automated system.

To monitor all of these changes related to the automated system, the reference librarian will continue to use the procedures outlined for use in the planning and implementation stages of the automated system.

— The process of automation should periodically be reviewed and compared to what is happening in the library. Questions should emerge from this process, such as: Are labor costs dropping in the library?
— The global question should be asked again and again, to test the significance of new ways of incorporating the automated system into the library operation.
— Specific questions must be developed to probe questionable procedures being proposed for the automated system. For example, a cataloging proposal which would remove the call numbers from all of the serials listed in the on-line catalog, while the catalogers change the classification system, could be one which reference librarians would wish to explore in some detail.

Automation can open new vistas for the user. Yet without continual monitoring and control, the library operation can begin to move in undesirable directions. Automation must remain the servant of the library user. The reference librarian is the staff member most concerned with assuring that the servant serves the user as economically and effectively as possible.

NOTES

1. Since 1980 reference articles relating to computers are divided into the following categories.

> 75% Database searching for reference patrons.
> 2% Database searching interview.
> 5% Bibliographic utilities as support for reference.
> 1% Online catalogs as a support for reference service.
> 2% Database searching by reference patrons.
> 3% New reference technology.
> 4% Microcomputers in support of reference.
> 1% Technology to manage reference service.
> 7% Special local database.

This listing was compiled from *Library Literature*, covering 1980 through most of 1985.

2. These principles of automation are derived from the history of automation in the textile industry.

3. Goodrum, Charles A. *The Library of Congress.* New York, Praeger, 1974. pp. 229-230.

PREPARATION FOR REFERENCE SERVICES

Microcomputer Applications
for Teaching Reference Services

Bernard Vavrek

The glow (normally identified as the bloom) is starting to leave the screen. Before long, an increasing number of analysts will conclude, e.g., that computer literacy was another one of those trends to be endured before other alternatives are considered. Who knows, perhaps educators—including librarians—will begin to champion "library literacy" as a healthier and more significant long-range concern than turning every school age kiddo into a computer programmer. But this essay is not a critique of our technological society, regardless of the fascination associated with that subject. Rather, the purpose of this article is to describe the practical applicability of utilizing microcomputers in the instruction of reference activities.

This author has spent "some years" attempting to cope with the challenges of teaching reference services to new Library Science recruits. The difficulties revolve around the need to orient students to both the philosophy of service and the practical aspects of library resources. In the latter case, "learning by doing," at any level of intensity, is frequently precluded by class size. That is, there are never enough copies of the basic reference works to make them available individually. With an introductory class, moreover, it has been my belief that students should be made sensitive to reference/information service as it is facilitated by the communications act, even at the expense of learning bibliographies of resources. While not every student of reference librarianship agrees with that view, this author continues to have belief in its conceptual soundness. On the other hand, at the advanced level of course selection, whether

The author is head of the Center for the Study of Rural Librarianship and on the faculty of the School of Library Science, Clarion State College, Clarion, PA 16214.

213

these offerings are labeled "Bibliography of . . ." or "Advanced Reference in . . . ," there is clearly a need to deal fairly intensively with resources. For the record, however, in case anyone checks the catalog of the College of Library Science with which the author is associated, the course "Advanced Reference" deals with problem issues, i.e., ethics, evaluation, etc., instead of resources.

Adequately instructing reference services has always been an elusive thing. Added to the challenges of what and how to teach is the prerequisite need to keep things as interesting as possible. Hopefully, e.g., we have seen the last of instructors who drone-on unnecessarily about each and every nuance of a reference title. Over the history of reference education, one may note the use of a variety of teaching techniques. In addition to the human annotator approach, teaching strategies have included role-playing, videotaping reference encounters, hide and seek (i.e., questions and answers), programmed texts, student reporting on reference books, etc.

Pedagogically, one of the most creditable applications for reference teaching was the use of the case study approach initially suggested by Tom Galvin and then by others. This educational paradigm, although conceptually supporting the interpretive approach, i.e., the problematical aspects of reference services, could also be lent to deal with those issues pertaining to resources. In my view, the major reason for abandoning this case study methodology was the inability to conveniently modify the content of the cases. This, presumably, was a problem both for authors of case study texts and as well as for those attempting to utilize these instructional episodes for classroom instruction.

THEORY VS PRACTICE

In hindsight, the inability to conveniently utilize a case study dimension in reference teaching has helped to emphasize the wrong things for future reference librarians. It has had the effect of glamourizing bibliographical tools including online systems at the expense of understanding theoretical context. Of course, for the record, it should be stated that the case study is not necessarily the only technique for developing a perspective on reference problems. Directed class discussion, for example, can also play an important role to that end. In any event, whether directly attributable to the singular absence of case study analysis or not, reference training has frequently lacked an analytical emphasis. It is the author's belief that the proper application of technology can be instrumental in helping to overcome those areas of reference education which continue to be neglected.

First, it is possible to develop a taxonomy of these "interpretive" omissions, but the most serious one relates to the failure of not having students develop written statements of reference policy. Without an information policy, which assumes the presence of strategic planning, there is little ability to determine the library's meaningfulness as a viable institution. While it is relatively commonplace, e.g., for library science students to be encouraged to master the "rigors" of book selection policies, collections development as well as all other library functions must now be considered in the context of an information policy. Some reference librarians are annoyed at the prospects of attempting to circumscribe that which they perceive to be a truly creative process. Unfortunately, this interpretation of high drama has been less important for the library's clientele than the reference staff. A reference policy, while making provisions for dynamic and simple change, enables the public as well as the library staff to understand the range and limit of information service. A particularly salutary benefit of producing a written policy is to eliminate the tendency of most librarians, who out of a real sense of professional commitment, constantly want to do more for their clientele. At the same time, however, these individuals fail to consider the fact that there are limits to what can be reasonably expected or accomplished. No policy statement, written or otherwise can compensate for the lack of personal service. But students of reference service need to be reminded that policy is a prerequisite to the execution of the service itself.

Second, as a consequence of not stressing planning through reference/information policies, students have not been taught that meaningful goals and objectives are basic to a functioning reference service. The document, *Commitment to Information Services: Developmental Guidelines*, is a seminal publication for students to consider and emulate—at least to the extent that it provides an outline of those things to be included in a written policy. But it is less than perfect when specifying the need for setting goals and objectives. Although the inference is suggested, indirectly, that through planning, analysis, etc., that performance objectives must be established.

REFERENCE NORMS

The cumulative thinking that led to documents such as *The Planning Process*, or *Commitment to . . .* helped to establish an important norm for reference librarians. Philosophically, these publications implied that neither the American Library Association, or one's own state association were the centers of the universe when considering expected information services. Quantitative standards, on the other hand, which in my view continue to have usefulness in small libraries, had the effect of creating obedience to a mythical library model, i.e., implying that all libraries of a certain type, whether school, academic, special, or public, were the same regardless of the individuality of the state or region where located. This tack also implied, of course, that setting goals and objectives were superfluous—the only appropriate direction was that promulgated from Olympus.

Third, another important area in reference education which continues to be overlooked is that of reference evaluation. This, clearly, is also an extension of neglecting to have planned directions of service. A great price has been paid, and not in a rhetorical sense, by librarians and library customers because of the confusion over how to evaluate information services. We have frequently sought national evaluative criteria when the issue relates directly to the evaluation of services at the local level.

If there has been any issue confusing to reference librarians, how to evaluate services has been at the top. A great deal of the library literature simply concludes that evaluation is impossible, or at least highly "iffy." The thinking has been that there are far too many variables to consider and that the whole matter is entirely subjective. There can be no doubt of the subjectivism associated with evaluating reference situations, but the key is quite simple. Evaluation is based first on planning and then setting measurable goals and objectives. This is one instance, e.g., where concerns for theories of service have tended to cloud a very simple process for determining the effectiveness of service.

The three aspects described above, i.e., reference policy, setting goals and objectives, and evaluation of reference services, have existed as lingering concerns during our present century. What is now different, however, in addition to changes in society itself is the influence of technology for educational purposes. This array of technology offers us unique approaches at meeting the challenges posed in training new reference librarians.

Enter the microcomputer. While there are justifiable reasons to be skeptical about what precisely can be gained, as opposed to lost or traded-off, by utilizing microcomputers in library education, current technology provides us with new technical opportunities in training reference librarians. The current availability, e.g., of word processing, project manager, idea processing programs, etc., offer us options to rejuvenate not only the case study approach but a variety of other simulations for library education. Virtually any word processing program and microcomputer can be employed to easily prepare, change, enhance, and up-date case studies. And as suggested earlier, in this way, emphasizing the interpretive aspects of reference services. Some microcomputer programs provide greater ease than others, of course. My personal favorite is "WordPerfect," which may not necessarily be without faults, but it provides every feature that most mortals need. Another with potential is "Think Tank," which is essentially an idea, i.e., outline processor.

WORD PROCESSING OPPORTUNITIES

Regardless of the hardware/software to be used, word processing techniques provide the instructor with the opportunities of conjuring up case study simulations to challenge even the most experienced or articulate student. Not only can the case models be changed from semester to semester, within large classes subtle or significant differences can be offered by the instructor with little technical challenge. Where several microcomputers are available for student use, the instructor might combine the objectives of reference education along with computer competencies, and distribute case study simulations on floppy disks. Students, in like manner, would be expected to analyze those conceptual models and also to respond on disk. In this way, students would not only be maximizing reference objectives, but also practicing word processing and microcomputer use at the same time.

In educational institutions where many machines are accessible, either through personal ownership or laboratory situations, the instructor might consider a local area network approach linking everyone in the educational chain together. Simulated examples of reference models could be networked to the students who are then expected in similar fashion, to electronically submit their analyses to the classroom instructor for review. This last suggestion would also be a benefit for students who are unable to immediately complete class requirements because of mitigating personal reasons. For example, this would be feasible on campuses where students have their own personal microcomputers in the dorms. For those who are physically away from the campus, one could use a microcomputer to microcomputer linkage, with a simple modem hookup, for transferring and sharing data—and assignments.

Perhaps, this last example, i.e., using telecommunications, would also have the potential to reach the marketplace of those individuals who are much interested in developing their educational skills, but are located hundreds of miles from schools of library and information science. There is a desperate need, e.g., to reach individual staff members who live in rural areas and provide them with opportunities to upgrade their reference experiences. The research conducted by the Center for the Study of Rural Librarianship consistently shows that the need for the augmentation of reference teaching is one of the key problems to be assuaged. In addition, reference service is consistently identified by rural librarians to be the number one choice for workshop themes.

With the reader's permission, the author would like to digress long enough to discuss the nature of geographical isolation for one who may be unaware of the vagaries of attempting to provide information services in that type of environment. Not all of the problems, e.g., deal with the landscape itself. The typical rural library ("rural" is defined by the U.S. Census Bureau to include populations of 2500 or fewer people) consists of a collection of approximately 25,000 volumes, is staffed by three people, and has an annual budget of $41,000. There is a fifty percent chance that the librarian is not academically certified. Our library is 50 miles away from a city of 25,000 or more people, and the odds are strong that no other library is available in the area for support. While 20% of the libraries we have surveyed have microcomputers, about 5% of America's rural libraries are still without telephone service. The most significant problem in providing reference service is the absence of specialized resources. Finally, membership in the American Library Association includes only one-third of the rural librarians in the country. This has had the tendency of helping to keep the needs of rural librarians distinct from the consciousnes of American librarianship. The needs are immense.

AVAILABLE TECHNOLOGY

For the first time, however, we have the technology available to overcome these professional concerns and to mitigate the negative effects of geographical remoteness. Undoubtedly, the most pressing issue for those interested will be to determine some strategy through which individuals may receive academic or continuing education credit or some other form of official recognition for their online training when not in residence. Although, it has been this author's experience that record keeping means less to the people involved than the opportunity for them to extend their knowledge, attitudes, and skills. The most difficult audience to whom these concepts must be sold is the one responsible for the accreditation of library science training. The possibilities are most fascinating, however, even on paper.

The presentation of reference problems via case studies and microprocessors, will be made even more dynamic in the near future because of the application of inter-active video components, i.e., slow-scan television, video encapsulated information, and other microprocessed linkages. These will provide the instructor with opportunities to offer unique examples of reference situations both through text and visual stimulation. For instance, videotapes or videodisks portraying reference encounters could be displayed to the student, who then must answer a series of questions utilizing a word processing program.

To this point, the author has used considerable space in this essay describing the potential of the case study approach in educating future librarians. Word processing programs also have applicability in relation to other aspects of teaching reference services, however. Another use would enable students to practice what we have come to describe as the "reference interview." While it doesn't quite give the reality, for example, of using videotapes of students enacting this temporary social encounter, microcomputer simulation has the potential of creating exciting learning exercises and at the same time attempting to convey the nuances of interviewing techniques. Students can be asked to create their own interviews, or instructors can provide a type of template to which the correct responses must be made. By template, the author is suggesting an outline of the type of questions that might be encountered in the "typical" reference inquiry. For example, "Where is the encyclopedia of stamp collecting?" would be a likely candidate as a question with the expectation that the student would then factor its continuing narrative. If the esthetics of the reader are troubled by the idea of seeing a type of multiple question—response outline to which the student provides the missing information, one might then use individual files that could be retrieved as the student completed the interview. Students would be instructed after responding to "Where is the encyclopedia of stamp collecting?" to then call-up the next file on disk (or whatever storage medium is used) which then simulates the inquirers next response. And so on. While this approach might strike one as similar to the reported instance of the gourmet, who owns two bottles of wine, buying a piece of software that is intended for the management of a wine cellar, our intent is to provide hands-on experience in the use of microcomputers while relating this practice to reference librarianship.

VARIATION ON A THEME

A variation of the simple technique discussed above would be for the classroom instructor or graduate assistant to provide real-time excitement in our "interview episodes," by using a multitasking microcomputer in the creation of a local area network. This was also suggested earlier in relation to the development of case studies. The reference interview could be conducted online in the format of "electronic mail" access. It would be less expensive, however, to use floppy disks.

As an alternative approach for the use of turn-key software, one who is experienced in programming might consider the construction of source code similar to the very popular "Eliza" program. "Eliza" seems to provide an almost real pattern to its response of user's input, and encourages the operator to "Tell me more about . . ." This type of inter-active program would provide a wonderful reality to modeling the reference encounter.

Microcomputers can also be utilized in reference education in relation to the development of resource skills. Admittedly, this is the most difficult part of reference training. Unfortunately, word processing or individually fashioned programs do not overcome the practical machinations of "learning by doing," but there is potential in these approaches. The simulation suggested here, if it isn't clear, is for the instructor to develop a series of model questions in relation to which the student is expected to develop typical strategies or solutions. The actual techniques to be utilized would not vary much from those already suggested.

Although word processing software has been emphasized in this paper, other types of application software also have particular relevance. One could make a case, e.g., for the use of a spreadsheet program such as "SuperCalc3," to provide for the manipulation of reference data. This would be particularly useful in reference evaluation and in the simple handling of reference statistics for both internal analysis as well as for reporting functions. "SuperCalc3's" graphing capability is especially suited for a no nonsense approach in preparing information for annual reports. While it will seem immodest, the author would like to "plug" another piece of software that is intended for data collecting and manipulation, i.e., "OUTPUTM." It doesn't rival "SuperCalc3" or the other well known products, but it is an effective program for anyone who is in need of collecting output measures for public libraries. It was produced by the Center for the Study of Rural Librarianship in cooperation with the State Library of Pennsylvania.

NEW WAVE

In addition to the software mentioned above, a new wave of managerial programs is currently being made available which provide the (library) manager with the opportunity of dealing with the variables for decision making. These programs are being touted as forms of artificial intelligence. Undoubtedly, other types of sophisticated software will follow. In fact, given the rate and speed with which microcomputer programs are being offered in the marketplace, teaching strategies and course syllabi may have to be changed significantly every semester (or during the semester) to keep current.

The intended message of this article is not very complicated. It merely suggests the obvious, i.e., that microprocessing technology provides us with flexible options to simulate and stimulate the teaching of reference services. Simultaneously, we must acknowledge that there is a lot of nonsense and over-exaggerated hype associated with today's microcomputer society. Nicely summarizing the concern, I believe, is the following comment. "If Dante had used a personal computer, he might never have gotten past the third cycle; he'd have been too busy figuring out why his printer couldn't handle italic letters."[1] There is little question but that microcomputers are distracting. They (intended personification) force us to deal with unimportant factors such as disk drives, serial ports, baud rates, etc. Our challenge is to shed the minutia of technology but use its enabling power to create a learning environment that is as exciting as today's libraries.

NOTE

1. Art Kleiner. "The Ambivalent Miseries of Personal Computing," *Whole Earth Review* Number 44 (December, 1984/January, 1985): 8.

Communicating With the New Reference Librarian: The Teaching Process

William F. Young

Staff development, as that term normally relates to reference librarians, refers to programs aimed at enhancing reference skills so that the reference librarian may develop some competence in all those areas where library users might reasonably expect information or service. There is much written on this topic and many institutions have developed formal staff development programs.[1] This is an encouraging trend if we, as professionals, are indeed serious about implementing our common goal of providing more effective reference service. Curiously, few topics have been less written about or discussed than the training of new reference librarians.[2] This is indicated from the paucity of literature on the subject and corresponds to a surprising disregard of the issue in both academic and public libraries.

As far as can be determined, few institutions in the United States have developed formal training programs for reference librarians. By training programs we are not referring to professional education within library schools, although library school education has an obvious relationship to the problem addressed here. Training programs seek to prepare new reference librarians in order that they might competently serve the public within a particular institution. We are addressing here the training of the professional librarian: the new MLS, the librarian transferred to reference from another library department, the experienced reference librarian moving from one type of library to another or even from a similar category of institution. The obvious fact is that each library, having variations in user populations and services offered, is unique.

In the case of academic libraries the demand on reference librar-

Mr. Young is Coordinator of Reference Services, State University Of New York at Albany, NY, 12222.

223

ians is naturally determined by the variant course programs offered at the institution. A very experienced academic reference librarian moving to a similar institution will likely have to rediscover long forgotten reference sources and learn new ones. The issue becomes particularly acute in large academic libraries where a large number of librarians may have an assignment of reference hours.[3] With such numbers one can expect a certain degree of turnover and hence the issue of standardized training increases in importance.

A reference training program may be defined as an in-depth and long term program of education for reference service suited to the specific needs and circumstances of a particular institution aimed at implementing the service goals established by that institution. Such a program is different from orientation. The latter relates to familiarizing persons with people, the location and function of departments and the physical whereabouts and arrangement of resources. What passes for training programs in many institutions is in fact orientation occasionally coupled with placing the new reference librarian in the care of a more experienced colleague. At other times the newcomer may be left alone entirely or alone as soon as possible. The attitude is that one learns best "by doing." Such an approach, however, places the burden of training on the patron and contradicts any reference department goal (one would hope) of providing a better quality of reference service.

SPECIAL LIBRARY LEADERSHIP

It is noteworthy that the best article, indeed the only truly relevant piece describing a reference training program is derived from a special library or, more precisely, a commercial and technical reference department in a British public library. In such a library, one may surmise, much is expected in terms of quality of work and competence. Special librarians consistently deal with other specialists in a particular field. Such a client group, unlike most public or academic library users, have the expertise to judge the quality of library reference service. Julian Isaacs, the author of this very brief article writes that "under no circumstance is the trainee allowed direct contact with clients until towards the end of the training course."[4] Ideally, the training period lasts for six months. At this particular library all reference questions, including telephone queries and correspondence, are recorded on a special form. The form indicates if the answer was found and space is provided for a digest of the answer and a list of the sources checked. These inquiry files reflecting, over a period of years, the actual daily workings of the department form the major basis of the training program. These questions are selected and divided into "papers" which encompass forms of sources which must be made use of: directories, statistical sources, periodical indexes, etc. Trainee and librarian carefully go over each completed paper thereby, says Isaacs, imparting a tutorial element to the program. Among the advantages claimed for this method are greater realism, since the questions are grounded in the realities of everyday reference work, the ability to distinguish those who have or lack an aptitude for reference and, most importantly, the result of more efficient service.[5]

Among academic libraries, McGill University in Montreal is a pioneer in the development of a true reference training procedure. A manual, now in a second edition, has been developed outlining their program.[6] The emphasis is directed to "on the spot demonstration techniques relying heavily on the principle of learning by example."[7] Training is required by everyone new to McGill's professional reference staff. An individual program, with varying emphasis, is worked out for each person with those new to Montreal and the University given special attention particularly in "regard to local resources and vocabulary."[8]

The first week is devoted to "Initial Training" which is in fact physical orientation combined with an introduction to library staff and functions as well as some preliminary reference training. A session with the Head of Reference focuses on the "philosophy of the Department" along with a discussion of such aspects as public relations, the reference interview, dealing with reference questions and ethics.[9] During this initiation the newcomer is introduced to the Library's reference telephone service and spends time in observing how telephone queries are answered. The trainee is also provided with *The Reference Manual* which is "the basic written guide and record of the Reference Department's policies and procedures." Throughout the entire training period as the new reference librarian is introduced "to people places and policies" sessions are devoted to reading specific parts of the manual so as to reinforce and supplement what was recently learned.[10]

FURTHER TRAINING PROGRAM

After the first week comes a period of "Further Training" which may last from two to three months. The major component here is from four to five hours per day of work at the reference desk with another librarian or on the telephone.[11] Another important element is five hours of training in using and mastering the complexities of MUC (the McGill Union Catalog) and the subject catalogs. This largely consists of checking interlibrary loan requests and reference book orders in "the MUC" as well as a session with the Head of Reference who explains the peculiar intricacies of McGill's public catalogs. Similarly there are sessions devoted to reviewing telephone queries which are recorded onto slips of paper:

FINISHED TELEPHONE SLIPS   7 hrs.

> You will be assigned a total of seven one-hour sessions with one of the slip checkers to review finished telephone slips. The purpose of this is to demonstrate thought and work processes. The previous day's slips will be most relevant to you as you will probably have had some input into them. Finished telephone slips are invaluable to the training process. You may wish to use them to retrace the steps of a question or familiarize yourself with a particular reference work. You will also be encouraged to develop the habit of looking through the finished slips when time permits especially those you took down, started work on, or contributed to—just to see that the work does get completed and how problems are resolved.[13]

During the extended period there are further in-depth opportunities scheduled for orientation and training sessions with non-reference librarians who explain their function in relation to the work of the Reference Department. For example, the Interlibrary Loan Librarian provides an introduction to the policies and procedures of that department "stressing ILL relationships with the reference desk and ways in which the reference librarians can be of most help to ILL and to the requestor after hours."[14] In addition there are ten hours of "subject specialty tours" in the reference stacks with other reference librarians who indicate the location and discuss the relative strengths of various works. These sessions also give the new librarian an opportunity to become more acquainted with his colleagues in the Reference Department.[15]

McGill's training program is self-described as physically and mentally "taxing." The training is indeed intensive. Each "session" consists of one hour and each hour of the working day is filled with some specific activity. Care is taken however that the trainee is given an opportunity to "browse and digest" in order "to reinforce the verbal explanations of department functions as well as to emphasize the best use of classic reference tools and services."[16] Ten hours devoted to browsing are therefore scheduled into the extended training period.[17] In addition at least once every week there are "Feedback and Follow-Up" sessions in which the newcomer has an opportunity to discuss his experiences and progress with the librarian who conducts the training.[18]

Like McGill, where fourteen staff members serve some hours at the reference desk, the State University of New York at Albany's (SUNY-A) reference service is a complex operation. Fifteen librarians are spread out over seventy-seven hours of weekly reference service. With such a large staff, a uniformed training program was deemed essential both in terms of efficiency and as one practical means of meeting the library's goal of providing consistent quality service. The reference training program at SUNY-A, begun in 1982, is a continuous state of evolution and development. The main components have, however, been well established.

The first two to three weeks comprise a basic training schedule. Each newcomer is given a written schedule in which the preliminary objective is clearly stated: "To familiarize [name of new reference librarian] with reference and government publications materials and sources as well as other persons and services related to the reference process." The emphasis here is on meeting other staff members in sessions usually lasting for several hours. A two hour appointment is, for example, scheduled with the head of our Computer Search Unit (online searching) "to receive an introduction and orientation to the operations of the Unit and its staff. The relationship of CSS to traditional reference work will be emphasized i.e., when and how patrons are referred from the reference desk for a computer search, when quick 'ready reference' computer searches are performed at the reference desk etc."

USEFUL METHODOLOGIES

During "basic training" a number of methodologies are also used to acquaint the librarian with the reference sources with which he may be possibly unfamiliar or perhaps made use of only occasionally in a previous position or library. He is given lists of some of the more esoteric indexing and abstracting services which he is asked to examine carefully. In addition, in-depth and lengthy sessions are arranged with our bibliographers. The emphasis here is normally on science, technology, business, law and, perhaps most important for reference service at SUNY-A, extended sessions on state, national and international documents. More generalized reference "tours" are scheduled with the Head of Reference who points out those works ordinarily made use of in daily work. In addition, the trainee works on a number of "self-instruction" question sheets. These are questions which have been actually asked at the desk over a period of years. Many relate to informational and locational queries unique or nearly unique to SUNY Albany. For example, "Where can one buy out of town newspapers in Albany?" "Where can I find a copy of New York State's current budget?" "Who lives at 710 Madison Avenue in Albany?" "Does the Library have an index to the Albany Times-Union newspaper?" "What is the University of the State of New York and how does it differ from the State University of New York?" The answer to these as well as less parochial queries contained on the question sheets provide an excellent basis for further dialog between the trainee and Head of Reference. This tutorial element is extended through the next phase of the training period when the trainee observes designated librarians at the reference desk. As the new librarian prepares to actually provide reference service he and the Head of Reference carefully go over SUNY-A's *Reference Service Training Manual*[19] and our newly developed *Reference Service Policy Statement*. The former is entirely procedural in scope dealing with such mundane matters as opening and closing the reference desk, reporting problems with the card catalog, taking statistics, explaining the telephone and intercom connections as well as containing a host of other routine procedures and explanations of the numerous aids and materials kept at the reference desk. The policy statement is more philosophical in tone. Its stated purpose is to outline "general guidelines for providing reference service of the highest possible quality and to insure, as far as possible, that this service will be performed according to a uniform standard."[20] The policy contains categorical statements as to what level and quality of service is expected and what the responsibilities of the reference librarians are in terms of professional development and behavior. For example on the subject of "Approachability and Attitude":

> Librarians may bring work to the desk or telephone office, such as memoranda, materials related to collection development duties, etc. The reading of professional literature is also

acceptable. All such activity must not, however, interfere with the process of service. Staff must be careful not to become so engrossed in other work that they fail to see readers in need of assistance in the reference area or at the public catalog.[21]

Obviously, from a training and policy point of view, it is essential that the precepts contained in such a document be absorbed by the new reference librarian.

When the new librarian is finally assigned to desk duty the reference schedule is devised so that the trainee serves on the desk with the Head of Reference or another experienced librarian. It is made clear that the "in training" status remains in effect for at least one semester and the trainee's initial performance evaluation will not be based on the more rigorous standards of performance expected from senior reference staff. At the same time the new librarian is provided with a written list of "points to consider" which the Head of Reference uses to evaluate reference librarians. Among these are such evident criteria as knowledge of reference sources, "reference technique" (i.e., finding sources which will successfully answer questions), communication skills with patrons and colleagues, use of computerized systems as they relate to reference. Evaluative guidelines will necessarily differ from one institution to another. It is important however, as well as only fair, that the trainee be made aware of specific objective standards upon which he will be judged.

What all the above training programs have in common is that they are structured and lengthy programs which evidently have been carefully thought out. It is training based on the realities of reference work in a given institution and involves a teacher-student relationship between the new librarian and one or several more experienced librarians. The great advantage of such programs is that they will, if efficiently carried out, at the very least provide uniformity and thoroughness in both training and orientation. No detail will be overlooked since the written components of a training program will serve as a checklist. Obviously, formulation and implementation demands commitment. Earlier it was pointed out how the issue of training new reference librarians has largely been ignored. An assumption that the master's degree in library science qualifies one to practice reference librarianship anywhere and anyplace perhaps accounts for the lack of attention to this subject. More likely it is the expense of such programs, in terms of time and personnel, and the inherent difficulty in making reference librarians accountable for their performance. Since reference librarianship is a creative process involving a personal, independent and usually anonymous interaction, poor reference work is often not readily detectable. Hence, particularly in academic and public libraries, there are normally few repercussions if a reference librarian is consistently providing inferior service. This situation has now become a major concern within our profession. The often cited unobtrusive studies of reference service in academic and public libraries indicate that we reference librarians are failing in our primary function: providing information completely and accurately.[22] The initial training period for the reference librarian is a crucial time which may be taken advantage of. It is an opportunity. In many institutions it is the only period when the work of a reference librarian is actively and closely supervised. It is the point where good or bad habits might be formed. A formal and actively supervised training program together with continuous staff development programming may provide at least one key to a much needed remedial process.

NOTES

1. See, for example, Lynn Elliott, "Professional Staff Development in Academic Libraries," *Journal of Librarianship* 14 (October 1983): 237-53. A survey of the recent literature is provided.

2. This article is based on a presentation I made at the Fall meeting of the Eastern New York Chapter/Association of College and Research Libraries, Rensselaer Polytechnic Institute, Rensselaer, New York, September 24, 1982. Anne Roberts made use of some of my points in a presentation made at the Association of College and Research Libraries, Third National Conference, Seattle, Washington, April 4-7, 1984.

3. For example the number of reference staff serving at a selection of main library reference desks within the State University of New York system: Albany 18, Oswego 18, Binghamton 11, Stony Brook 16.

4. Julian Isaacs, "In-Service Training for Reference Work" *Library Association Record* 71 (October 1969): 301.

5. Ibid, p. 302

6. Lillian M. Rider, "Training Program for Reference Desk Staff," 2nd ed., (Montreal Reference Dept., McLennon Library, McGill University, 1979). ED 175486.

7. Ibid, p. 3.

8. Ibid, p. 4.

9. Ibid, p. 5.

10. Ibid, p. 6, 10.

11. Ibid, p. 6

12. Ibid, p. 6, 7.

13. Ibid, p. 11.

14. Ibid, p. 13.

15. Ibid, p. 15.

16. Ibid, p. 4.

17. Ibid, p. 10.

18. Ibid, p. 9.

19. John Mielke and William Young, "Reference Service Training Manual", (Albany, N.Y.: State University of New York at Albany, University Library, Reference Services Division, 1984). ED 2457000.

20. William Young, "Reference Service Policy Statement," (Albany, N.Y.: State University of New York at Albany, University Library, Reference Services Division, 1984), p.1.

21. Ibid, p. 13.

22. We get it right just about 50% of the time according to Terence Crowley and Thomas Childers, *Information Service in Public Libraries: Two Studies* (Metuchen, N.J.: Scarecrow Press, 1971). These findings are supported by Marcia J. Myers and Jassim M. Jirjees, *The Accuracy of Telephone Reference/Information Services in Academic Libraries* (Metuchen, N.J.: Scarecrow Press, 1983).

Training Preprofessionals
for Reference Service

Beth S. Woodard
Sharon J. Van Der Laan

INTRODUCTION

As more libraries attempt to identify functions traditionally performed by professionals which can be managed by nonprofessionals, the use of nonprofessionals at the reference desk increases. Boyer and Theimer report that 69% of small-to medium-sized academic libraries use nonprofessionals in providing reference service.[1] The question of how those nonprofessionals are trained has become increasingly important. This is particularly apparent in public service as it effects not only the service the patron receives, but the patron's perceptions of the library as a whole. Courtois and Goetsch citing Halldorsson and Murfin[2] and Aluri and St. Clair[3] establish the fact that "well-trained nonprofessionals are capable of answering many, if not most, patron queries."[4] "In light of the judgments nonprofessionals must make in deciding when to refer a patron to a librarian, training is an important factor; however, few institutions reported having a systematic training program to prepare nonprofessionals for answering and referring questions."[5] Properly trained assistants can obviously provide better public service than those who have received little or no instruction. Further, "properly trained nonprofessionals with an understanding of reference service and a clear-cut referral relationship may enhance the job roles of both nonprofessionals and professionals."[6]

We as librarians who have received little formal education for our

Beth S. Woodard is Central Information Services Librarian, Reference Library, University of Illinois at Urbana-Champaign, Urbana, Illinois. Sharon J. Van Der Laan is Reference Librarian, Grand Valley State College, Allendale, Michigan, formerly Reference Librarian, Reference Library, University of Illinois at Urbana-Champaign, Urbana, Illinois. Both authors served as supervisors of graduate assistants at the Reference Library at UIUC and contributed to the development of this program.

roles as managers, supervisors, and instructors have received even less in our role as trainers. There are numerous examples of libraries' responses to training and instruction in automated systems and online catalogs, but not nearly enough to training for providing public service. Boyer and Theimer report more than 80%[7] and Courtois and Goetsch report 73%[8] of libraries provide no formal training for nonprofessionals, although some of Courtois and Goetsch's 73% did provide some orientation. A number of articles have appeared in recent years about nonprofessionals providing public service in academic libraries which have demonstrated the concern felt by practicing librarians, many of which are cited in this paper. Difficulties in training and supervising nonprofessionals may in many cases be traced back to failing to consider the conditions necessary for learning, primarily motivation.[9]

Motivation is not a problem, however, among graduate students in library science. This frequently overlooked group of preprofessionals is motivated to learn and perform well because librarianship is their career goal. Graduate students in library science are a tremendous resource with great potential for providing high quality public service. The combination of a high level of motivation, interpersonal skills, positive attitude toward working with the public, and thorough training enables graduate assistants to provide public service in an effective and professional manner. This article will discuss training this unique group to provide public service.

Specific examples will be drawn from the Reference Library at the University of Illinois at Urbana-Champaign (UIUC) where, beginning in 1980, four graduate assistants participated in a training program. The number of participants in this continuing program has doubled since then. The immediate goal of this program is to train graduate assistants to provide service at the Information Desk where they answer directional, quick reference, card catalog, and online catalog questions, in-person and by telephone. During the course of the program graduate assistants are also trained to provide in-depth reference service at the Reference Desk. Since assistantships run concurrently with library school course work, the training program can deal almost exclusively with institutional applications.

SELECTING TRAINEES

Examining the application files of prospective library school students who are interested in assistantships is the first step in the selection process. While there may be a large pool of applicants, it is well worth the time and effort to thoroughly consider each one. A fairly rigorous selection process makes it possible to appoint reference graduate assistants who not only are highly-motivated because they gain experience directly related to their career goals as reference librarians, but who are also enthusiastic with a strong commitment to public service.

In considering the applicants, it is important to discover each applicant's reasons for entering librarianship, attitude toward the profession, professional goals, potential to make significant contributions to the profession, and commitment to public service work. A Personal Statement—required in the application—that addresses each of these points, reveals a great deal about the individual.

The application files also contain important information about the candidate's experience. Library experience is not essential. An applicant with no library experience may be an excellent candidate, if, for example, he or she has worked with the public in another setting. Furthermore, a candidate who has a variety of experiences such as study abroad, extra curricular activities or creative accomplishments could have much to offer. The authors have been committed to seeking out promising individuals who have not had library experience, but who have the potential to succeed in public service work and who deserve an opportunity to gain experience.

The type and quality of the applicant's academic background is also of interest even though no specific undergraduate degree is desirable over another. In fact, diversity in backgrounds may enrich the collective character of the final group. Past academic performance may be an indication of general intelligence and ability.[10] However, grade point average and GRE scores, often used to predict future performance, should be considered with caution; they should not be the sole basis for hiring.

What others say about the candidate's abilities, accomplishments, attitudes, level of motivation, potential to succeed, personality, and ability to relate to others is also important. This information can be gleaned from letters of recommendation or personal contacts with references. Letters which discuss only past classroom performance are not as revealing as those which discuss work performance or involvement in a special project.

After reviewing the applications and considering all the relevant factors, candidates are selected for personal interviews. At UIUC the authors contact each promising candidate to ask if he or she plans a campus visit and if he or she would be interested in interviewing for a reference assistantship at that time. "Possibly the most important step in the selection process is the interview."[11] Frank validates the authors' experience in interviewing applicants: "Since attributes such as attitude, character, and initiative are not easily measured, the supervisor's ability to appraise/judge candidates during the interview is crucial."[12] The authors have found Lyle's comment about interviewing student assistants applicable to graduate assistants as well: "The interview should be relaxed and informal. The student's personality traits, personal appearance, attitude, and responsiveness can best be appraised from the interview. These are sometimes the determining factors in the employment of students."[13] The interview should also attempt to ascertain if the candidate has a commitment to public service, enjoys working with the public, has an outgoing personality, a professional manner, and good communication skills. The interviewer must also give the candidate the opportunity to verbalize his or her reasons for entering the field of librarianship.

The responsibilities of a reference graduate assistant and the expectations of the supervisor should be described during the interview. The type of work schedule, the number of hours per week of work, salary and benefits should be outlined. At UIUC, reference graduate assistantships are quarter time positions (ten hours per week) which carry a tuition and fee waiver in addition to the salary. Since the Information Desk is staffed all the hours that the Library is open, graduate assistants' work schedules vary and include evening and weekend hours. During the interview, it should be explained that the assistantship is a preprofessional position which will offer many opportunities for gaining experience (e.g., leading library tours, providing term paper counseling, participating in library instruction projects, attending weekly meetings to share information on the library, the profession, and topics useful in performing the responsibilities of a graduate assistant). It should be explained that weekly meetings are mandatory since they promote open channels of communication and encourage the exchange of information, questions, and problems common to graduate assistants. The supervisor should ascertain if the responsibilities, demands, and challenges of this type of position appeal to the candidate.

Based on the interviews and written documentation in the files, graduate assistants who are highly motivated, have a strong commitment to public service, an outgoing personality, and the potential to succeed should be selected. To balance the group, an attempt should be made to select some graduate assistants with library experience and some without. Selecting graduate assistants with diverse backgrounds and experiences may prove to be an asset to the group as a whole. An attempt should also be made to select a cohesive group comprised of compatible personalities that will complement each other. Having carefully selected a group of graduate assistants who meet these criteria, supervisors must channel these strengths by providing training for public service. Properly trained, graduate assistants will provide high quality public service with enthusiasm and confidence.

ORIENTATION VS TRAINING

The terms orientation and training are often used interchangeably in the literature. However, they are actually two separate components necessary for any program. The *Oxford English Dictionary* defines orientation as "adjustment, position, or aspect with respect to anything; determination of one's 'bearings' or true position in relation to circumstances, ideas, etc."[14]

The majority of the initial sessions for new graduate assistants should be devoted to orientation. Since many graduate library school students at the University of Illinois at Urbana-Champaign are new to the campus as well as to the assistantship position, an orientation to the university, the library, and the department, as well as the specific job is necessary. As Frank states, the orientation "incorporates a physical description of the library with an emphasis on the role and goals of the library within the college/university environment."[15]

In an orientation to the library, graduate assistants must be given an overview of the library system, including a tour, a brief history of the library, and a description of services, branches and library organization. Cottam describes the purpose of orientation to the library for student assistants; his comments are also applicable to graduate assistants—perhaps even more so because of the larger role graduate assistants generally play:

> The purpose of orientation is to help a new student assistant become quickly familiar with policies and procedures of a library, to help him know his job in relation to others and to become acquainted with fellow staff members. Orientation provides a student assistant with perspective and attitude that

he might not otherwise acquire for some time—if at all. It acquaints him with facts he should have about the library, such as internal policies and standards, library objectives, physical facilities, library resources, personnel organization, and general working conditions. Student assistants should not receive any less orientation as new employees than full-time staff. They are hired to fill a particular need, and they become part of what should be a unified organization, working to achieve common objectives.[16]

Thus this part of the orientation should integrate graduate assistants into the larger library organization as a whole. In addition, this segment of orientation should also cover compensation, benefits, and safety information.

The next phase of orientation should serve to integrate graduate assistants into the department. Graduate assistants should learn through orientation how and where they fit into the workings of the department. They should be presented with the specific objectives, activities, and structure of the department; they should be given a detailed explanation of policies and procedures unique to the department and an introduction to all departmental employees.[17] Frank substantiates this idea with the following comment that also applies to graduate assistants: "An understanding of the purpose of the department and of the relationship of the student's specific role or position to other roles/positions in the department will give the student aide a sense of perspective. Hence, students are more aware of where they fit into the scheme of departmental operations."[18]

Furthermore, it is necessary for graduate assistants to become well acquainted with the librarians in the department. In the reference graduate assistant program at UIUC, the authors have encouraged and promoted a collegial relationship between the librarians and graduate assistants. Graduate assistants are asked to view each librarian as a resource person from whom they can learn. For example, graduate assistants are instructed to consult with one of the reference librarians if they are unsure how to approach a question posed by a patron. It has been apparent to the authors that graduate assistants who have a clear understanding of their role in the department and who have a collegial working relationship with the librarians in the department, perform more successfully than those who do not.

The next portion of the orientation should provide the graduate assistants with information about the specific responsibilities of their position. The supervisor should carefully state the job description and give a detailed explanation of job duties. Graduate assistants should be informed about specific procedures and provided with specific guidelines for performing responsibilities. Nothing should be assumed to be common knowledge since the responsibilities are completely new to the graduate assistants. At UIUC, reference graduate assistants, for example, are informed that attendance at all meetings is required.

The supervisor should also clearly outline his or her expectations of the graduate assistants as public service preprofessionals. In particular, the importance of conscientiousness and accountability in providing information and reference services should be stressed. Reference Library graduate assistants are explicitly instructed to be approachable, to treat all patrons courteously and politely, and to treat all requests for assistance as equally important. They are taught that it is essential to document answers to all questions and to cite the source used to answer reference questions.

Orientation to the university, the library, the department, and assistantship responsibilities is incomplete without socialization. Each of the elements of orientation described above should foster the socialization of new graduate assistants. Socialization is the process each graduate assistant must go through to adapt to the new organizational climate or culture of the library and to the attitudes, standards, practices, and acceptable behavior patterns unique to the library.[19] The authors agree with Hollmann that "even a top-notch orientation program will not result in complete socialization for there are simply too many pecularities of organizational life that can only be assimilated over time and through experience."[20] However, a systematic and comprehensive orientation program can at least begin the process, which is a step in the right direction.

Over the course of the assistantship, it will be necessary to review with graduate assistants some of the areas covered in the orientation. However, with the orientation as a foundation, graduate assistants should be ready for training. The *Oxford English Dictionary* defines training as "systematic instruction and exercise in some art, profession, or occupation, with a view to proficiency in it."[21] How does orientation differ from training? While orientation primarily aims to assimilate the preprofessional into the library organization, training provides the skills needed to perform a specific job. The purpose of training preprofessionals "is to develop within trainees the body of facts, ideas, concepts, methods, and procedures to enable them to visualize mentally and physically what it is they must do and why it must be done.''[22] Orientation is generally applicable to all library employees; training is job-specific.

SPECIFYING TRAINING NEEDS

''Good training is synonymous with relevant training. By defining the duties, responsibilities, tasks, knowledge and skills which make up a job—and specifying training accordingly—relevance must result.''[23] To determine training needs, then, is an essential step in any training program.

There are many approaches to identifying training requirements, such as comparing job descriptions and applicant specifications with skills of employees, analyzing performance appraisals, analyzing personnel records, analyzing operating problems through observation, interview, questionnaires or group conferences.[24] Other approaches include use of checklists, consultants, informal talks, self-analysis, simulation and factual data.[25] However, ''the right strategy whenever new recruits are being trained for a job which already exists''[26] is the job-related approach.

If training is based on memory or speculation rather than on job data, irrelevant material may be included or essential content omitted resulting in inadequately trained or overtrained employees. Before needs can be specified, it is necessary to analyze the job performed and the circumstances in which it is performed and to break the job down into component skills. A detailed study of the responsibilities, duties and the tasks carried out must be conducted by the supervisor.

Since most service desks keep some kind of statistics concerning work performed, statistics sheets are a good starting point for breaking tasks into general categories. Using the UIUC Information Desk statistic sheets, general categories are easily identifiable: online catalog, card catalog, ready reference, directional, in-depth reference questions, and referrals. Since data for these categories is compiled for both in-person and telephone queries, interpersonal skills, reference interview techniques, and telephone communication skills can be inferred as related skills that are essential to performing the tasks. From these general categories, specific tasks that preprofessionals perform are identified. An example of a specific task at the

UIUC Information Desk might be: Given the title of a serial and a volume number, the preprofessional should find the location in the library using LCS, the automated circulation portion of the online catalog.

WRITING PERFORMANCE OBJECTIVES

"Job analysis produces a list of tasks essential to the performance of a job, but task descriptions alone do not provide the degree of detail needed to select the subject matter necessary to their performance."[27] This list of tasks does not describe what the graduate assistant needs to know or to be able to do. It does not address the characteristics that the preprofessional should have in order to perform these tasks successfully. A further analysis allows the identification of characteristics such as knowledge, skills and attitudes.

The knowledge required could be about machines or terminals to be operated, the materials or equipment to be used, the procedures to be followed, or may refer to problems that will occur and how they should be handled.[28] It involves recalling facts, names, places, rules, formulas, definitions or concepts. In the Information Desk example above, the preprofessional needs to be able to recognize if LCS is working properly and if the terminal is responding correctly, and needs to know the procedures used to identify the problem and report it. The Information Desk preprofessional would also have to know that not all title changes are cross-referenced on LCS, and that it may be necessary to check the Serial Record portion of the card catalog to correctly answer the patron's question.

Necessary skills—manual, intellectual or mental, perceptual or social—that enable knowledge to be used effectively, must also be identified. Skills include identifying symbols; classifying objects, symbols, and concepts; using principals and rules; discriminating and detecting differences; using verbal information; decision-making; and problem solving, as well as manipulative activities such as using terminal keys or catalog cards. Attitudes, or the disposition to behave or perform in a certain way, are not observable, but are reflected in the decisions or choices people make, such as the decision to direct someone to the Shelflist or to accompany him or her. Knowledge, skills, and attitudes necessary to successful job performance are identified through task analysis.

After considering these tasks and the characteristics necessary to perform these tasks, a "competency description"[29] is written. This "competency description" states the expected behavior of a competent staff member, including what skills must be mastered and what knowledge must be acquired. It should describe the performer, not the jobs to be performed. In addition to including basic knowledge and skills, it describes areas where deep understanding is required, and covers behavioral and affective aspects of job performance as well as cognitive aspects. The "competency description" then serves as a basis for learning objectives.

Performance competencies are stated in objectives for training. "Breaking the training task down into steps consists of defining each major teachable punctuation point in the progress from present condition of behavior to the desired condition and defining indicators of successful achievement."[30] These written objectives must specify exactly the kind of behavior that is expected after training occurs, preferably in measurable terms. The most specific and meaningful objectives will include "the conditions under which the behavior will be expected to occur and how well the participant must perform,"[31] as suggested by Mager.[32] Further, these standards of performance should be set in levels, "identified as 'minimum qualifying' or 'go, no-go'."[33] This makes it very clear if the trainee has acquired the necessary behavior stated in the objective. An example might be: Given a citation to a periodical article, the preprofessional can correctly identify if the library holds the title and the particular volume the patron needs, and can tell the patron where the volume is located. The graduate assistant may use all appropriate tools, LCS or FBR and their accompanying manuals, the Serial Record, the Card Catalog, the Shelflist, a periodical abbreviation list, or Ulrich's to identify the title. If he or she cannot locate the title within a short period of time, an appropriate referral to the reference desk is made.

Trainers and educators both stress that "the specification of a set of criterion measures (measures of desired outcomes, results, or performances)"[34] is essential. This standard can be described in terms of speed, accuracy, quality, or quantity. Additionally, if a standard exists in another source, the objective can refer to this criteria.[35] Further, the criterion for determining successful performance "can consist of situations that require trainees to demonstrate the learned behaviors, under appropriate conditions (simulated, if necessary) and to the standard prescribed in the objective."[36] This is particularly important when attempting to determine if trainees have acquired abstract concepts. Observed performances that will be accepted as an indication of mastering a concept or skill must be written into the objective.

IDENTIFYING AND SEQUENCING TRAINING CONTENT

The content of the training program then is the difference between trainees' present level of skills and the desired level of skills as stated in the written performance objectives. The next problem is to identify the present level of skills. Most of the training literature advocates some sort of pretesting to determine present skill level. The Houston Public Library in its basic library skills workshop for Library I's uses a pretest for knowledge of reference tools,[37] as do the SUNY Albany Libraries for their clerical staff development workshops.[38] Training in industry often uses performance evaluations as a method to identify trainees and to identify skill levels both present and obtained after training.[39] These would be good methods to use when training existing employees.

With new employees, however, no previous performance evaluations exist. Much of what graduate assistants at UIUC do is institution specific, such as giving directions and using the Library's on-line catalog; these things could not have been learned through previous employment in another library. Some skills obviously can be brought to the job, such as interpersonal, communication, interviewing and telephone skills, knowledge of ready reference sources, and use of a card catalog. Unfortunately with the exception of the last two, these are very difficult to test in a way which would give accurate results of performance on the job. Since even the most carefully screened group of trainees will have a wide variety of skill levels, necessity dictates that some information presented will be repetitive for some trainees. The biggest problem is whether the skills were actually learned through the training program, or whether trainees had them in the first place. Johnson maintains that "if the consequences of error on the job are great, then it is better to lean toward including unnecessary training."[40] Therefore, to avoid erroneous assumptions, "general training specifications for new starters or for workers transferred to new jobs normally assume no previous knowledge or experience."[41]

Once training content is identified, it is important to present the subject matter in a logical sequence to produce the most learning in the shortest amount of time. Broad concepts and terms which are generally applicable throughout the training session must be presented early in the sequence, accompanied closely by practical application of concepts and principles. Any skills or concepts which are essential portions of later training sessions must be reviewed and practiced.

Training sessions which rely or build on previous knowledge or skills in other areas must be deferred until the prerequisites are acquired. Advanced materials which require complex or cumulative skills, such as exceptions to general searching rules for special types of publications, advanced searching techniques, special internal files, and troubleshooting techniques are presented late in the sequence. Sequences can be hierarchical, chronological, problem-centered, or in the order performed on the job. Identifying the proper sequence for the presentation of this information is a necessary part of the planning process.

It is also important to identify subject areas where most of the information will come from external sources. The graduate library school curriculum and the assistantship program have a hand and glove relationship. They complement each other in such a way that both would be lacking without the other. The assistantship provides graduate assistants with the opportunity to apply and to use material presented in classes, such as to use reference tools discussed in class to answer the questions of real patrons or to dial into and practice searching on OCLC. The assistantship experience combined with library school classes, assignments, and research contributes to the growth and development of graduate assistants as preprofessionals.

SELECTING APPROPRIATE METHODS

Identifying the appropriate methods to present the training subject matter can be very difficult. Too often the most convenient method, rather than the most appropriate one is used. The strategy chosen must be consistent with a large number of factors, including the subject to be presented, the training objectives, and the appropriateness of the method, and must take into consideration budget, facilities, space, time, equipment, instructional materials, trainee population, instructional staff, and the kind of participation desired.[42] Another factor to be considered is variety, as research shows that "adults respond to a variety of teaching methods."[43]

How then can a relatively inexperienced trainer-librarian choose the appropriate techniques? Librarians involved in bibliographic instruction, of course, have some knowledge of learning conditions and techniques which would be useful. After carefully considering the factors involved, the wide variety of methods should be explored.[44] William Tracey has published a very helpful table entitled "Guide to the selection of instructional strategies," which gives suggested primary and alternative techniques based on training objectives and other relevant factors.[45] Our professional colleagues in training and industry are making available some useful data to aid in the critical decisions involved in designing training programs. Two surveys have been conducted which give perceived effectiveness of different training methods by training professionals.[46] It is helpful to examine what methods other trainers and trainer-librarians feel are effective when choosing approaches, although it is beyond the scope of this article to present all the factors to be considered or the advantages and disadvantages of each instructional method.

Reference Librarians at the University of Illinois must present a great deal of information in a very short time for preprofessionals to perform at even a minimum level. The lecture/discussion format is used heavily as an appropriate means to introduce policies and subjects, to indicate their importance, and to present an overview of their scope. Managers and supervisors from other departments are called upon to present introductions to their areas of responsibility. This maintains accuracy in content and provides variety in the program. As much of the information is subject to change from one year to the next, these oral presentations with accompanying handouts are less time-consuming to change than would be other types of formats.[47]

"Demonstration is the technique of telling or showing a trainee how to do a job and then allowing him to get on with it. It is the most commonly used—and abused—training method."[48] Demonstrations of the online catalog are vital for an introduction to the Library's automated systems. Difficulties arise in presentation to a large group such as this, particularly with equipment and facilities. Librarians also demonstrate advanced searching techniques and reference and interviewing skills at the Reference Desk. Graduate assistants work with experienced professionals at the Reference Desk and are encouraged to view the librarian as a resource person and to observe their behaviors. Demonstrations of dial-up procedures and sample searches of OCLC for reference purposes are also performed. However, demonstrations must be accompanied with explanations and allowance for practice if skills are to be acquired.

Hands-on exercises are used to allow preprofessionals to practice manipulation of terminal keys and to apply knowledge they have gained of the online systems. Since their active response is critical to acquiring expertise, practice sessions are scheduled so that each preprofessional can use an online catalog terminal located in the Information Desk area. Two supervisors are available to answer questions as they arise and give feedback. This also allows the trainees to complete this phase of training at approximately the same time.

Programmed instruction is becoming more popular as libraries seek alternatives to the vast amount of professional time necessary to administer good training programs.[49] Programmed learning has several advantages in that it can accommodate large numbers of trainees, it requires trainees to respond in some way, and it requires little professional time once it has been developed. The UIUC reference graduate assistant training program utilizes a programmed instruction handbook to teach card catalog filing rules for the main card catalog which closed in 1979. Since these rules will not change, there is no need for constant revision. Another advantage is that trainees can work at their own pace, with ample time for review, if necessary. Programmed instruction has proven effective in knowledge acquisition, to teach concepts, principles or theories.[50]

Another application of programmed instruction utilizes current computer technology. The University of Evansville, for example, has developed a computer-aided instruction program for circulation assistants.[51] This would seem to be a particularly useful medium for teaching the use of an online catalog since the simulation of the actual process would be accurate. Rawlins also points out that advantages of computer-aided instruction include the possibility of generating a printed list of responses to each question, the responses of an individual student, an account of actual time online, or which individuals had used the instruction program.[52]

Role playing could be an effective and successful technique for teaching reference interview questioning strategies as most trainers rate it highly for teaching interpersonal skills.[53] This technique has been used successfully in training programs by San Diego State University Library and the Library Networking Committee of the Consortium for Continuing Higher Education in Northern Virginia.[54] Both these libraries used this technique for small group practice in communication skills.

Video taping as a method of giving immediate feedback for role playing situations would greatly enhance this type of program. The Northern Virginia Consortium program taped individuals and then asked them to evaluate their own performances.[55] Video taping is also used by the Undergraduate Library at the University of Illinois to train preprofessionals to present research skills instruction sessions. Obviously, if equipment is already owned, then no additional equipment costs are incurred. But most libraries could not consider purchasing video tape machines for this purpose alone.

Lists of reference sources to examine are given to graduate assistants to help them with sources frequently used at the reference desk, and an effort is made to include discussions of them in general meetings. Graduate assistants are introduced to reference materials by using the lists as a guide and become acquainted with the sources through regular use.

MAINTAINING DESIRED BEHAVIOR

One of the most difficult problems with this type of training program is its urgency. The "overload design"[56] method must be used to give a crash course on the necessary information and skills, so that graduate assistants can perform on very short notice. For this reason, continuity, which is essential in any training program, has assumed greater levels of importance in the UIUC Reference Library program.

"Too many trainers look upon a formal program as the end of training. It really represents only the beginning. Unless formal programs are followed up with less formal types of training, full return on the initial training investment cannot be realized."[57] Neil Rackham reports on a Xerox Corporation study which showed that 87% of skills changed by a training program were lost due to lack of follow-up. He goes on to discuss the "results dip" which is an awkward period immediately following training where newly-acquired skills feel unnatural and do not bring results. He concludes that "without coaching, very few people can maintain a newly acquired skill."[58]

Coaching has been used very effectively in the University of Illinois Reference Library training program. However, coaching is not the only means of maintaining these new skills. "Maintenance of behavior is anything which keeps an acquired skill or knowledge up to a performance standard, e.g., getting feedback on the quality of one's work, and having the opportunity to use the skills."[59] In addition to coaching, practice, buddy systems, on-the-job positive reinforcement by the supervisor, job aids, performance appraisals, self-checking, and conferences with the immediate supervisor are other activities which can be used to maintain behaviors.

Some of the feedback techniques used at the UIUC Information Desk include a mandatory weekly meeting, a question log where staff can address questions to the supervisors as they arise, formal conferences, and exit interviews. It is essential to establish communication lines, both formal and informal during the orientation and training process. Supervisors have an open door policy and encourage graduate assistants to approach them with all concerns and problems whenever they arise. Careful analysis of backgrounds provides information used in staffing the first few weeks of the program. In an attempt to create an informal buddy system, every effort is made to schedule those without any library experience with those who have library experience at another location or have experience in this system.

"The preparation of manuals, training guides, and outlines is the best means the organization has to insure that the skills of its most capable workers will be preserved."[60] Job aids include manuals in each of the automated systems, an Information Notebook with all training and orientation materials and duplicated materials distributed at meetings illustrating special problems and a card file with the answers to common questions and problems. The card file also serves as a quick index to the Information Notebook. Work is now being done on a troubleshooter's guide to solving certain recurring problems. Having invested a great deal of time, effort, and money into a training program, the supervisor must take all the necessary measures to ensure that the trainees retain what they have learned and can use it on the job.

EVALUATING THE TRAINING PROGRAM

In order to find out if the entire training program is effective (i.e., if the training objectives of competent job performance have been reached), it is important to measure and analyze results. Only by measuring the results of the training program and analyzing those measurements can trainers gain feedback on the training system and answer some important questions: Did the trainees acquire the skills and knowledge necessary to perform on the job? More importantly, do preprofessionals perform as they are expected? While measuring and analyzing results can be time-consuming and tedious, "training managers must realize that competent evaluation is not an academic exercise."[61]

Since "learning depends on reactions,"[62] Hamblin suggests that "trainees must react favorably to training. This does not necessarily mean that they should *like* the training; it means that their reactions to it should not be incompatible with the learning objectives."[63] Therefore, the first level at which results should be measured and analyzed is reactions.[64]

Reactions can be measured in several ways—by using reaction scales or comment sheets for each training session, expectation evaluations, end-of-course reaction forms, and post-course reaction questionnaires and interviews.[65] Obviously, the type of techniques used depends on exactly what you wish to measure and the amount of time available. Measuring reactions for each session can provide detailed information about the effectiveness of each part of the program and suggestions for improving these sessions. Hamblin suggests that "if one evaluated reactions at the end of a training programme rather than during it, this means that one is viewing the whole programme as a *unit* for evaluation purposes; reaction objectives are specified in terms of *terminal* reactions only."[66]

Each spring semester since 1983, graduate assistants have completed an eight-page open-ended questionnaire which solicited their opinions and reactions to initial orientation and training sessions, weekly meetings, continuing training, and the assistantship experience as a whole. Because nine months have elapsed since the initial sessions, comments have tended to be vague about specific items, but positive overall. The authors have found this format to be very useful in assessing the program as a unit.

Kirkpatrick points out that "it is important to recognize that favorable reaction to a program *does not assure* learning."[67] Just because a movie, book, or lecture is accepted by a group or is enjoyable or entertaining, does not mean that anyone in the group understood, absorbed, or acquired the principles, facts, or techniques presented. In order to assure that learning has taken place, a second level of measurement is taken. Kirkpatrick suggests that before and after tests should be used to assure that learning which does take place can be related to the training program and that a control group which does not receive training should be used for comparison.[68]

The use of a control group which would acquire all skills on the job would be "at least partially destructive of the image of competence to demonstrate to the general public that learners are being used."[69] However, as most of the hourly student assistants, who also staff the UIUC Information Desk, have been hired after the initial orientation session, there has been consistent evidence, which has been reinforced by peer evaluations and individual conferences, that the individual training given student assistants is not as adequate or thorough as that given to the group of graduate assistants before the semester starts.

Kirkpatrick urges trainers to build evaluation of learning into the training program, using classroom performance or demonstration as evidence of learning skills and paper-and-pencil tests as proof of learning facts and principles.[70] Evaluation of learning should be an integral part of the training program, not a separate action or an afterthought.

However, what reference librarians have to be most concerned with is the third level of measurement, actual job behavior or *application* of principles and techniques learned. As is sometimes quite painfully obvious, a person can know the proper procedures to follow and still not apply them to the job. Actual behavior on the job or job performance needs to be appraised, using the training objectives as a basis for this evaluation.

Who should make these job appraisals? Kirkpatrick stresses that performance appraisals should be made by as many of the following groups as possible: the person receiving the training, his or her superior or supervisor, the trainee's subordinates (if any), and the trainee's peers.[71] Another often overlooked group to be involved in performance appraisals is the patron.

"There are many types of methods by which job behaviour can be investigated and evaluated, but they are all variants on two themes: *watching* and *asking*, or observations and questionnaire/interview."[72] One of the best methods of job appraisal involves direct observation of job behavior by the supervisor. The obvious problem in any public service unit is that the observing supervisor often gets involved in helping patrons and answering questions. While a useful technique, it is not entirely appropriate at reference or information desks due to the high number of interruptions.

Another method suggested but spurned by Hamblin is what he calls "keyhole" observation,[73] or what is popularly referred to in the literature of librarianship as unobtrusive methodology. This is the method whereby surrogate patrons are used to ask and record answers and to evaluate the efficiency of a service. Hamblin's quarrel with this methodology stems from the fact that most often it is applied without the knowledge of the person being evaluated. Since the evaluation process itself changes the behavior of the person being evaluated (called the Hawthorne effect), keyhole observation negates this potentially useful effect. Since the patron's viewpoint of staff performance is important, an unobtrusive study of the service of the University of Illinois Information Desk is being planned. However, preprofessionals and paraprofessionals involved will have prior knowledge of the study.

Questionnaires completed by the preprofessional and his or her peers are also useful, as are conferences and interviews. In December 1985 nonprofessionals at the Information Desk participated in peer evaluations. Individual conferences were held to discuss these peer evaluations and to informally discuss the training program. Exit interviews are held prior to the preprofessional leaving the assistantship. Although an enormous amount of time is expended on these conferences, we feel they are well worth the time and effort, both in terms of the information gleaned and reinforcement of attitudes.

CONCLUSION

The authors believe that libraries have failed to recognize graduate students in library science as a tremendous resource with great potential for providing high quality public service. More libraries should be willing to establish ties with library schools and to invest in the development of training programs for graduate students in library science. A library which implements a careful selection process will be rewarded with motivated, conscientious, and enthusiastic staff members who can make significant, although short term, contributions to achieving the library's service mission. Such training programs provide service-oriented preprofessionals with the opportunity to gain reference experience while attending library school. The authors believe that this mutually beneficial relationship will only result from a thorough training program.

The supervising librarian is faced with the challenge—to provide the means for the preprofessionals to realize their potential. Through careful analysis of the jobs performed, meticulous planning of orientation and training sessions, conscientious follow-up, and competent evaluation, the supervising librarian can develop an effective training program. Such a training program will enable preprofessionals to provide reference service capably and confidently.

NOTES

1. Laura M. Boyer and William C. Theimer, Jr., "The Use and Training of Nonprofessional Personnel at Reference Desks in Selected College and University Libraries," *College and Research Libraries* 36 (May 1975): 195.

2. Egill A. Halldorsson and Marjorie E. Murfin, "The Performance of Professionals and Nonprofessionals in the Reference Interview," *College and Research Libraries* 38 (September 1977): 385-95.

3. Rao Aluri and Jeffrey W. St. Clair, "Academic Reference Librarians: An Endangered Species?" *Journal of Academic Librarianship* 4 (May 1978): 82-84.

4. Martin P. Courtois and Lori A. Goetsch, "Use of Nonprofessionals at Reference Desks," *College and Research Libraries* 45 (September 1984): 385.

5. Courtois and Goetsch, p. 389.

6. Courtois and Goetsch, p. 391.

7. Boyer and Theimer, p. 197.

8. Courtois and Goetsch, p. 389.

9. Richard B. Johnson, "Determining Training Needs," in *Training and Development Handbook*, ed. by Robert L. Craig and Lester R. Bittel (New York: McGraw-Hill, 1967), p. 36.

10. Guy R. Lyle, *Administration of the College Library*, 3d ed. (New York: Wilson, 1961), p. 226.

11. Lyle, p. 227.

12. Donald G. Frank, "Management of Student Assistants in a Public Services Setting of an Academic Library," *RQ* 24 (Fall 1984): 53.

13. Lyle, p. 227.

14. *Oxford English Dictionary*, 1933 ed., 1961 reprint, s.v. "orientation."

15. Frank, p. 53.

16. Keith Cottam, "An Experiment with Student Assistance," *Utah Libraries* 12 (Fall 1969): 26.

17. Robert W. Hollman, "Let's Not Forget About New Employee Orientation," *Personnel Journal* 55 (May 1976): 246.

18. Frank, p. 53.

19. Hollmann, p. 247.

20. Hollmann, p. 247.

21. *Oxford English Dictionary*, s.v. "training."

22. Louis V. Imundo, *The Effective Supervisor's Handbook* (New York: AMACOM, 1980), p. 62.

23. Michael Armstrong, *A Handbook of Personnel Management Practice* (London: Kogan Page, 1977), p. 132.

24. See William R. Tracey, *Designing Training and Development Systems*, Revised Edition, (New York: AMACOM, 1984), pp. 62-72, for a detailed explanation of these and other approaches.

25. Johnson, pp. 17-31.

26. A.C. Hamblin, *Evaluation and Control of Training* (London: McGraw-Hill, 1974), p. 47.

27. Tracey, p. 227.

28. Armstrong, p. 133.

29. Stephen Becker, "The 10 Sequential Steps of the Training Process," *Training* 17 (January 1980): 42.

30. G.S. Odiorne, *Training by Objectives: An Economic Approach to Management Training* (New York: MacMillan, 1970), p. 156.

31. John S. Randall, "You and Effective Training; Part 1," *Training and Development Journal* 32 (May 1978): 11.

32. Robert F. Mager, *Preparing Instructional Objectives*, 2d ed. (Belmont, California: Fearon Publishing, Inc., 1975), p. 21.

33. Tracey, p. 45.

34. Jonathan S. Monat, "A Perspective on the Evaluation of Training and Development Programs," *Personnel Administrator* 26 (July 1981): 48.

35. Mager, p. 74-86.

36. Tracey, p. 44.

37. Houston Public Library, "Basic Library Skills Workshop," Houston, n.d., (Mimeographed).

38. Jacquelyn Gavryck, "Library Instruction for Clerical Staff: The Rest of the Iceberg," *The Journal of Academic Librarianship*, 11 (January 1986): 344.

39. R. Bruce McAfee, "Using Performance Appraisals to Enhance Training Programs," *The Personnel Administrator* 27 (November 1982): 31-34.

40. Johnson, p. 46.

41. Armstrong, p. 134.

42. John W. Newstrom, "Selecting Training Methodologies: A Contingency Approach," *Training and Development Journal* 29 (October 1975): 12-16 and Chip R. Bell, "Criteria for Selecting Instructional Strategies," *Training and Development Journal* 31 (October 1977): 3-7.

43. John S. Randall, "You and Effective Training, Part 2: The Learning Process," *Training and Development Journal* 32 (June 1978): 11-12.

44. See Armstrong, Appendix F, pp. 386-399, for a list of training techniques with a discussion of advantages and disadvantages, and *Training and Development Handbook*, ed. by Robert L. Craig and Lester R. Bittel (New York: McGraw Hill, 1967), Chapters 6 through 17, pp. 113-337, for discussions of training methods.

45. Tracey, pp. 277-289.

46. Stephen J. Carroll, Jr., Frank T. Paine, and John J. Ivancevich, "The Relative Effectiveness of Training Methods—Expert Opinion and Research," *Personnel Psychology* 25 (Autumn 1972): 495-509 and John W. Newstrom, "Evaluating the Effectiveness of Training Methods," *Personnel Administrator* 25 (January 1980): 55-60.

47. Tracey, p. 277-289.

48. Armstrong, p. 386.

49. Sandra F. Mitchell, *Development of a Handbook for Student Assistants in the Memorial Reference Room at Mankato State University* (Master's Thesis, Mankato State University, 1981; Bethesda, Md.: ERIC Document Reproduction Service, ED 212 256, 1981) and Nathan M. Smith, "For Student Assistants—Programmed Training," *Utah Libraries* 14 (Fall 1971): 13-15.

50. Carroll, Paine, and Ivancevich, p. 497.

51. Susan M. Rawlins, "Technology and the Personal Touch: Computer-Assisted Instruction for Academic Library Student Workers," *Journal of Academic Librarianship* 8 (March 1982): 26-29.

52. Rawlins, p. 28.

53. Newstrom, "Evaluating the Effectiveness of Training Methods," p. 58.

54. Kathleen Coleman and Elizabeth Margutti, "Training Nonprofessionals for Reference Service," *RQ* 16 (Spring 1977): 218 and Donna R. Bafundo, *In-Service Training Pro-

gram for Library Paraprofessionals: A Report (Bethesda, MD.: ERIC Document Reproduction Service, ED 207 536, 1981), p. 22-39.

55. Bafundo, p. 28-29,38-39.
56. Hollmann, p. 245.
57. Tracey, p. 17.
58. Neil Rackham, "The Coaching Controversy," *Training and Development Journal* 33 (November 1979): 14.
59. Donald F. Michalak, "The Neglected Half of Training," *Training and Development Journal* 35 (May 1981): 22.
60. Samuel B. Magill and John E. Monaghan, "Job Instruction," in *Training and Development Handbook*, ed. by Robert L. Craig and Lester R. Bittel, (New York: McGraw-Hill, 1967, p. 127.
61. Monat, p. 47.
62. Hamblin, p. 18.
63. Hamblin, p. 18.
64. Hamblin, p. 18 and Kirkpatrick, p. 88.
65. Hamblin, p. 178.
66. Hamblin, p. 83.
67. Kirkpatrick, p. 96.
68. Kirkpatrick, p. 96.
69. Magill and Monaghan, p. 122.
70. Kirkpatrick, p. 97.
71. Kirkpatric, p. 101.
72. Hamblin, p. 116.
73. Hamblin, p. 70.

THE REFERENCE LIBRARIAN

Accountable Reference Librarians

Patrick R. Penland
Aleyamma Mathai

To those directly involved daily in providing information services for real people engrossed in their own style of life, it may seem presumptuous to discuss accountability beyond the everyday fluctuations between survival and burnout in the reference room. But of all the evaluative statements that could possibly be made in the post mortem phase to a library program, the one once made by a librarian at the end of a community study is particularly revealing:

> As a result of this experience, for almost a year of great effort, I have learned to sit quietly every morning before the work schedule begins. I use these few minutes to think about what I can accomplish today to meet professional objectives.

Any person involved in such a "what-to-think-about" event may of course lapse into reverie and wishful fantasy. But the process can be deliberately used to focus on client-centered response patterns and objectives. Successfully mature reference librarians have continuously used reflective thinking to improve performance in a responsible manner. Self-directed individual learning is a unique characteristic of the accountable librarian and, unfortunately remains almost unattended as an area of empirical research investigation.

BACKGROUND

As one reviews the literature of the field a number of anomalies and inconsistencies appear; but some major omissions are especially disturbing. *First*, it appears that there is no formal psychological understanding of the client in librarianship who is involved in the in-

Professor Penland is at the School of Library and Information Science, University of Pittsburgh, Pittsburgh, PA 15260. Aleyamma Mathai is Principal Librarian, East Orange Public Library, East Orange, NJ.

257

formation processing behavior of decisioning, learning and communicating. Even the "needs" assessment and "user" surveys give little attention to the matter—patrons of course are described as library users but not as human information processors. The profession has not given attention to such psychological matters as to how the awareness of people (not "library users") is aroused, or as to how information is created and verified before it is used in everyday life (Dervin 1976).

Secondly, it is puzzling to find that there are few, if any articles calling for an integration of client-centered professionalism into a coherent mode of information facilitation and *service* delivery. Apparently, in practice, there are several discrete service bureaus into which the patron service environment is partitioned: reference, library use instruction, readers' advisory, bibliotherapy, etc. Obviously the profession lacks an overall concept of client-centered facilitation and does not know at what psychological and behavioral moments various service modes could be introduced in the interpersonal encounter.

Underlying these areas of concern is a *third* omission: no adequate discussion appears to be held over the length and developmental nature of the interview itself. One would have hoped that librarians were able to conduct professional interviews for periods of time longer than 5 minutes—a "quickie" transaction beyond which librarians apparently become increasingly uncomfortable. They begin to panic over what to talk about, or even not talk about, and desperately fill up time with anything—even advice and conversational "tid-bits" in abhorrence, like mass television, of any silences whatsoever.

Given such irrational and unprofessional behavior, the librarian is at a serious disadvantage with the administrator. It is impossible to negotiate for the time required to hold interviews that may last up to 60 minutes, especially when administrative changes are seldom made without a rational and research-based proposal for doing so. Of course some patrons may chatter away the time, in mimicry of such an indepth interview, and many librarians love to lecture and give directions to people. Nevertheless until steps towards professional accountability are taken it is not likely that librarians will adequately address the interpersonal dimensions of their work nor develop a mature psychological sensitivity to the developmental need of people even though the image of a learning consultant is a currently fashionable one.

Another *fourth* concern that has escaped much if any professional attention is the value and pricing of information. Librarians have been immersed, for all too long, in the information welfare system which has grown out of the traditional state-supported knowledge acquisition and storage system or bibliographic network. No concept exists of what a financial charge could possibly be for a reference interview, *qua* interview service. But a clinical counselor has to make charges, so does a psychiatrist and even fee-based entrepreneur librarians, or else they will not survive financially.

This fourth area could well be a professional dilemma whose "moment of truth" has come. What is the professional ability of a reference librarian worth financially? It seems that in practice not much of anything is ever actually priced out and charged for the data assembled or product delivered. The nurturing ministration of a sensitive facilitating professional appears to be of no account, except as a dole in the information welfare system, or as a "freebie" prelude to the cost of online connect and searching charges.

Fifthly, the lack of a proactive model of reference service is nowhere more evident than in the neglected attention to the reference interview in information and referral services. The concepts of advocacy, exchange and negotiation remain unattended such as they are embedded in an interpersonal resource network that is supported by information and referral clearinghouses and switching centers. Despite the information policy research of the National Commission on Libraries and Information Science (NCLIS 1975) and the information psychology research recommended by the Airlie House Conference (Cuadra 1982) librarians adhere to the reactive model of data retrieval, assembly and product delivery.

PERCEPTUAL APPREHENSION

The librarian's discipline, based on archival and subject classified prescriptions, is at variance to a humanly behavioral "discipline" stemming from the negotiations and the roles people actually play in real life. Not knowing much about information processing behavior in everyday life, as derived from research investigation, they are at a loss as to what to do but suffer in burnout "martyrdom." On the other hand, the librarian may be a desperate soul, eager to show off "professional" response capabilities almost regardless of client concerns especially those whose problems can be easily talked away.

The common practice of using nonprofessionals at the reference desk reduces professionalism in the eyes of the public to a lowered status with disastrous effects on the professionalism of the so called reference interview. It is all too easy to say: "Surely you can't expect much more from such clerks as these than a conversation or at most a question and answer quiz." Spread thin, then, over various functions and levels of professional competence, and suppressing their own feelings of ambiguity and self-doubt, librarians should not be surprised that conflict and burnout occur.

The issue of the *Reference Librarian* on "Conflicts in Reference Service" (Katz & Fraley 1985) may serve to help some librarians to achieve professional catharsis and do a great deal to release pentup emotions. Perhaps, in addition, this issue will do more for professional ethics than what the various codes have done and which have been largely ignored (Rothstein 1982). At the least, let us all hope—desperately—that librarians will put their own behavioral "house" in order before the public and its authorities step in to purge the atmosphere.

Librarians will continue to burnout, and perhaps not realize they deserve it, until the profession comes to terms with itself. How can a profession integrate its services while tolerating—in subprofessional acquiescence—the behavioral disorder of the times (Katz & Fraley 1985) even to the point where elementary courtesy and conversational niceties are abandoned? Can the profession continue to function coherently and intellectually when the disorder is high? Or can the *professional* librarians serve collectively as mentors and thus become an ameliorating influence?

If librarians had only a modicum of educational or instructional training they might be able to keep better discipline as some teachers have done in the classroom by environmental control, atmospheric management and ergonomic prescriptions. The point is often made that the reference desk(s) is the focus for an understanding of the professional climate in the library environment (Nielson 1982). Certainly all of the conflict reduction seems to swirl around the reference staff, perhaps because they are presumed to be skilled at client-centered negotiations, regardless of whether their negotiative ability is apparent or real. The high burnout rate in some libraries would suggest that appearances do not always match reality.

The hysteria of the reference services in most libraries has begun to "educate" the American public and especially users to a dysfunctional notion of the role of the professional librarian. It would seem that librarians get what they deserve in their image as a "doormat" by tolerating every possible disorderly behavior. Submissively accepted, behavioral deviation concatenates until the librarian is deadened by the sheer immensity of the problem, and the gargantuan bedlam of occurrences.

The problem of the reference interview and reference service is embedded in the conceptualizations and the subject nomenclature derived from knowledge, resources and intelligence. Regardless of whether the model is expressed as content or process, intermediary or instruction, the scope of the entity (reference) being defined, explicated, evaluated or researched is largely limited to the coterminous subject, topic or knowledge being retrieved.

Other evidence of the librarian's general intolerance of ambiguity and the consequent desperate need for control—based on an infrastructure of classified and chain-indexed books—is evident in the job descriptions and personnel policies of libraries. Almost no attention is given to the role and personality characteristics of the reference librarian, as derived from client-centered expectations; unless one finds it possible to take hope in what seems to be the resemblance of positive advances in this regard from Ricking & Booth (1975), through Debons (1981) to King Associates (1985).

Almost unique in the literature of the profession is the work of the Central New York Regional Library Service (Kordalewski 1982, pp. 15-22) done to train facilitating professionals to acquire and practice the roles and behaviors that clients expect them to have. Each facilitator is evaluated by the client using client-centered criteria that are embedded in the end-of-contact assessment form. This procedure was useful to the individual librarian and the supervisor because it engaged learning consultants in client-centered self-assessment, provided guidance for training, and introduced greater uniformity to the processes.

It has remained the contribution of the librarian as learning consultant to turn this limited perspective of the reference model around and to derive competencies for professionals from human expectations, not knowledge and subject resources. Instead of the usual input-output measures based on hard-core knowledge containers (Powell 1984), it is the developing behavior of a human being that creates and provides the situation within which reference activity can be more meaningfully considered.

The aim of such client-directed learning services is to assemble a unique combination of counseling, facilitating and assessing functions that are meaningful to people in everyday life. Response to the situationality of their involvement is the focus of the learning consultant's approach to client self-discovery, goals clarification, options consideration, priority setting, decision making, and self-confident follow through (Kordalewski 1982, p. 13).

The volume of literature on the reference process would seem to indicate that librarians have convinced themselves that they have finally found a uniquely distinct role for themselves. The flush of enthusiasm is infectious even though philosophically significant questions could be raised over the possibility that the retrieval function can be so easily differentiated from any other professional activity. Not only has the clamor of rejoicing become so strident as to exhibit locked-in defensiveness, but it seems to have been forgotten that machines can be almost as effective as the professional intermediary. To paraphrase a statement made by Babbage (1864, p. 122), it may be more effective to directly reconstitute information from language/knowledge processing than in retrieving it from the document store (Farradane 1974, p. 73).

Research in reference service is no better or worse than the models upon which its theoretical constructs are based. If reference is the central core of librarianship, then the models of the process proposed and developed for research purposes (Powell 1984) are at variance with other major professional recommendations (NCLIS 1975; Cuadra 1982). It appears that the librarians retrieval model remains dependent, at least in part, on the now largely discredited user studies of the past.

Instead of the traditional classified subject paradigm of knowledge-based reference retrieval, the fact that people need ''life information'' for day-to-day living was assigned a priority level of number one at the Denver Conference (NCLIS 1975). The need for research in the psychology of everyday information processing was among the top recommendations of the Airlie House Conference (Cuadra 1982). But these recommendations have fallen on deaf ears and reference librarians seem to be unaware of the research done in lifestyle information processing within environmental and situational constraints (Mick 1980).

TOWARDS DIRECTIONAL ANALYSIS

No responsible accountable research investigator or academician can ignore the totality of the situation within which client-centered professionals operate. It is not sufficient to limit empirical advances to the analytical method, tearing out elements of a completely human process for investigations of the minutiae of single subcomponents. Analysis may be the essense of specific research studies but until the findings of several of them are integrated around an application, the impact on professional practice is negligible.

The purpose of the interface between client and librarian cannot be limited to a conversational mode although many of those elements may be present in the discourse. Nor is the objective a discursive interchange where each person in the dyad seeks verbal gratification and refreshment—human processes so common in the multitude of everyday affairs. Of course in the professional interface a facilitating librarian may have to take all of these factors into consideration.

Of course, such elements as those of negotiation, of control and of persuasion may occur in particular circumstances. But mature facilitating professionals have learned to avoid becoming so trapped in any such conversational tactics as to be locked into a psychological "grounding," or shunted into the role of salesperson. All too soon, such compliances begin to undermine and destroy any semblances of the role of mentor, whether as intermediary or as instructor, if that is what librarians conceive their social function to be.

Fortunately, or unfortunately, the most persistent role that librarians feel comfortable with is that of direct control over the interface process. The sources of control may be various; but for most librarians they stem from the subject-organized collection of materials and the subject-organized indexing structures. In this latter instance—the most controlled—the so-called professional interface is largely a quiz session employing "what" and "why" questions about formal word descriptors and their rigorously classified relationships.

Known as the "procrustean method," the patron inquiry—if it can be articulated at all—is attacked and pulverized until its structure could be remolded into the architecture of the classification scheme operable in that particular library. That few patrons ever submitted themselves to such interrogations did not dissuade librarians of the day as to its efficiency in effecting a retrieval. To some extent this subject inspired imitation of the "skinnerian" approach has not disappeared from the librarian's method.

Of course, today, directives such as these are modified in discussions of the evaluation of the reference interview. Instead of the "procrustean" prescriptions, a "good" reference interview must be organized to achieve a particular outcome. It is above all else coherent, progressing speedily towards its goals as constrained by subject content, form and end product. By means of such a model, the interview can be judged for its conformity and efficiency rather than the quality of its interpersonal climate (Penland 1983).

Over the last decade, there has been a peculiar and unhealthy fixation on the knowledge-base of the reference interview to the exclusion of all other aspects of human information services. This preoccupation permeates the reference librarian journals and the various professional conferences sponsored by the bibliographic "pentagon." It is "understandable" when two facts are taken into consideration (1) the drive for status by creating an information "science;" (2) the reluctance to seriously consider integrating extra-library information processing theories.

There are signs that the prescriptive nature of the data-driven reference interview is being questioned. Some librarians have faced such unthinkables as losing control at the reference desk (Goodyear 1985) and facing up to the "anathema" of self-disclosure (Thompson 1980). Control is variously described as the competencies required to: (1) freeze human performance into archival structures, and (2) keep emotion out of the interface. However, to lock objective reference service into a technically rational model—apparently held today as a generally acceptable standard—dooms librarians to continuous guilt "trips" over the learning facilitations they are so readily inclined to use in practice.

It is of course easier on the librarian's emotions and psychic powers to remain aloof and in direct control of process through the use of rigorous problem solving rules and procedures. These paradigms however are more effective with computers and highly specialized experts—not everyday people experientially involved in the opportunities and constraints of real life. The human concerns expressed in coping-skills information and situational resolution remain largely unattended despite the information and referral movement (Childers 1984) and the recommendations of the NCLIS Task Force (1983).

Other signs of the times seem to indicate that a humanistic and psychological renaissance is underway in client-librarian interpersonal behavior (Zweizig 1984; Fine 1984). If so, many of the serious questions being raised (Chene 1985) about the librarian's role in advanced technology applications may be answered, especially as the prototype of so-called "machine-assisted" reference work is augmented by the findings of research in expert systems and artificial intelligence.

To many librarians any interest let alone concern over expert systems and artificial intelligence may seem unfounded. But these advanced technology applications represent a proactive treatment of knowledge resources and natural language indexing. Unfortunately, the typical reference librarians' hang-ups blind them to the realities of access to info-sphere resources (Toffler 1980) now available in the postrevolutionary telecommunications society.

Perhaps there are some values in being "hooked on books"— conforming oneself to vicarious experience and reactive message treatments. But the danger lies in the fact that reference librarians will be left out of the mainstream of contemporary information processing whether by humans and/or machines. Commercial information entrepreneurs stress the person-centered values of immediate and low cost access to textual databases from the home. Regardless of what librarians do, this "education" of the American citizen towards having personal computers in a home-based media center goes on continuously through the mass media.

RESEARCH AND DEVELOPMENT

Conceptually, if not practically, one can consider most retrieval activity, stemming from the reference interview, as the generation and selection of alternative solutions. Even random trial and error, which is not usually considered intelligent, can be viewed as generating a solution and then testing to see if the solution is correct. This has led one researcher (Dervin 1976) to point out that people (in general) *create* their own information and then consult sources other than libraries (Chen & Hermon 1982) for verification and validity.

It appears that American librarians are hung-up on knowledge control not educational control. Such control is vested in the power of organized knowledge and classified indexing to change human nature for the better. If this control is humanly beneficial, it is surprising how seldom if ever reference is made to any "psychology" whatsoever (Ford 1979, a&b) to improve the rigor of the theoretical constraints employed in research investigation.

Despite the cliche, "no person is an island," librarians continuously operate as if their professional roles with clients could be developed without reference to learning psychology and instructional theory (Hilgard & Bower 1975) or to the findings of cognitive styles research (Witkin 1974; Messick 1976). It may be the case that information processing, as defined by librarians, has a unique manifestation and practice without basis in comprehensive psychological or philosophical positions. In practice, however, this retreat from a systems approach has resulted in a continued proliferation of miniature "models" focusing on measuring the flow of knowledge production and dissemination, and on constructing the "mathematical" equations thereof.

These micro-analyses tend towards the amassing of evidence to support particular propositions rather than in helping librarians select facilitation modes and in integrating them around the wholistic and humanistic purposes of real people in everyday life. As Ford has shown (1979 a&b), this regression from the psychologies and philosophies has increased the likelihood of "burnout" problems among practitioners trying to synthesize and use variant client-centered roles.

Facilitation is a purposeful activity, focused on client-centered expectations. This goal-set may be to disseminate knowledge, create a nurturing situation or develop cognitive processes. The approach may be behavioral and task oriented, or humanistic and cognitive. But whatever the objective, librarians begin—knowingly or unknowingly—from one or more philosophical or psychological frameworks and plan, however loosely and unprofessionally, for some desired effect.

The reconciliation of the implications of the variant theories—behavioral, task analysis, cognitive construct, humanistic—can be a rewarding experience for professional librarians. It is not simply a matter of which is right or even which is most appropriate for a given situation. During any client-centered facilitation, there are times when one or another theory or some combination may be appropriate and should be used. The question of reconciliation is one of combining the strengths of each group (Snelbecker 1974).

A facilitation theory is largely concerned with practices that lead to the improvement of the librarian-client interface. A facilitation theory is prescriptive dealing with real life processes that are broader than the boundaries of variant psychologies—behavioral, task analysis, cognitive, humanist. The behavioral and task analysis psychologies complement one another as do the cognitive and humanist. In regard to goals, strategies and self-assessment, librarians have many choices. But the worst choice of all in regard to an interdisciplinary approach is to ignore the psychological work in other fields.

On the one hand, the behavioral and task analysis approaches may appeal more strongly to the librarian used to exerting control over the helping process based on the step-by-step analysis of subject categories and "chain index" relationships. Certainly the behavioral emphasis on hierarchical order and sequenced advances according to logical prescription will sound familiar to librarians (Gagne & Briggs 1979). In addition, there is a strong emphasis on the structure of knowledge and the topic-aspect matching or arranging of patron verbal behavior in conformity with the "logic" of the retrieval file.

On the other hand, despite the fact that the cognitive and humanist positions rest on very little empirical evidence, public opinion tends to favor such positions (Snelbecker 1974). These psychologies focus on creating a climate or a web of situations within which significant emotional events can occur. The procedures employed tend to be eclectic based on goals that are independent of specific subject matter such as learning-how-to-learn and assuming responsibility for one's own self-development. The humanists endorse a view of the human potential that would lead to fundamental changes in librarianship (NCLIS 1975; 1983).

The differences between the behaviorists or task analysts and the cognitivists or humanists can be considered as one of degree—a dimension related to that of artificial intelligence. Each of the polar positions can be productively associated with the psychologies necessary to develop expert systems and natural language access. Librarians have skills, probably better than most, applicable to artificial intelligence research and to the subsequent "nth-generation" software especially relevant to their demands for vertical systems and modular components (Smith 1980; Davies 1983).

CONCLUDING OVERVIEW

The objective is to encourage research that will range all across the interview control dimension from knowledge production, dissemination and utilization (KPDU) to the cognitive and humanist positions. Such a range of inquiry will force librarians to think about the purposes of client-centered facilitation and how to accomplish these goals. This continued focus—on problem-solving, creativity, self-development, other aspects of the affective domain such as goals, and the view of the client as an active information-processor and a developing emotional human being—will enrich professional service for some time to come.

For example, the potential exists to develop goal-weak theories using the methodology of behavioral or task analysis. In this instance, the apex of an affective domain taxonomy might be something to the effect that: "Each client creates within the self a positive internal environment." Here the focus is on individual self-development and creative problem-solving. Yet such a goal has the beginnings of an operational definition within a systems approach to taxonomic development (Steinaker & Bell 1979).

While there may be no one comprehensive facilitation theory, there are a number of points of agreement which can be used to guide research and practice. Some of these areas of mutual agreement (Hilgard & Bower 1975) are familiar to traditional librarianship and may serve as assumptions upon which further advances can be made. Maturation in information processing is based on:

— Actively involved and personally responsible individuals.
— Use of repetition and reinforcement to ensure consistent follow through.
— Essential organization of knowledge from simplified entities to more complex wholes.
— Generalizability and longevity of acquiring knowledge with understanding.
— Importance of goal setting and the transfer of competences.
— Effects of situational atmosphere and attitude on the processing of information.

Much of what occurs in librarian-provided services is experiential, intuitive, and based on common sense. If for no other reasons than these, the KPDU model of librarianship should be enriched. Client-centered facilitation is so complex that theory combinations and research constructs must address a host of practical issues—motivation, attention, perception, interaction patterns, as well as the state of a philosophical orientation or belief about the purposes and goals of librarian-client interaction.

Finally, in conclusion, one may observe that the reference interview has a 110-year history of development untainted by psychological theorizing and research. Why take such a radical departure now? There is probably no reason for doing so if librarians want to give up the struggle and lapse back into a handmaiden role—however much expertise they may have developed in online retrieval.

For years, the advances in reference services did keep pace with research in subject analysis and classification theory. Has the time now come for librarians to rest on their laurels and let the AI professionals take over building expert systems and natural language access? Or can we expect librarian-providers to take their craft seriously enough not to be manipulated by unexamined assumptions?

REFERENCES

Charles Babbage. *Passages from the Life of a Philosopher*. London: Longman, 1864.

Dorice D. Chene, "Online Searching by End Users." *RQ*, 25: 89-95, Fall 1985.

Ching-chih Chen and P. Hermon. *Information Seeking: Assessing and Anticipating User Needs*. New York: Neal-Schuman, 1982.

Thomas Childers. *Information and Referral: Public Libraries*. Norwood, NJ: Ablex Publishing, 1984.

Cuadra Associates. *Library and Information Science Agenda for the 1980's*. U.S. Department of Education, Office of Libraries and Learning Technologies, 1982.

Roy Davies, "Documents, Information or Knowledge." *Journal of Librarianship*, 15 (1): 47-65, January 1983.

Anthony Debons. *The Information Professional*. New York: Marcel Dekker, 1981.

Brenda L. Dervin. *Development of Strategies for Dealing with the Information Needs of Urban Residents*. School of Communications, University of Washington, 1976.

J. Farradane, "Necessity for Semantic Analysis for Information Retrieval." *Informatics 1*. London: ASLIB, 1973.

Sara F. Fine, ed., "Behavioral Perspectives." *Drexel Library Quarterly*. 20: 1-102, Spring 1984.

Nigel Ford, "Cognitive Psychology and Library Learning." *Journal of Librarianship*, 11 (1): 25-38, January 1979A.

Nigel Ford, "Toward a Model of Library Learning in Educational Systems." *Journal of Librarianship*, 11 (4): 247-60, October 1979B.

Robert M. Gagne and Leslie J. Briggs. *Principles of Instructional Design* (2d ed.). New York: Holt, Rinehart & Winston, 1979.

Mary L. Goodyear, "Are We Losing Control at the Reference Desk: A Reexamination." *RQ*, 25: 85-8, Fall 1985.

Ernest R. Hilgard and Gordon E. Bower. *Theories of Learning*. 4 ed. Englewood Cliffs, NJ: Prentice-Hall, 1975.

William Katz and Ruth A. Fraley, "Conflicts in Reference Service." *Reference Librarian*, 12: 1-236, 1985.

Donald King, ed. *New Directions in Library and Information Science Education*. Rockville, MD: King Research, 1985.

Jean B. Kordalewski. *Regional Learning Service: an Experiment in Freeing Up Lives*. Syracuse, NY: Regional Learning Service, 1982.

Samuel Messick, et al. *Individuality in Learning*. San Francisco, CA: Jossey-Bass, 1976.

Colin K. Mick. "Toward Usable User Studies." *Journal of the American Society for Information Science*. Vol. 31 (5): 347-56, September 1980.

NCLIS Task Force. *Community Information and Referral Services*. Washington, DC: National Commission on Libraries and Information Science, 1983.

National Commission on Library and Information Science. *Library and Information Service Needs of the Nation*. Washington, DC: U.S. Government Printing Office, 1975.

Brian Nielsen, "Teacher or Intermediary." *College and Research Libraries*, 43 (3): 183-91, May 1982.

Patrick R. Penland, "Information Interview Patterns." *International Journal of Instructional Media*, 10 (2): 95-106, 1982-83.

Ronald R. Powell, "Reference Effectiveness: Review of Research." *Library & Information Science Research*, 6 (1): 3-19, January-March 1984.

Myril Ricking and Robert Booth. *Personnel Utilization in Libraries: A Systems Approach*. Chicago: American Library Association, 1974.

Samuel Rothstein, "Where Does it Hurt?" *Reference Librarian*, 1-6 (4): 1-12, 1982.

L. C. Smith, "Artificial Intelligence Applications in Information Systems." *Review of Information Science and Technology. Vol. 15*. New York: Knowledge Industry Publications, 1980.

Gerald E. Snelbecker. *Learning theory, instructional theory, and psycho-educational design*. New York: McGraw-Hill, 1974.

Normal W. Steinaker and Robert Bell. *The Experimental Taxonomy: New Approach to Teaching and Learning*. New York: Academic Pr., 1979.

Mark J. Thompson, "Proposed Model of Self-Disclosure." *RQ*, 20: 160-4, Winter 1980.

Alvin Toffler. *The Third Wave*. New York: William Morrow Co., 1980.

Herman A. Witkin et al. *Field Dependent and Field Independent Cognitive Styles and their Educational Implications*. Princeton, NJ: Educational Testing Service, 1974.

Douglas L. Zweizig, "Lifelong Learning and the Library." *Public Libraries*, 23: 70-5, Fall 1984.

Reference:
Rewards or Regrets,
Believing Makes It So

Nathan M. Smith
David T. Palmer

It's 7:30; the alarm sounded an hour ago. Jim must get out of bed; he is due at the library at eight. His head hurts. His body has not rejuvenated overnight. He feels drugged, although he went to bed early. For Jim, facing another day at the reference desk is difficult. He thinks, "If I am not plagued with inane directional questions, then it's ungrateful, demanding patrons, who sneeze on me and infect me with their germs; I have already had four colds in the last three months. I would like to take a six-month Caribbean cruise—if only I had the energy and the money." Jim is already looking forward to the end of his day at the library when he can stop at Joe's Bar and unwind.

In another part of the city, Janet, Jim's partner at the reference desk, was up at six o'clock, went to her aerobics class, showered, and has just finished a good breakfast. She sings along softly with the radio as she finishes getting ready to leave for the library and the work she likes to do. She enjoys most of the patrons and tries not to let herself be upset by the few who are rude. During the day she will take several breaks and for lunch she will get away from the library to eat with a friend who lets her talk about "deep" concerns as well as idle chit chat. Her friend is a good listener. On the days she doesn't meet her friend, Janet walks through the shopping mall, or goes to a hobby store to make her favorite crafts. Sometimes she just finds a quiet place away from the library where she can read. Janet enjoys being a librarian, but sometimes wishes the job was better paid.

Nathan M. Smith, Ph.D., is Director, School of Library and Information Sciences, Brigham Young University, 5042 HBLL, Provo, UT 84602. David T. Palmer is Research Assistant, School of Library and Information Sciences, Brigham Young University, 5042 HBLL, Provo, UT 84602.

Jim sounds and acts burned out; however, his symptoms could also be a sign that something has gone wrong in his body. He needs to have a physical examination from a physician before choosing to treat his symptoms as burnout. Although Jim may be burned out, Janet does not seem to have been afflicted even though she is in the same work place. How is it that one will burn out and another does not? How did Viktor Frankl survive a World War II German concentration camp while others around him were succumbing to death?[1] Nearly five years of checking librarians for signs of burnout has revealed that over a third of some populations are experiencing high levels of burnout. During this time library researchers discovered and reported some personal characteristics common to high burnout librarians.[2] They also reported some of the causes and symptoms of burnout, and suggested how librarians could protect themselves against burnout. In this article, we will briefly review some of this previous material and connect new information on the cause and prevention of burnout in librarians.

THE MASLACH BURNOUT INVENTORY

Maslach and Jackson described burnout as ". . . a syndrome of emotional exhaustion and cynicism that occurs frequently among individuals who do 'people-work.'"[3] To measure burnout they created the Maslach Burnout Inventory (MBI). Birch, Marchant and Smith used the MBI to gather information from reference librarians in public libraries.[4] The MBI measures burnout out in three areas: emotional exhaustion, personal accomplishment, and depersonalization (see Table I).

Professionals in the helping professions become emotionally exhausted when they feel they can no longer care or feel empathy for their clients. They feel that their clients are somewhat deserving of their problems and hence are angry at their pleas for help.

In order to protect themselves from caring too much, they change themselves. They become emotionally calloused and bury their humanity deep inside where it will not be bruised by clients who keep asking for more. This is depersonalization.

The negative feelings they have for their clients begin to come back at them. They feel they are accomplishing less and less. To compensate for this, they often work longer and harder with fewer results. Their self-esteem suffers correspondingly, and they feel little sense of personal accomplishment.

TABLE I

Subscales of the Maslach Burnout Inventory*

A. Emotional Exhaustion
    Sample items:
        I feel used up at the end of the workday.
        I feel fatigued when I get up in the morning and have to face another
            day on the job.
    Frequency patterns:
        High burnout--several times a month or more
        Low burnout--several times a year or less

B. Depersonalization
    Sample items:
        I've become more callous toward people since I took this job.
        I worry that this job is hardening me emotionally.
    Frequency patterns:
        High burnout--once a month or more
        Low burnout--once or twice a year, or less

C. Personal Accomplishment
    Sample items:
        I feel I'm positively influencing other people's lives through my
            work.
        I have accomplished many worthwhile things on this job.
    Frequency patterns:
        High burnout--less than once a week
        Low burnout--several times a week or daily

WHO BURNS OUT?

It is not possible to say of a person, he has certain characteristics and therefore he will burnout. Stress is always a factor. Most stress, however, is not caused by the great tragedies of life; it comes from the accumulation of minor irritants that steadily grind us down over the years. We determine the amount of wear and tear that day to day pressures cause by our attitudes and the choices we make.[5] Librarians who burnout, however, tend to have certain characteristics in common.[6] Demographic studies show that a librarian's gender has very little correlation with tendencies to burnout, but marital status or an individual's choice of intimate relationship did. Maslach found that those who were both married and had children were at less risk for burnout.[7] Singles were found to be more at risk than marrieds for each of Maslach's categories, but singles were at considerably less risk than those who indicated alternate lifestyles, such as live-in lovers, or homosexual partners. Sixty-seven percent of those who checked "Other" for the marital status question were in the high burnout category for emotional exhaustion.[8] This supports Maslach's findings that families offer some immunity to burnout.

Full-time librarians were found to be slightly more at risk for the emotional exhaustion and depersonalization categories than those who worked part-time, but were at about the same high burnout percentage for personal accomplishment. Increasing age appeared to be a buffer against burnout, as older librarians showed less burnout. This finding could be misleading, however, if young librarians who burned out left the profession.

Smith, Birch and Marchant also found levels of burnout increase with level of education.[9] Their findings suggest that more education may increase an individual's expectations beyond that which is reasonable, thus increasing risk to burnout. Interestingly, Maslach reported that burnout was higher in workers who had only a bachelor's degree than in those with graduate degrees.[10] She suggested that those without the additional training were less prepared to deal with actual on-the-job situations. These conflicting results may suggest a difference between the profession of librarianship and those studied by Maslach.

VALUES AND BURNOUT

One area that has been overlooked so far with regard to burnout is that of the values held by those tested for burnout. Fortunately, Neil A. Yerkey has done a survey of the values held by library school students, librarians, and library administrators.[11] He found that librarians and library administrators rated personal accomplishment as that which they most value and that library students most value self-esteem. Self-esteem often follows from a sense of personal accomplishment. Therefore, the three groups in Yerkey's study have a similar priority in values. A third of the Maslach Burnout Inventory (MBI) deals with personal accomplishment and it is in this category where up to 35 percent of librarians register high levels of burnout.[12] The other two categories registered levels not nearly as high (see Table II).

While a sense of personal accomplishment is a strong value for librarians, and many who burn out do so because of a low sense of

TABLE II

Burnout Percentages, by Category, for 533 Public Reference Librarians

			Burnout Levels		
Burnout Factors	M	SD	%Low	%Mod.	%High
Emotional Exhaustion					
Frequency	20.793	10.805	43	36	21
Intensity	29.055	13.015	38	39	23
Personal Accomplishment					
Frequency	36.563*	6.807	14	56	30
Intensity	38.684*	6.457	22	43	35
Depersonalization					
Frequency	8.589	5.894	36	34	30
Intensity	11.225	7.185	30	40	30

*High scores indicate low burnout.

personal accomplishment, this cannot be said to be an exact cause and effect situation. Something else seems to be operating between the cause (valuing personal accomplishment), and the effect (burnout from a low sense of personal accomplishment). This other factor which we believe is a rational belief system, lets some librarians successfully deal with a goal of personal accomplishment and the reality of a job that isn't going well. A rational belief system may be absent in those librarians who do burnout from a low sense of personal accomplishment.

REWARDS OR REGRETS

To understand more about burnout and its association with a rational belief system, we asked colleagues in reference service, "What are your rewards and regrets associated with reference

work? What are the major stresses you feel?'' All of those interviewed, without exception, described their reward feelings first. But
for a few long lists of regrets or heavy sighs evidenced burnout or
near-burnout. For most of those interviewed the major reward was
(1) the appreciation of a grateful patron or (2) the personal satisfaction of knowing one had confronted the library collection and found
the correct answer. Note the different locus of control in these two
reward feelings. In the first statement the librarian relies on an *external source*, the patron, for a rewad. Psychologists warn that self-
worth cannot be verified by others; you must give yourself worth by
saying it is so. If you depend on others for your value it is not self-
worth, it is other-worth.[13] In the second statement the librarian's
reward comes from within, through an *internal locus of control*
which psychologists indicate is more healthy.

The regrets listed by our colleagues were particularly interesting.
Our intent was to (1) search the comments for evidence of shifting
responsibility for one's happiness to external sources and (2) check
for evidence of what Albert Ellis calls irrational beliefs.[14] We want
to emphasize that our search was similar to that which a doctor performs when searching for the cause of some physical symptom,
such as a stomachache. Before the source of the stomachache can be
determined the symptoms must be described. We are not interested
in making moral judgments about the goodness or badness of a librarian's belief system. But before burnout can be understood, the
psychological aspects of the stress and distress associated with it
must be known. Some psychologists in explaining these psychological aspects of stress and distress are adamant that one's emotional
upset is caused by one's self-talk.[15]

BELIEF SYSTEMS

When burnout symptoms are not the result of physical causes,
one's self-talk should be examined. Harper and Ellis, expanding on
an idea posited earlier by the psychologist Alfred Adler, describe
how the self-talk associated with one's belief system leads to unhap-
piness and neurosis.[16] Their ABC Model describes how this happens
through *A* an activating event, *B* one's belief system, and *C* the consequent behavior after *A* and *B*. At point A, The *A*ctivating event—
such as an angry patron—is processed through one's *B*elief system—
people should not get upset with me when I am doing my best, how

dare they, this is awful—which leads to one's *C*onsequent behavior —such as getting upset. While most people are not consciously aware of the content of their belief system, "B," once recognized, the recognition allows them to take responsibility for their beliefs; they created them, they maintain them, and therefore through disputing the irrational beliefs have the power to change the belief system and consequently change the resulting emotions. Emotion does not exist outside of an individual. It is self-created in response to an outside pressure: a stressor. Because emotion is self-created one can change or redirect the thoughts which create personal stress. Stress management doesn't mean getting rid of all stress or emotion. Rather, it means making thoughtful decisions about which stress to keep and which to let go.[17]

Some stress is beneficial, but when overdone, or created irrationally, stress leads to distress. In a stressing situation, it is not the stressors that will produce stress, but rather one's way of thinking that will produce feelings leading to anxiety about personal accomplishment. Thoughts that begin with "Isn't it awful that . . . ," such as "Isn't it awful that I don't get more satisfaction from my reference work." Or, "People should have more appreciation for all that I do for them. It is terrible when people don't appreciate my hard work."

Ellis developed rational-emotive therapy (RET) in order to help his clients deal rationally with their emotions by pointing out their beliefs that lead to feelings of distress.[18] In RET, clients learn how their thinking can produce disturbing emotions. Once a client recognizes that he operates from a belief system that is irrational, he can learn to accept what cannot be changed, come to grips with a "worst case scenario" and realize that even then, though that scenario may not be desirable, he can cope with it. This will include saying to oneself, "I enjoy receiving appreciation; I let myself feel good when I receive it. I do not have to feel terrible, however, when it is not given." It is our belief that in a stressing environment this kind of rational dealing with the stressors and one's emotions can be the difference between burning out and not burning out.

Lists of irrational ideas that lead one to emotional disturbance, even neurosis, are not unique to Harper and Ellis. Regardless of the list chosen, each item in any of the lists contains a belief which is irrational and leads to emotional upset. We have incorporated the essence of the beliefs found in several lists[19] and submit them for librarians as follows:

1. I should be loved and appreciated, especially by my patrons and those with whom I work.
2. My director/supervisor should appreciate my hard work and give me proper recognition.
3. I must be thoroughly competent in my job before I can be considered worthwhile.
4. Anyone, patron, fellow worker, or supervisor who disagrees with my ideas is "bad" and becomes an opponent to be scorned, rejected, or anathematized.
5. I should become upset with patrons who ask dumb questions.
6. It is awful and catastrophic when patrons and the library do not behave as I believe they should.
7. My happiness is caused by patrons or the library and I have little or no ability to control my emotional reactions.
8. Until the patrons and the library straighten themselves out and do what is right I have no responsibility to do what is right.
9. There is a right, precise, and perfect solution to human problems and it is catastrophic if that solution is not found.
10. People should give me my own way.
11. Life should be fair.
12. My past is all important; because someone in the past said I was incompetent, I must continue to be influenced by their judgement.
13. Life should be easy. I should have happiness just because I want it.

The above irrational beliefs can be seen in action in a number of comments offered by unhappy, burning out librarians. Contributing factors might be low pay, powerlessness, bad library politics, lack of appreciation, and tasks considered inappropriate to their training and position. In each case an irrational response is to assume that things *have* to be the way one thinks things *should* be before one can act constructively or find satisfaction in one's work. The rational response is to see what one can do with what one has (or else consider the option of leaving the job).

Mark Twain is reported to have said, "Man is the only animal that blushes, or needs to." Blushing is an emotional reaction to a judgment on reality. Animals only known how to accept reality as it is without judging it. They are incapable of being embarrassed about anything. Only we humans victimize ourselves by our beliefs about reality. A list of words and phrases follow which represent judgments that simply do not exist in reality, but many people would find their existence impossible without them.[20]

disasters	a perfect person
a depressing game	bad manners
mistakes	a guarantee
a dreadful dress	the right way
a bad odor	a gorgeous hairdo
terrible language	a good boy
a nice day	improper grammar
a successful career	a magnificent human being
a beautiful woman	a stupid patron
a bad accident	a disgusting display

Dyer asserts that these concepts do not exist in reality. Each, however, represents a judgment about reality and are listed here to emphasize again it is one's belief system which leads to upsetness and possible burnout. Insofar as these judgments are self-defeating or victimizing, they should be abandoned and replaced with reality based beliefs that are self-enhancing.

UNIVERSALITY OF PERSONAL ACCOMPLISHMENT VALUES

A high priority on personal accomplishment and self-esteem is not unique to librarians. Psychologist Abraham H. Maslow describes a hierarchy of human needs that must be satisfied and satisfied sequentially for one to be a happy, self-actualized individual.[21] The need for self-esteem is near the top of Maslow's hierarchy. At the base of the hierarchy are basic physiological needs: air, food, water. According to Maslow, before an individual can move up to the next plateau in the hierarchy the basic needs must be satisfied. At the next step is safety-security, both physical and psychological. The third level of the hierarchy is the need to belong and be loved. Only when these lower level needs have been satisfied can one move on to achieve the need for self-esteem.

Welch, et al.[22] use Maslow's Hierarchy and substitute accomplishment as a synonym for self-esteem, which suggests again the association of accomplishment and self-esteem. They suggest that one way for us to enhance our self-esteem is to become more aware of our strengths and accomplishments through keeping a diary in which we record accomplishments. The diary is to be reviewed at the end of each day.

For the term self-actualized, they substitute creative innovation, indicating this highest level of need can be met by refusing to allow a job to become routine and boring. Here again, we must take charge of our belief system. Life is boring when we choose to be bored. Boredom is an inability to use up present moments in a personally fulfilling way. Boredom can be replaced by engaging in some creative or innovative activities. They can be as simple as changing a routine, rearranging furniture, writing for publication, creating a workshop, etc. The innovation can be large or small—the important thing is the creative activity which must be done daily. These activities are one way of disrupting the irrational thinking which is central to burning out.

SUMMARY

Regrets and concomitant burnout stem in part from an irrational belief system that demands more of the world than it is willing to give. For example nearly a third of reference librarians score in the high burnout category on the Maslach Burnout Inventory for feelings of personal accomplishment. To think of so many reference librarians experiencing the anguish which accompanies a feeling of little or no personal accomplishment is sad. There is, however, an encouraging side to this because feelings about personal accomplishment are an area where learning to dispute one's irrational beliefs may bring very positive results.

NOTES

1. Viktor E. Frankl, *Man's Search for Meaning: An Introduction to Logo Therapy* (New York: Pocket Books, 1963).

2. Nathan M. Smith and Veneese C. Nelson. "Burnout: A Survey of Academic Reference Librarians," *College and Research Libraries* 44: 245-250 (May, 1983); Mary Haack, John W. Jones, and Tina Roose, "Occupational Burnout Among Librarians," *Drexel Library Quarterly* 20: 46-72 (Spring 1984); Nathan M. Smith and Laura F. Nielsen. "Burnout: A Survey of Corporate Librarians," *Special Libraries* 75: 221-227 (July, 1984); Nathan M. Smith, Nancy E. Birch, and Maurice P. Marchant, "Stress, Distress, and Burnout: A Survey of Public Reference Librarians," *Public Libraries* 23: 83-85 (Fall, 1984); and Nancy Birch,

Nathan M. Smith, and Maurice P. Marchant. "Perceived Role Conflict, Role Ambiguity, and Public Reference Librarian Burnout." *Library and Information Science Research* 8: 53-65 (1986).

3. Christina Maslach and Susan E. Jackson, *Maslach Burnout Inventory Manual* (Palo Alto, Ca.: Consulting Psychologists Press, Inc., 1981). p. 1

4. Nancy Birch, Maurice P. Marchant, and Nathan M. Smith, "Perceived Role Conflict, Role Ambiguity, and Reference Librarian Burnout in Public Libraries," *Library & Information Science Research* Vol 8:55-57 (Winter, 1986).

5. Donald A. Tubesing, *Kicking Your Stress Habits: A Do-It-Yourself Guide for Coping With Stress* (Duluth, Minnesota: Whole Person Associates, 1981).

6. Smith, Birch, and Marchant, "Stress, Distress, and Burnout," p. 83-84.

7. Christina Maslach and Susan E. Jackson, *Burnout: The Cost of Caring* (Englewood Cliffs, N.J.: Prentice Hall, 1982), p. 60.

8. Smith, Birch, and Marchant, "Stress, Distress and Burnout," p. 84.

9. Ibid.

10. Maslach and Jackson, *Burnout: The Cost of Caring*, p. 61.

11. Neil A. Yerkey, "Values of Library School Students, Faculty, and Librarians," *Journal of Education for Librarianship* 21: 127-34 (Fall, 1980).

12. Birch, Marchant and Smith, "Perceived Role Conflict," p. 57.

13. Wayne W. Dyer, *Your Erroneous Zones* (New York: Avon, 1977).

14. Albert Ellis and Robert A. Harper, *A new Guide to Rational Living* (No. Hollywood, Ca.: Wilshire Book Company, 1975).

15. Ibid.; Lewis E. Losoncy, *You Can Do It!: How To Encourage Yourself* (Englewood Cliffs, N.J.: Prentice-Hall, 1980; and David S. Goodman and Maxie C. Maultsby, *Emotional Well-Being Through Rational Behavior Training* (Springfield, Ill.: Charles C Thomas, 1974).

16. Ellis and Harper, *A new Guide to Rational Living.*

17. Tubesing, *Kicking Your Stress Habits.*

18. Ellis and Harper, *A new Guide to Rational Living.*

19. Ibid.; Jerry Edelwich, *Burnout: Stages of Disillusionment in the Helping Professions* (New York: Human Sciences Press, 1980); and Don Dinkmeyer and Lewis E. Losoncy, *The Encouragement Book: Becoming a Positive Person* (Englewood Cliffs, N.J.: Prentice-Hall, 1980).

20. Wayne W. Dyer, *Pull Your Own Strings* (New York: T.Y. Crowell Co., 1978), p. 187.

21. Abraham H. Maslow, *Motivation and Personality* (2nd ed., New York: Harper & Row, Publishers, 1970), p. 35-47.

22. David I. Welch, Donald C. Medeiros, and George A. Tate, *Beyond Burnout: How to Enjoy Your Job Again When You've Just About Had Enough* (Englewood Cliffs, N.J.: Prentice-Hall, 1982), p. 278.

The Courteous Librarian:
Helping Public Service Employees
to Keep Smiling

Catherine Suyak Alloway

It's 7:50 p.m., near closing time at the reference desk. You have an awful headache and are worrying about your latest bounced check while a stack of interlibrary loans begs for attention. Suddenly he's standing before you, asking for statistics on "the number of cheetahs bred in captivity" for a term paper due the next morning. How do you respond?

Hopefully you restrain yourself from being too harsh or curt to the patron. But what about those occasions when you or someone on your staff lose control in a public service situation? Unfortunately, I have witnessed many such occasions when I have cause to be on the receiving end of library service. Library staff behavior often lacks the "well-mannered conduct indicative of respect of or consideration of others" that *Webster's Third* defines as "courtesy," and I am made to feel that my routine requests are an imposition and intrusion. Many other librarians have expressed similar complaints to me.

In a related vein, how many times this week have you been the victim in a service transaction? As Miss Manners observes, "one can easily encounter a dozen provoking rudenesses on the way to work in the morning," and worse yet, "counterrudenesses are escalating, sometimes beyond rudeness itself into violence."[1] Librarians are all too familiar with the stresses and strains of public service, but not with the strategies that can help them maintain a friendly, courteous demeanor in a demanding, pressure-cooker

The author is Public Services Librarian, Harris-Stowe State College, 3026 Laclede Ave, St. Louis, MO 63103.

The author wishes to gratefully acknowledge the assistance of Muriel Lindsay, Librarian, and Robert Hightshoe, Training Manager, Auto Club of Missouri; and Patty Slocombe, Librarian, Maritz Inc., in the research for this manuscript.

283

world. This article will examine some ways to start helping public service staff to "keep smiling"—that is, to develop and exercise that elusive good to be known here as "courtesy."

WHY BOTHER TO BE COURTEOUS?

Traditionally, public services in libraries include reference, circulation and other activities involving regular contact with patrons. The truly successful outcome of these services requires that library staff use their knowledge of resources to meet the patron's information needs, and *that they do so in a pleasant, courteous manner.* Why my emphasis on courtesy? Common sense and personal experience should tell you that people perceive service to be best when it is delivered with a willing, attentive and responsive demeanor. A successful businessman has knowingly labelled the interactions between customers and the people or systems delivering a service as "moments of truth," and those moments of truth are crucial to successful service management, according to management consultant Karl Albrecht.[2] Another expression of the power of politeness is found in the philosophy of champion car salesman Joe Girard. "Girard's Law of 250" is based on the unscientific observation that a typical person has about 250 relationships in a lifetime. As Girard explains the law in action:

> Can you afford to have just one person come to see you and leave sore and unsatisfied? Not if just an average person influences 250 others in the course of his or her life . . . if I see 50 people in a week, and only two of them are unhappy with the way I treat them, at the end of the year there will be about 5,000 influenced by just those two a week . . .[3]

Hopefully you've been persuaded to examine the "courtesy quotient" in your library. To be fair, I should not throw stones without confessing that I, too, have sinned. Therefore, I'll begin by asking, "what are some of the things that keep me from being nice to the public?"

There are many factors that can prevent a staff member from being at his/her best with the public. These factors can be divided into two groups: those related to the individual and those related to the situation. Moreover, some factors are temporary, others of a more permanent nature. Figure One summarizes some prevalent reasons for discourteous service behavior. Some of the variables that can put staff "off the mark" such as illness or personal stress cannot always be resolved through library intervention. However, other variables are manageable, and to that end I have outlined a six-step action plan designed to help library staff learn the importance of courtesy and employ positive behaviors in service routines. Two comments on the plan: first, these activities are meant to enhance, not supercede, interview skills, communication skills, and knowledge of the library and its resources. Secondly, some of these activities may seem to belabor common sense; yet, I ask, if they do, then why does there seem to be so many discourteous librarians?

SETTING THE STAGE
FOR COURTEOUS SERVICE BEHAVIOR

Step One: Establishing a Patron-Oriented Service Philosophy

The secret of every profitable service business lies in the words, "the customer comes first." When library goals and objectives focus on this basic principle, a patron-oriented climate is established, and there will be a foundation and rationale for courteous behavior. Of course, the implementation of a service philosophy involves more than just paying it lip service in memos and meetings. All library staff, especially management, must understand, support and implement the service culture. Towards this end, steps 2-6 will help put the "Golden Rule" into action.

Step Two: Design User-Friendly Service Systems

As Karl Albrecht notes:

The delivery system that backs up the service people must be designed for the convenience of the customer, rather than the convenience of the organization. The physical facilities, policies, procedures, and communication processes all say to the customer, "This system is here to meet your needs."[4]

Yes, it is possible to work in a library that accommodates patron convenience while maintaining the integrity of services and collections. Begin by evaluating current service systems, soliciting input from all appropriate staff, especially front line clerks and student aids.[5] For example, you might question renewal procedures: Do you allow patrons to renew materials that haven't been requested by others? If so, do you make it easy by allowing telephone renewals? If there are numerous renewals, could the lending period be too short?

Next, analyze the nature and number of service interactions in your library. Flow charts of service systems and service desk activity will provide information essential to a successful service management program. Among the things you should know are:

— Who are the library's patrons? Why do they come to the library?
— How many staff interact with a typical patron during one visit? What services are performed by those staff?
— Which staff have contact with the public?
— How many different patrons do those staff serve in the course of an average day? How many hours do those staff spend with the public on an average day?
— What number of interactions involve simple, routine service? Complex, judgemental, or prolonged service?
— How many service interactions involve "problem patrons" or exceptional stress?

Finally, initiate the necessary changes in facilities and processes that will make things easier for patrons without creating extraordinary demands on staff. You might even set guidelines for bending the rules if it benefits the patron without creating extraordinary demands on staff. What, you may ask, does all this have to do with courtesy? Establishing public services on the basis of value and convenience to the library user, rather than to the library, demonstrates that you really mean "the patron comes first," and it will create an atmosphere conducive to courtesy for both staff and patrons.

Step Three: Establish Service Interaction Guidelines

Etiquette books aside, there are few exact standards or measurements of courtesy, even though there is no mistaking rudeness for politeness. To complicate things, there are matters of individual personality and style. I know many courteous librarians and each has a unique service manner, ranging from an almost-cloying Little Mary Sunshine style to a distant, professional facade. Moreover, as Elizabeth Post points out, people do not all agree on the type of service like, thus, "a clever saleswoman must have different methods with different customers."[6] Nevertheless, there is some value in defining courtesy and setting guidelines for appropriate service behavior.

Examples of actual library reference service manuals show that courtesy is a matter that is appropriately addressed in written policies and procedures:

> The attitude at the desk should reflect approachability . . .

> Courtesy, patience, sensitivity and tact are important in all interactions with library users . . .

> Library users will return to request further assistance if the librarian is courteous and helpful . . .[7]

Unfortunately, many libraries don't have procedure documents, which serve many useful purposes related to training and other management functions. In the absence of formal policies and procedures, one beneficial exercise is for staff to identify some of the primary attributes and behaviors of the courteous employee, for example:

— *Kind, thoughtful, considerate* to ALL patrons.
— *Attentive* to patron's requests and comments.
— *Responsive, takes action immediately.*
— *Patient* with those who need assistance, instruction.
— *Tactful* in difficult situations.
— *Friendly, cheerful* disposition that is . . .
— *Natural*, not forced or fake.
— *Concerned* about patrons' needs and complaints.
— *Sympathetic* with patrons' difficulties in finding information.

Identifying the nature of courtesy will be a good starting point for service behavior evaluation and training.

Bear in mind that there are 3 types of patrons that tend to render courtesy guidelines worthless. First there is the "problem patron" who is insulting or at worst, verbally or physically abusive. Then there is the "demander" who expects service above library capabilities and norms. Last but not least is the "lonely heart" who pours out his/her soul to library staff. Although it is true that "the cobra will bite you whether you call it cobra or Mr. Cobra," it is also true that "there can be no defense like elaborate courtesy." However, staff should be taught when it is appropriate to adopt a more assertive stance with patrons; a good rule of thumb is when someone is interfering with service to others.

MANAGING SERVICE BEHAVIOR

Step Four: Evaluate Service Behavior

One of the implied objectives of this courtesy plan is to improve the performance of service employees, and this can only be done if such employees desire and see the need to change. Evaluations of service behavior can help provide an impetus for change by informing employees that their performance is not up to expectations. Unfortunately, the evaluation of service behavior and courtesy is problematic because courtesy is a subjective quality and is difficult to assess in a library where most employees interact one-on-one with patrons. Moreover, the process of evaluation imposes a burden on employees called "emotional labor" and there can be a dear price to pay for its inherent stresses.

Emotional labor is defined as "the management of feeling to create a publicly observable facial and bodily display."[8] There are 3 characteristics of a job entailing emotional labor: (1) There must be facial or vocal public contact; (2) The employee is required to have an effect on the emotional state of clients (i.e., waiters foster "pleasure," bill collectors, "fear," and so on); (3) The employer controls the employee's emotional activities through training and supervision. Public services library staff bear a certain amount of emotional labor as they try to affect positive emotions in patrons by satisfying information needs. However, since librarians do not usually have direct supervision of their service behavior, they do not meet all the criteria for emotional labor. Like social workers, doctors, and other professionals, library employees tend to monitor their own emotional labor by considering internal and professional norms, the expectations of the patron, and constraints of the situation. To replace this self-regulation mechanism with strict library control of service behavior would demand true emotional labor of staff, eventually lowering employee self-confidence, morale, and ultimately, service behavior. This, however, does not mean that all evaluation and training activities related to service and courtesy need be abandoned. Obviously there is a need for some supervision and education in these areas, as noted previously. The objective is to employ activities that will indirectly influence behavior and strengthen self-supervision of service interaction and courtesy skills.

Formal supervisory reviews are often conducted in for-profit service businesses that depend largely on emotional labor. Unobtrusive monitoring of service can provide accurate feedback on staff performance but is considered unethical by some and has a negative effect on employees. Even when there are warnings, covert observations of service desks foster a "big brother" atmosphere that temporarily incites good behavior but fosters stress. In addition, the logistics of unobtrusive monitoring usually require personnel and resources beyond the means of many libraries. Even open monitoring of service behavior can be stressful, as well as being a less accurate measure of performance, as the employee tends to "perform" during the review period. Given the drawbacks, formal evaluations of service behavior seem inappropriate for libraries.

One relatively non-stressful and productive gauge of service behavior is patron comments. They have limitations in that surveys have shown that dissatisfied customers do not usually complain but simply take their business elsewhere.[9] This would imply that written and oral comments should be analyzed in the context of total library activity, yet, this is problematic, for decreases in activity can be due to a number of factors, not just discourteous staff. Despite these problems, patron complaints still tend to be influential service management tools because they provide information that can be used for both evaluation and motivation purposes. This suggests that libraries would benefit from active solicitation of patron comments. Surveys and questionnaires are very useful; less time-consuming methods include comments boxes or notebooks, especially those that include a board or space for public display of patron remarks and library replies. Do encourage positive as well as negative comments whatever method is used.

Another recommended evaluation technique is peer review. There are a number of different forms of peer review; for our present purposes it is best to use more informal and congenial methods. One such activity is "team service," where a team or pair of librarians work together, sharing comments and ideas on each other's service technique. An extension of this idea is the "peer coaching" concept, which has been successfully adapted by a public library. According to an item in *Library Journal*, teams of 3 to 5 librarians met and shared information on specific reference behaviors including greeting and smiling. Team members then observed each other in actual reference interviews which led them to "help each other . . . by providing encouragement and suggestions."[10] The promise of peer coaching thus goes beyond mere feedback to include elements of team-building and training.

Whatever technique used, do not overlook the importance of assessing staff service behavior. The objective of this activity is to aid—or perhaps remove from public service—rude employees who do not reflect the service orientation of the library.

Step Five: Train and Motivate Employees to be Courteous

The most direct way to show library staff the importance of courtesy is through a training program. Training is also one of the activities most often recommended by researchers for burnout, which is a common problem in public services.[11] Although staff development can be a costly and time-consuming affair, even the smallest effort in service-technique is bound to benefit employees and improve the overall quality of library service.

Specific training methods and topics will depend on individual library needs and resources, and should highlight the necessity for courtesy, demonstrate appropriate service behavior, and provide practical information that can be easily integrated into existing behaviors and library routines.

One successful training method has already been mentioned, the "peer coaching" technique. Group activities like peer coaching are highly recommended for service-technique training, not only because of the social nature of courtesy, but also because of the benefits of participant input and the tendency for groups to reinforce behavior conformity. Other group activities such as role-playing and discussion of case studies also seem well suited to the subject of service behavior. It is not possible here to go into detail about the design and methodology of staff training programs; fortunately there are many good books available on the subject.[12] As for the specific topics of service training programs, some topics I think need to be addressed include "telephone and desk etiquette," "defusing anger," "listening skills,"—or whatever else is identified as an area of concern in your organization.

The greatest challenge lies in determining content and finding appropriate resources—experts, print and audio-visual aids—that fit the library's needs and budget. Traditionally, libraries tend to recruit educators and trainers from their own ranks. However, in regard to service behavior, the business world is light years ahead of us, and we would do well to tap their resources. It is easy to find commercial, pre-packaged material on service behavior, for as one management expert observes, "getting employees 'turned on' has become a major industry."[13] A recent issue of the journal *Training* contained numerous advertisements for training and motivation programs focusing on service. There are even businesses that specialize in the production of staff development seminars and audio-visual programs; a catalog from one such organization describes programs on courtesy-related topics such as "How to Handle People with Tact and Skill" and "Telephone Techniques for Customer Service Representatives."[14] Although much of this material associates service quality with profits, a great deal of it seems applicable to libraries.

When recruiting speakers from the business community, try a local chapter of the American Society for Training and Development. In addition, local business organizations can often provide lists of recommended consultants. Keep in mind, however that because service industries are at the forefront of business activity, related training has become expensive. Your personal network may provide a lead that is within the library's financial reach. Another approach is to see if fellow librarians in corporate settings can recommend co-workers in customer service or training departments who are experts on service behavior. Some company representatives may be permitted to provide some assistance to library staff as a public service gesture.

A warning in regard to commercial offerings: much of it is not worth the price. Do not spend large sums of money for speakers, films, or aids without previews or personal recommendations. Particularly beware the "smile management" packages that offer quick solutions or that equate quality service and courtesy with a grin. Good service doesn't come easy, and library staff would surely find smiley-face presentations superficial and insulting.

A good training program should help motivate employees to change or improve their service behavior. But what initially motivates people to act courteously? Much has been written on motivation, but I found 3 principles that seem particularly relevant to courtesy.

MOTIVATING PRINCIPLES

(A) *There is emotional and value commitment between person and organization; people feel that they "belong" to meaningful entity and can realize cherished values by their contributions . . . there must be a "culture of pride."*[15]

Steps One and Two in this paper stem largely from this principle and from the related finding that a service-oriented philosophy will inspire courtesy in employees. Related to this principle is the practice of "reminder campaigns" in businesses that employ flashy slogans, posters, buttons or whatever it takes to reinforce the concept of good service. Although most libraries may not want to pursue such aggressive motivation programs, well-placed memos or signs can strengthen employee perception of the service philosophy.

(B) *The things that get rewarded get done.*[16]

What rewards do you receive when you are courteous? Perhaps you feel pleasure when people are nice to you in turn . . . or you enjoy the immediate gratification of helping others . . . or you see courtesy as a display of your professional status or power. Each employee has their own rationale for courteous behavior which drives them more strongly than any external incentive. Therefore, the best way to motivate library employees is to identify and support these self-motivating factors. Unfortunately, internal drives sometimes falter under the circumstances described in Figure One. Therefore, external or library-instigated incentives must supplement personal reasons for courteous behavior.

Promotions and raises are two obvious incentives for good work, but are major actions that are usually based on more than service performance. Other rewards such as increased job responsibilities or special project assignments are not always feasible. So what is left?

(C) *Feedback is the breakfast of champions.*[17]

A study of corporate librarians revealed that lack of positive feedback was one of the major factors contributing to burnout. The study revealed that "those who received a great deal of positive feedback felt rewarded, while those who received no feedback or who had to deal with considerable negative feedback felt frustrated."[18] Feedback on service skills is most meaningful when it comes from patrons. It is very important for library management to share complimentary patron comments with all staff as tangible evidence of work well done. Of course personal praise from supervisors and peers should not be overlooked.

Another feedback mechanism is recognition, a practice long utilized by service businesses. Recognition can take many forms, including the familiar "Employee of the Month," or a twist on the idea such as Kroger's program that awards roses to employees who demonstrate "outstanding service above and beyond the call of duty." If these kinds of incentives seem too gimmicky for your library, especially for professionals, more appropriate recognition might include plaudits in a staff newsletter or nomination for a professional organization award. Overall, recognizing and rewarding courteous behavior takes extra efforts, but is well worth the trouble to supplement personal motivation for good work.

Step Six: Maintain Quality Through Service Management

So far we have determined that courteous behavior will be encouraged by promoting a service philosophy, providing user-friendly systems, establishing service guidelines, and evaluating, training, and motivating staff. The final step is to maintain the quality service you have initiated through service management, which includes the ongoing process of evaluation, training and motivation just discussed, as well as coaching or problem-solving activities. To illustrate the problem-solving process, some solutions are suggested for a few of the service behavior problems in Figure One not yet discussed.

Personal illness, worry and stress may not be alleviated through library intervention, but their effects on service behavior can be minimized. Open communications and a spirit of teamwork will support the need for desk assistance or reduced public service time when warranted. When library staff are rude because of *negative encounters with patrons* or *stereotyping*, many times it is a subconscious or emotionally-charged reaction. In such a situation the employee must be helped to acknowledge the existence of negative feelings, and then appropriate coping skills can be reviewed. A common problem of this nature is the problem patron or situation that makes a librarian feel frustrated or angry. Some practical techniques for handling anger are listed in Figure Two.

FIGURE ONE

Reasons For Discourteous Public Service Behavior

Individual

— Illness
— Worry or stress
— Negative encounters with patrons
— Stereotyping of patrons
— Lack of personal motivation
— Lack of knowledge, experience in public service
— Personality not fond of, or unsuited to, public contact
— Burnout

Situational

— Long hours
— Work too difficult, too much work
— Work too easy or repetitive
— Lack of proper supervision
— Lack of feedback on performance
— Lack of incentives
— Lack of rewards or measures of accomplishment
— Library goals and objectives not people-oriented or service-
oriented

It is much more difficult to face the fact that an employee with chronically rude behavior may simply have a *personality unsuited for public contact.* Hopefully, people who don't want to work with the public will avoid those types of jobs in the first place, although librarians in tight job markets may have to take whatever position they can get. Continuous service behavior problems may also signal burnout; in either case there is often an urgent need to remove the employee from public service either temporarily or permanently. Other strategies for dealing with burnout are covered in several well-researched papers,[17,18,19] although one service business executive I consulted warned, "burnout is more often than not a 1980's term justifying copout."

If there are numerous *situational factors* causing below-par service behavior, measures should be taken to provide better overall working conditions. Reducing desk duty, encouraging team service, and assigning a wide variety of tasks to each employee are particularly constructive measures that counteract the stress of public contact. In addition, it is essential that public service employees have some private space that lets them hide from patrons—and even colleagues!

SUMMARY

"Hail, ye small, sweet courtesies of life! For smooth do ye make the way of it," wrote Laurence Sterne. True as that may be, courtesy is often overlooked as an important aspect of library service. Library staff are susceptible to numerous forces that may cause them to lose enthusiasm and kindness in their dealings with the public. Although they may have some legitimate reasons for feeling

FIGURE TWO

Keeping Your Cool With a Difficult Patron

These suggestions were adapted from comments made by flight attendants as reported in *The Managed Heart* by Arlie Hochschild.

1. Increase your tolerance of annoying customers by pretending they are children or that something traumatic has happened to them.
2. Empathize with the customer. Try to identify the source of their behavior and defuse it.
3. Express your anger in a non-offensive way: take a walk, chew gum, talk to yourself.
4. Remember that anger is exhausting—get it out of the way.
5. Try to relax: deep breathing, count to ten.
6. Remind yourself not to take insults personally.
7. Be thankful you don't have to go home with the offenders!
8. Beware of sharing your anger with a colleague—it can produce 2 angry employees. Try to find someone who will calm you down, not support your anger.
9. Inflate your sense of humor. "Laughter is the best medicine."

poorly, there are few excuses for being rude to patrons. A service management program that promotes the importance of courtesy, like the one outlined here, will bring old-fashioned quality to the library work of the new information age.

NOTES

1. Judith Martin, *Miss Manners' Guide to Excruciatingly Correct Behavior*. New York: Warner Books, 1983, p. 4.

2. Karl Albrecht, "Achieving Excellence in Service," *Training and Development Journal* 39: (Dec. 1985) 64-67.

3. Joe Girard, *How to Sell Anything to Anybody*. New York: Warner Books, 1977.

4. Albrecht, p. 65.

5. Sandra H. Neville, "Organization Support for Direct Service Functions," *RQ* 21: (Summer 1982) 384-390.

6. Elizabeth L. Post, *Emily Post's Etiquette* (14th edition). New York: Harper and Row, 1984, p. 564.

7. Bill Katz and Anne Clifford, editors. *Reference and Online Services Handbook*. New York: Neal-Schuman, 1982.

8. Arlie Hochschild, *The Managed Heart*. Berkeley: University of California Press, 1983.

9. Direct Selling Education Foundation, "Customers Mean Business . . ." (pamphlet). Washington D. C.: Direct Selling Education Foundation, 1982.

10. "Peer Coaching in Maryland Improves Reference Service," *Library Journal* 111: (Feb. 1, 1986) 30.

11. Nathan M. Smith and Veneese C. Nelson, "Helping May Be Harmful: The Implications of Burnout for the Special Librarian," *Special Libraries* 74: (Jan. 1983) 14-19.

12. For starters: Barbara Conroy, *Library Staff Development and Continuing Education: Principles and Practices*. Littleton, CO: Libraries Unlimited, 1978. Matthew B. Miles, *Learning to Work in Groups*. New York: Teachers College Press, 1981.

13. Philip B. Crosby, *Quality Without Tears: The Art of Hassle-Free Management*. New York: McGraw-Hill, 1984.

14. *Catalog of seminars and audio cassette programs* from Associated Management Institute, Inc., 1125 Missouri St., Fairfield, CA 94533.

15. Rosabeth Moss Kantor, *The Change Masters: Innovation for Productivity In the American Corporation*. New York: Simon and Schuster, 1983.

16. Michael LeBoeuf, *GMP: The Greatest Management Principle In the World*. New York: Putnam, 1985.

17. Kenneth Blanchard and Robert Lorber, *Putting the One-Minute Manager to Work*. New York: Morrow, 1984.

18. Nathan M. Smith and Laura F. Nielsen, "Burnout: A Survey of Corporate Librarians," *Special Libraries* 75: (July 1984) 221-227.

19. David S. Ferriero and Kathleen A. Powers, "Burnout at the Reference Desk," *RQ* 21: (Spring 1982) 274-279.

Theory and Practice
of Library Client Interaction

Robert J. Merikangas

THE INDIVIDUAL'S THEORY

It has been said that there is nothing so practical as good theory, and I believe it. This is *not* to say that writing and reading articles on reference theory will result in improved practice. Such writing and reading *may* be helpful, especially as individuals work to clarify their goals and policies, roles and models. Articles in journals such as this may report useful data, analyze what we do, propose new visions or activities. All these materials may contribute to each individual's ability to have a good model for answering questions and to use as a check on one's behavior, especially when what one is doing doesn't seem to work, that is, have the intended consequences.

Much of the theory for good reference service is what might be called microtheory, theory that deals with the core process: question, negotiation of question, search for answer, delivery of answer. A usable theory based on studies on this level is one which can be used as a direct aid by the librarian in answering questions, by providing a structure for the transaction and even a checklist, to keep performance up to an expected standard. A good example of a microtheory tested in a real setting, leading to a useful checklist, is the Maryland study, reported by Ralph Gers and Lillie J. Seward.[1] What is especially noteworthy about their report, however, is their realistic assumption that it is not sufficient, for *consistent* good service, for reference librarians to know the microtheory and have the checklist in hand (or in mind). In addition, of course, continued practice is needed, so the intended behaviors become habitual. Beyond this, both peers and clients are involved in *testing* (one might

---

The author practices his theory as Reference Librarian, The Library University of Maryland, College Park, MD 20742.

297

say) the behavior. The librarian should ask peers to observe and report data:

> If each librarian who provides reference service would "contract" with a trusted colleague to observe one another in action and provide specific, descriptive feedback regarding the model behaviors, they should become an integral part of his/her repertoire.[2]

Feedback from the client is also built into the model, by the emphasis on asking each time the follow up question: "Does this *completely* answer your question?"

WHERE DO WE STAND NOW?

The long history of the literature on the characteristics of this library-client interaction has been reviewed by Charles A. Bunge.[3] Although much of the writing has dealt with the specific interpersonal behaviors, which can be made available in the form of a checklist or model, Bunge indicates that larger contexts have been put forward. These larger contexts come into play especially when the interaction moves beyond the simple question-answer situation. Even though the more complex situations may be less common than the short-answer type, they are certainly significant, and provide most of the major issues confronting reference librarianship today. It is the more complex question and its larger context that demand a macrotheory, and ways to discuss the alternative macrotheories.

As Bunge points out, in the more complex situation we pay greater attention to the *user*: the psychology of the user, and the place of the reference librarian in the user's general information-gathering project. The needs and expectations of the user become more ambiguous, and numerous proposals have been made that we need serious research on user behavior, not just on-the-spot observation.[4] In addition to the user's behavior and mind, we need to pay attention to the library-client interaction, and the *policies* inherent in that interaction. It is at this point that we encounter strong disagreements, it appears, concerning the proper and ideal role of the reference librarian.

Mention of some recent critiques of the way we do things may help delineate the levels we need to consider in seeking a practical theory. One critique, by Constance Miller and James Rettig,[5] portrays current reference service practice in academic libraries as obsolete, and calls for a revised theory of service. They characterize the revised theory as client-centered, with a primary intention to save the time of the user, by delivering hard-to-locate information. Their theory of action would require reorganizing the library and reallocating priorities and budgets. Another critique, which has led to much discussion, is that of Stephen K. Stoan.[6] Stoan warns academic reference librarians that they may over-value the access literature (indexes, reference books, etc.) and under-value the primary literature (with its footnotes, bibliographies, etc.) because they do not understand research skills as opposed to library skills. Although the main thrust of his argument is toward a sounder basis for bibliographic instruction, a note that is heard throughout is how much "imagination, inspiration, intuition, and luck or serendipity [are] involved in scientific research."[7] Within this frame of reference, the librarian as intermediary would try to structure a search that should best be left unstructured. Certainly the librarian could not "deliver" the information, except as a clerk who locates and provides specific known items (as graduate students often do for professors).

Two other articles which have attracted much attention are those by William Miller[8] and Brian Nielsen.[9] Rather than recall their specific arguments, let us note what they are doing: urging us to reconsider our reference practice in a time when decisions on the best use of limited time have to be made. Miller calls for long-range planning, but sees obstacles in people's reluctance to be candid about limitations and failures, and in staff conflict. He also urges needs assessment that goes beyond current practice:

> Our current stock-in-trade is the administration of virtually useless questionnaires which ask people to tell us what they like and do not like about our services. At best, such questionnaires may tell us a little about what people think that they want, but very little about what they actually need. How dare we presume to differentiate between what people say that they want and what they actually need? The answer, one would like to think, is that we are professional librarians with a much better sense of the range of possibilities than those we serve.[10]

Miller urges analysis of use data; I will urge dialog with users in a way that allows us to confront defensiveness on all sides.

Miller does not ignore the impact of technological change upon reference, but Nielsen confronts it more thoroughly. As he writes in his abstract, "The development of a new model for practice, which transcends both the intermediary and teacher role, is proposed."[11] Realizing that we need more than new models, Nielsen suggests that we use a larger concept of professionalism—but we have to develop it. How do we do so?

> Undertaking the project of redefining appropriate helping roles for librarians will require the work of many individual librarians, experimentation and research in libraries, and much communication with users. Such redefinition cannot be merely a paper exercise practiced by authors in library journals.[12]

I concur heartily that it is this process of redefinition that we need, an examination of our macrotheories of service in action. I also concur that writing articles will not do it. In spite of my agreement, I am writing. However, I hope to clarify the process, and even begin it.

In a nested fashion, I will now present yet another theory or model (the two concepts are quite similar, with the model, perhaps in graphic form, presenting the parts of the theory). I will then ask questions: what shall we do with this model, or alternative ones we have on the table for discussion? I will propose that we can profitably use the works and approach of Chris Argyris to move to the new definitions we need for *practice*.[13]

As you read this position statement, reflect on your attitudes toward it: do you agree with the *governing values* it expresses? What do you think of the *action strategies* it presents? How would we *test* it, and check out the *consequences* of applying this in practice?

PROPOSED THEORY:
LIBRARIANS AND USERS
COOPERATE AS MAPMAKERS

It has been said that "where you stand depends on where you sit."[14] The position I propose in this paper is based on the view from my chairs as a reference manager. Seated in my office, I reflect on the multitude of duties and projects we reference librarians are engaged in. There is a measure of truth in what has been written, that "we have succeeded in pushing ourselves beyond our levels of comfort and competence."[15] Seated in another chair, the high stool at the reference desk, I reflect on the users who pour into the library, especially when the classes change. What do they *see* in the library, how effective are we in helping them get the most from their visits? A little later, seated on the edge of a table, I pause and invite questions in a bibliographic session. I reflect: how can I really assist these students in seeing the bibliographic world as I see it, so they can choose the most direct path to the places of knowledge they need?

From these several perspectives I have sought for a unifying concept which would enable me to integrate my broad range of concerns as a reference librarian and at the same time link all these concerns to the actual situations and needs of the library users, both faculty and students. Picking up from numerous hints and sallies in the literature, such as McInnis' "Mental Maps and Metaphors in Academic Libraries,"[16] I postulate that librarians may fruitfully be seen as *mapmakers* in two basic and interrelated ways. Using a general meaning of map from the OED, as a "mental conception of the arrangement of something," I see us as making maps through our library bibliographic systems and assistance and instructional systems, which in turn are best used by readers who have become mapmakers themselves, with our assistance, in that they create mental maps of our systems and devise pathfinding and problem-solving schemes by which they traverse the maps to the knowledge-places they seek. If, as I maintain, we are engaged in mapmaking and map interpreting *both* in our bibliographic systems and in our personal interaction with users, they we are engaged in a truly cybernetic endeavor: as we learn more about our readers' inner maps and search schemata, we can improve our bibliographic arrangements by making them easier to understand and more flexible in meeting the varied needs of users, and, most essentially, also *cumulative*: we learn to do better and so do the users, because we keep *adding* to our maps—we grow.

I am using the model and terminology of scheme theory because it enables us to picture more clearly the inner processes of users, so we can be concerned more effectively with our interventions with them as an aid to their growth. A good summary of scheme theory, which has numerous formulations in cognitive-motivational psychology today, is provided by Eckblad:

A central proposition in scheme theory is that schemes are organized in hierarchic means-end relations. In principle, all of a person's processes may be represented as a very large, more or less tightly organized, hierarchic system of schemes, the means-end structure. It is active from birth to death, starts as a fairly simple system of reflexes, but develops through the differentiation and extension of schemes. The structure serves as the perceptual and conceptual context into which the person's experience is assimilated, as a system of intentions and plans for action, and as a system of goals towards which purposive activity is directed.[17]

When schemes are conscious, they may be articulated by the person, especially in response to questions.

We have created or have available many maps which provide access to the world's recorded resources: how well can our patrons use them? The only way to find out, and thus be able to design better maps, and assist more effectively, is to dialog with the users. Our use studies, such as transaction logs and user surveys and circulation studies, may give us patterns of behavior, but not the *reasons* for the behavior, and usually not the maps or schemata for using them, in the minds of users. I am going to review some of the mapping systems we use: as I do so, let us think of having a dialog with each other about them and how we use them (see Appendix A).

Let us imagine a reader entering a university library and taking advantage of some of the systems. First, the reader needs to know where to go. We have campus maps showing the various libraries, floor plans of individual libraries, and orientation tours. We try to assist the reader in obtaining a good mental or cognitive map of the library as a spatial environment and can even measure some of the results of orientation by asking readers to fill in places on outline maps, as Trish Ridgway has shown, in "Library Orientation Methods, Mental Maps, and Public Services Planning."[18] Our signage systems obviously play an important role in showing locations—how well do they work?

The reader may move directly to the library catalog. Each form of catalog displays records: how do users conceptualize the structure of the catalog? Christine Borgman's dissertation, *The User's Mental Model of an Information Retrieval System: Effects on Performance*,[19] is a good example of a way to take the mental maps into consideration, so that we can direct our attention to them as well as to step-by-step behavior. The most systematic map of a library collection is the classification scheme itself, as Richard Gray has pointed out in his article, "Classification Schemes as Cognitive Maps."[20] Experiments are under way on classification systems as a library user's tool in online catalogs.[21]

Finding difficulty in searching a specific topic, the reader may consult a reference librarian. Marilyn White has outlined a model of the reference encounter which explicitly uses a scheme approach and enables us to see the importance of a match between the schemes or frames of each and the resulting common information base of user and searcher.[22] (See Figure 1.) Another use of the schemata analysis was in a study of the reference process by S.D. Neill.[23]

We may use and direct users to a resource that is more comprehensive than any bibliographic session—the research guide. As Barbara Bell has rightfully described it, "a research guide is a learner's map."[24] As Bell further adds, "considering the helpfulness of these maps, it is surprising that they are so little used."[25] Perhaps a major reason is that they are not made visible by librarians as a part of larger maps. Librarians have been alerted to these guides by a good survey in *Choice*, "A Guide to the Guides: Literary Maps of the Humanities, Social Sciences, and Sciences."[26]

Let us think next of the decision to try online bibliographic searching. Just as with the online catalog, here the nature of the database system and the ways to access it, as pictured by the user, are important. Search decisions are best guided, both in the user and assisting librarian, by a mental model of the performance of the system and the necessary trade-offs in using it. Marcia Bates gives a key example of the danger of a poor conception in her article, "The Fallacy of the Perfect Thirty-Item Online Search."[27]

Our inquisitive reader may be blessed with the opportunity for a bibliographic instruction session. What happens there? Instruction in maps and their use, of course: methods of mental mapmaking for the user's general or specialized pathfinding. The effectiveness of the instruction will depend on a mix of cognitive and motivational aspects, according to scheme theory: in the best situation, there is the highest degree of pleasure, interest, and absorbed attention. The learning activity "catches attention because there is the right kind and degree of match between the situation and one of this person's schemes, one that is capable of becoming spontaneously active."[28] Sharon Rogers expressed it in another way, in stating that "the suc-

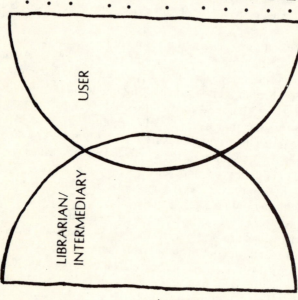

Librarian/Intermediary frames:
- Reference Interview Master Frame
- Search Strategy Master Frame
- User Frame
- Problem Frame
- Subject Frame
- Service Requirements or Information Frame
- Information System Frame Network
- General and Specific Source Frames

User frames:
- Problem Master Frame
- Search Strategy
- Reference Interview or Interview Master Frame
- Subject Frame
- Service Requirements or Information Frame
- Information System Frame Network
- Colleague Frames
- Own Collection Frame
- Library Frame
- Librarian/Intermediary Frame
- Reference Collection Frame
- Specific Book or Article Frames

FIGURE 1

cess of the instructional process may require translation of knowledge from the academic library experience into the conceptual
frameworks and habits of users."[29]

In this survey we are reminded that one of the major obstacles
facing our users is that our maps are many, usually self-contained,
and do not refer to each other and are not effectively interconnected.
We can imagine, after the model of expert computer systems,[30] a
single computer terminal which would offer a display of a variety of
maps, from floor plans to indexes to reference books.[31] One published recommendation moving in this direction is William Jarvis's
proposal on "Integrating Subject Pathfinders into Online Catalogs."[32] A working example is Bowling Green University's project
reported as "An Online Reference System."[33] No matter how
elaborate and complete a system which displays bibliographic
records and resources, the user may need and should always have
available *assistance* in making the connections between needs and
the system.

FUTURE DEVELOPMENT

I see a great opportunity before us, to use our knowledge of the
maps of literature to move more closely into partnership with researchers, especially those more sophisticated, such as those in the
realm of "bibliopoetics" as described by David Shupe,[34] so that we
can act in some way like a clearinghouse of research strategies on a
level more profound than our generalized search processes and our
concerns with college assignments. In bibliographic instruction we
have set up clearinghouses of teaching methods and guides. Perhaps
we need now to have local or individual clearinghouses by which we
can display a wider range of options.

In this proposal, have I merely increased our burdens, in an age in
which we seem to have not enough staff for good one-on-one reference service and not enough staff for comprehensive bibliographic
instruction programs? My position is that a focus on mapmaking, as
I have outlined it, would enable us to put into effect the principles of
the best-run institutions, as proposed in the challenging management
book, *In Search of Excellence*.[35] We would have a bias for action,
be constantly experimenting to see what works best, staying close to
users, with a hands-on, value-driven approach. Our users would be
telling us what helps most, and supporting those activities more and

more. Our metaphor of service as mapmakers would be an important part of the image that would be conveyed within the staff and to users.

I am not thinking that our closeness to users and service priority would mean that we would be merely reactive and responsive. As educators, we offer as options many knowledge maps that may go beyond what individual users may be seeking, but which may represent a more comprehensive awareness, a valuable and value-laden awareness (see Appendix B).

I have outlined a position, advocating the value of the mapmaking concept for our creative library activities. I am convinced that as we try to create better maps and schemes, our energies will be effectively directed toward our essential goals. Since we as librarians always work as a team, a real test of my position is whether the mapmaker concept can serve to bring us *together* in our service efforts. We need to test this possibility. To what extent can we agree on the fruitfulness and motivating efficacy of a creative life as mapmakers and map interpreters?

MOVING FROM THEORY TO PRACTICE

In our world of conflicting theories and diverse client groups it seems to be no easy task to deal with our practice. Frustrations and confusions are reported in the literature and in our conversations, and we observe clients who are quite unsure what to expect or to demand of us. Professionally, we have accepted the obligation to put our policies in writing so that users can both know them and challenge them. We believe in the Freedom of Information Act, and certainly can have no objection when it is applied to us. But: we live in a world in which it is difficult to confront issues among ourselves as professionals and between ourselves and our clients, whether we are intending to assist them, deliver to them, consult with them, counsel them, or intervene in their organizations and programs.

I am using, and recommending that we all use, the work of Chris Argyris as an aid. His interventions, as reported in his writings, try to integrate reasoning, learning, and action and make use of an action science which is "expressly designed to foster learning about one's practice and about alternative ways of constructing it."[36] In this article I am taking one of the first steps, in putting forth *my* theory and inviting a public testing of its validity and use. Just as I must involve peers and clients in giving me feedback in basic question-answering behavior at the reference desk, so I must get feedback from peers and clients concerning my theory and how I practice it. I would like to do this systematically, using Argyris' method: "action scientists engage with participants in a collaborative process of critical inquiry into problems of social practice in a learning context."[37] One of the methods used in action science (one might have surmised), is mapping, in which verbally or diagrammatically we represent the interrelationships among our working conditions and constraints, our customary actions, the binds we find ourselves in, and tacit reasoning we engage in. It is beyond the scope of this article to work this method out, but it may be useful to see Argyris's survey of methods that usually do *not* work in enabling an organization to examine its present situation and change.

In the chapter, "Seeking Help: The Literature and Consultants," in a recent book,[38] Argyris shows that defensive behavior routines normally interfere with the use of all the good advice in the literature (such as mine, here), and the interventions of invited consultants. The context goes beyond the institution:

> We, as a society, hold a theory in use that is basically oriented toward unilateral control, winning not losing, and face saving. This leads to defensive consequences such as miscommunication, self-fulfilling prophecies, self-sealing processes, and escalating error. It also leads to defensive reasoning. Defensive reasoning is characterized by the use of soft data, by reasoning that is privately compelling and privately testable.[39]

Of course, as Argyris has pointed out over the years, it is easier to see defensive routines in others than in ourselves, and easier to see them than to change others or ourselves. The main instrument Argyris uses, then, in his books, is the reporting and analysis of *transcripts* of meetings and interactions. He then can have directly observable data, and also the opportunity to question and make public the reasoning processes used by professionals and clients. This approach, interestingly enough, is similar to the method of protocol analysis which we as information scientists use to study user behavior and librarian behavior.[40]

The power of Argyris's method, however, is not only in its ability to help us see what we *are* doing, but also to "offer an explanation that describes what happened in a way that implies how it might be changed.''[41] We then go on to develop alternatives and paths for getting from here to there. All policies and alternatives involve norms, and it is certainly clear in library literature that norms and governing values are being applied. What is not present, usually, is a way of discussing them. When we discuss how and why to help a client we are applying ethical norms and judgements; as deliberate interventionists, which I believe us to be, we apply our norms. Conflicts between proponents of reference and library instruction are based on norms as well as on theories of information science.

All of this implies that we begin our discussion of my theory (or any similar theory, from the literature or put forth in our institutions) by being aware that we will all tend to be defensive and such defensiveness will block our effectiveness. Going beyond the defensiveness requires a *learning* process. It is here that we see the crucial link between theory and practice. Good theory and good advice (based on all the relevant data we could imaginably acquire) become applicable to our actual practice only as a result of a personal learning process. In the simpler reference situations the handy checklist of behavior may seem to be the necessary and even sufficient aid. In dealing with the more complex questions of users and of our service policies we need ways to achieve a breakthrough to vital aspects we tend to label as undiscussable and try to bypass. I propose the theory and method of Argyris as a way to achieve this breakthrough. Let us test my proposal.

A summary statement: if we are to design systems of *maps*[42] for our personal clients and general users, and then dialog with them about the use of such systems, as advisors, consultants, and intermediaries, we need to *know* their information-gathering patterns and needs better. This includes more research into *use behavior*, such as the studies by Bulick,[43] Metz,[44] and Cullars.[45] More than this type of research however, it means more personal interviewing, taking advantage of ways to remove defensive routines, between librarians and clients and librarians and other librarians.

Another way to put it would be this: our rational analyses and technological systems need to be *more* personal and sensitive. Given these polar needs, we need to integrate them on two levels: in the single reference encounter, and in the reference management context, where the macrotheory is discussed and priorities are set. I am attracted to a synthesis that may be called ''an integrated development strategy,'' after the book by the Asplunds.[46] The Asplunds spent many years trying to work out their initial insight: "to understand fully what happens when a group of people formulate a business strategy, it is necessary to examine both rational decision-making processes and group dynamics, and to integrate insights from both these areas."[47] Just as the Asplunds used the work of Chris Argyris to work with their integration, so we can too. I suggest if we do this task thoroughly, we may make our reference theories supremely practical. This *making* will be based on our own *learning*.

NOTES

1. Ralph Gers and Lillie J. Seward, "Improving Reference Performance: Results of a Statewide Study." *Library Journal* (Nov. 1 1985), pp. 32-35.

2. *Ibid.*, p. 35.

3. Charles A. Bunge, "Interpersonal Dimensions of the Reference Interview: A Historical Review of the Literature," *Drexel Library Quarterly* 20 (Spring 1984), 4-23.

4. See, for example, D.J. Foskett, "User Psychology." Proceedings of the *International Conference on Training for information Work, Rome, 15-19 Nov. 1971* (The Hague: International Federation for Documentation, 1972), pp. 385-396. A more recent plea is in Sara Fine, "Research and the Psychology of Information Use," *Library Trends* 32 (Spring 1984), 441-460.

5. "Reference Obsolescence," *RQ*, 25 (Fall 1985), 52-58.

6. "Research and Library Skills: An Analysis and Interpretation," *College & Research Libraries* 45 (March 1984), 99-109.

7. *Ibid.*, p. 102.

8. "What's Wrong with Reference: Coping with Success and Failure at the Reference Desk," *American Libraries* 15 (May 1984), 303-06, 321-22.

9. "Teacher or Intermediary: Alternative Professional Models in the Information Age," *College & Research Libraries* 43 (May 1982), 183-191.

10. Miller, p. 321.

11. Nielsen, p. 183.

12. *Ibid.*, p. 189.

13. The major works by Chris Argyris and his colleagues I have found helpful are these: *Theory in Practice: Increasing Professional Effectiveness* (San Francisco: Jossey-Bass, 1977) with Donald A. Schön; *Reasoning, Learning, and Action: Individual and Organization* (San Francisco: Jossey-Bass, 1982); and the recently published *Action Science: Concepts, Methods, and Skills for Research and Intervention* (San Francisco: Jossey-Bass, 1985), with Robert Putnam and Diana McLain Smith. I have not seen much use of Argyris in library literature, although some of his concepts were used by Mary Lou Goodyear in "Are We Losing Control at the Reference Desk? A Reexamination," *RQ* 25 (Fall 1985), 85-88.

14. Rufus E. Miles, Jr., "The Origin and Meaning of Miles' Law," *Public Administration Review* 38 (Sept.-Oct. 1978), 399-403.

15. Miller, p. 303.

16. Raymond G. McInnis, "Mental Maps and Metaphors in Academic Libraries," *The Reference Librarian* no. 10 (Spring/Summer 1984), 109-120. See also the highly significant essay by D.J. Foskett.

17. Gudrun Eckblad, *Scheme Theory: A Conceptual Framework for Cognitive-Motivational Processes* (London: Academic Press, 1981), p. 12. Another use of cognitive learning

theory for library service is by Harold W. Tuckett and Carla J. Stoffle, "Learning Theory and the Self-Reliant Library User," *RQ*, 24 (Fall 1984), 58-66.

18. Trish Ridgway, "Library Orientation Methods, Mental Maps, and Public Services Planning" (ED 247942) (1983).

19. Christine Borgman, "The User's Mental Model of an Information Retrieval System: Effects on Performance," *Dissertation Abstracts International* 45/01-A:4 (1984). See also Christine L. Borgman, "Performance Effects of a User's Mental Model of an Information Retrieval System," in *Proceedings of the American Society for Information Science 46th Annual Meeting*, vol 20 (White Plains, N.Y.: Knowledge Industry Publications, 1983), pp. 121-124.

20. Richard A. Gray, "Classification Schemes as Cognitive Maps," *The Reference Librarian* no.9 (Fall/Winter 1983), pp. 145-153.

21. Karen Markey, "The Dewey Decimal Classification as a Library User's Tool in an Online Catalog," in *Proceedings of the American Society for Information Science 47th Annual Meeting*, Vol. 21 (White Plains, N.Y.: Knowledge Industry Publications, 1984), pp. 121-125.

22. Marilyn Domas White, "The Reference Encounter Model," *Drexel Library Quarterly* 19 (Spring 1983), 38-55.

23. S.D. Neill, "The Reference Process and Certain Types of Memory: Semantic, Episodic, and Schematic," *RQ* 23 (Summer 1984), 417-423.

24. Barbara Currier Bell, *Tools in the Learning Trade: A Guide to Eight Indispensable Tools for College Students* (Metuchen, N.J.: Scarecrow Press, 1984), p. 77.

25. *Ibid.*

26. Donald C. Dickinson, "A Guide to the Guides: Literary Maps of the Humanities, Social Sciences, and Sciences," *Choice* 21 (Nov. 1983), 385-393.

27. Marcia J. Bates, "The Fallacy of the Perfect Thirty-Item Online Search," *RQ* 24 (Fall 1984), 43-50.

28. Eckblad, *Scheme Theory*, p. 55.

29. Sharon Rogers, "Research Strategies: Bibliographic Instruction for Undergraduates," *Library Trends* 29 (Summer 1980), 69-74.

30. *Building Expert Systems*, ed. Frederick Hayes-Roth and others (Reading, Mass.: Addison-Wesley, 1983).

31. Examples of indexing multiple reference books are: *DataMap: Index to Published Tables of Statistical Data, 1983*, by Jarol B. Manheim and Allison Ondrasik (New York: Longman, 1983) and Benjamin F. Shearer and Barbara Smith Shearer, *Finding the Source: A Thesaurus-Index to the Reference Collection* (Westport, Conn.: Greenwood Press, 1981).

32. William Jarvis E., "Integrating Subject Pathfinders into Online Catalogs," *Database* 8 (Feb. 1985), 65-67.

33. Janet Chisman and William Treat, "An Online Reference System," *RQ* 23 (Summer 1984), 438-445.

34. David A. Schupe, "Towards a Bibliopoetics: Contemporary Re-evaluations of the Scholarly Process and Their Implications for Academic and Research Libraries," in Association of College and Research Libraries, National Conference (2nd, 1981, Minneapolis, Minn.), *Options for the 80's: Proceedings of the Second National Conference of the Association of College and Research Libraries*, ed. Michael D. Kathman and Virgil F. Massman (Greenwood, Conn.,: JAI Press, 1982), vol. 1, part A, pp. 207-214.

35. Thomas J. Peters and Robert H. Waterman, *In Search of Excellence: Lessons from America's Best-Run Companies* (New York: Warner Books, 1984).

36. Argyris, *Action Science*, p. 237.

37. *Ibid.*

38. Chris Argyris, *Strategy, Change and Defensive Routines* (Marshfield, Mass.: Pitman, 1985).

39. *Ibid.*, p. 91.

40. See for example, Patricia Sullivan and Peggy Seiden, "Educating Online Catalog Users: The Protocol Assessment of Needs," *Library Hi Tech*, Issue 10 (1985), pp. 11-19.

Sullivan and Seiden refer to K. A. Ericsson and H. A. Simon, *Protocol Analysis: Verbal Reports as Data* (Cambridge, Mass.: The MIT Press, 1984).

41. Argyris, *Action Science*, p. 229.
42. Such as expert systems; see, as an example of an effort in this direction, W. S. Vaughan, Jr., and Anne S. Mavor, *Simulation of a Scheme Theory-Based Knowledge Delivery System for Scientists* (Technical Report by W/V Associates, Annapolis, MD, May 1981).
43. Stephen Bulick, *Structure and Subject Interaction: Toward a Sociology of Knowledge in the Social Sciences* (N.Y.: Dekker, 1982).
44. Paul Metz, *The Landscape of Literature: Use of Subject Collections in a University Library* (Chicago: American Library Association, 1983).
45. John Cullars, "Characteristics of the Monographic literature of British and American Literary Studies," *College & Research Libraries* 46 (Nov. 1985), 511-522.
46. Gisele Asplund and Goran Asplund, *An Integrated Development Strategy* (Chicester: John Wiley & Sons, 1982). Does this sound more mature than "High tech, high touch"?
47. *Ibid.*, p. ix.

APPENDIX A

Selected Maps In The University Library

1. Maps and floor plans
   — User develops cognitive map of spaces and locations
2. Library catalogs
   — User develops mental model of the bibliographic record system, and skills in using it.
3. Reference encounter and search for information
   — Librarian and user seek to create effective match between their interviewing and information "frames" or cognitive structures
4. Published research guides
   — "A learner's map"
5. Online bibliographic searching
   — Users search directly or through librarians as intermediaries: search decisions require mental image of the database and the results of each formulation
6. Bibliographic instruction sessions and library-produced maps of the literature
   — Effectiveness depends on both cognitive and motivational aspects
7. Postulated expert computer system
   — Display system linking all maps and bibliographic retrieval systems

APPENDIX B

Knowledge Maps To Be Made Available To Library Users

1. Maps of interdisciplinary materials and materials in many disciplines not immediately evident
2. Maps of materials that go beyond the course or curriculum or even the total offerings of a school
3. Maps of information from many kinds of sources: films and other media, direct correspondence and interviews with experts
4. Maps of resources from a variety of worldwide sources, such as those enabling Americans to see how they are seen by those in other countries
5. Maps of the many alternative publications, from religious and ethnic groups, from activist and special-interest groups, which provide information and insights not visible in the mass media of the United States
6. Maps of the publications of the variety of schools of thought within a single discipline, where each theoretical approach defines the scope and scale of its own map, its own paradigm
7. Maps showing cultural variations, especially in fields of human creativity (art, music) and human social forms (marriage, child raising, religion)
8. Maps which show users that they are not limited in their search for knowledge to the contents and control systems of our machines and megamachines